W9-CQN-652

undergraduate

LELAND STANFORD JUNIOR UNIVERSITY ★ ★ ORGANIZED 1891

book fund

contributed by
friends of Stanford

STANFORD UNIVERSITY LIBRARIES

WITHDRAWN

PLAYING THE GAME

PLAYING THE GAME

THE HOMOSEXUAL NOVEL IN AMERICA

BY ROGER AUSTEN

THE BOBBS-MERRILL COMPANY, INC.

INDIANAPOLIS / NEW YORK

PS
374
. H63.A9

The mention in this book of authors, dead or alive, should not be construed as incontrovertible indication of sexual orientation. The writers mentioned fall into four categories—announced homosexuals, unannounced homosexuals, bisexuals, and heterosexuals—and the reader is asked to keep in mind that there is no firm correlation between the degree of sympathy toward homosexuals in the writer's work and the sexual orientation of that writer.

Copyright © 1977 by Roger Austen
All rights reserved, including the right of reproduction
    in whole or in part in any form
Published by the Bobbs-Merrill Company, Inc.
Indianapolis   New York

Designed by Jacques Chazaud
Manufactured in the United States of America

First printing

Library of Congress Cataloging in Publication Data
Austen, Roger.
    Playing the game.
    Bibliography: p.
    1. American fiction—20th century—History and
criticism.   2. Homosexuality in literature.   I. Title.
PS374.H63A9   813'.5'09352   76-46228
ISBN 0-672-52287-X cloth
ISBN 0-672-52318-3 paper

ACKNOWLEDGMENTS

For directing me to the books, I would like to thank Hal Call, Nancy Mitchell of the San Francisco Public Library, Phyllis Lyon, Jim Denson, Dorr Legg, Don Slater, Ian Young, and especially Noel I. Garde. For offering suggestions on improving the manuscript, I am indebted to Dr. Samuel M. Steward, Dan Allen, Richard Girsch, and, most particularly, Steve Steinberg. And for just "being there" when no one else was, I would like to thank my friends Peter and Margaret Reed of Minneapolis.

CONTENTS

Tell all the truth but tell it slant,
Success in circuit lies. . . .

—Emily Dickinson

PREFACE

NEARLY TEN YEARS AGO, in his study of Gore Vidal, Ray Lewis White wrote, "It is to be regretted that no writer or scholar— renowned or otherwise—has yet been daring enough to study the possible literary and social value and influence of recent American fiction dealing with homosexuality."[1] In the meantime, many studies have been written about the special contributions made to our national literature by the more respectable minorities: Jewish, black, Chicano, Oriental-American and native American; moreover, it has gradually been revealed that some of our most important writers were or indeed are homosexual. A main reason that no one has fulfilled White's rather modest request is that gay writers and gay fiction have always been subjected to a peculiar set of rules rarely applied to other minority literature and never, of course, applied to "majority" literature. Until very recently a malicious and inequitable game has been played, with heterosexual critics and publishers making up the rules and, in most cases, with gay writers wanting to have their fiction published and praised in this country abiding by those rules. The name of the game is homophobia, and it has been played with appalling success on all sides. While nearly everyone now concedes that we have many gifted homosexual writers, few are willing to recognize that these writers have produced a body of homosexual fiction worthy of being taken seriously. No one has been daring enough to write a study of gay fiction in this country because, according to one of the cardinal rules of the game, the very existence of the homosexual novel in America is steadfastly denied. The reading public has been led to believe that while gay men dabble in poetry and write interesting plays and trenchant essays, the few novels they have written about themselves and their milieu have always turned out to be seriously flawed and second-rate.

It is time to stop playing this game and to expose the mischief and harm it has done over the last hundred years. Just as thousands of gay people in all walks of life are now leaving their closets and refusing to play the grim game of trying to pass, it seems to me to be an appropriate time to put aside all of the poses and masquerades of past decades and to declare that homosexuals, like members of other American minorities, have a literary tradition of which they need not be ashamed. It is immediately conceded that the rules of the game, as summarized in the following passage from the editorial in the recent gay issue of *College English,* have been so inhibiting that our homosexual literature is not all that it might have been.

One can, of course, simply refrain from writing on the subject that is nearest one's heart, and continue to accumulate notes for the work-in-progress for when the time is ripe. . . . One can write and then eschew publication, as did E. M. Forster with *Maurice.* One can arrange for private printings, as did many of the writers from 1890 to 1920. One can reverse the pronouns prior to publication . . . call one's lover Narcissus and transform oneself into a simple country swain . . . can leave pointers via Greek mythology . . . can talk about aesthetics and spiritual friendship . . . can tell a tale of woe and kill off a major character in the last chapter, thereby providing evidence of redeeming social value. One can do just about everything except utter the truth.[2]

But at the same time heterosexuals must concede that homosexual literature—particularly the homosexual novel—has existed in America for decades, often in spirited defiance of homophobia. An overview of this unexamined body of fiction seems to me long overdue.

The aim of this study is twofold. For heterosexual readers, especially English professors, literary critics, and book reviewers, I would like it to serve as a corrective to the past decades of shabby treatment that much gay fiction has received. It is time for these people to ponder the cause-effect relationships endemic to playing the game and to ask themselves whether any other minority writing, equally hamstrung by prohibitions against truth-telling, could have won any more praise than that which has been given to homosexual fiction. Gay readers, all too well aware of shabby treatment in their everyday lives, need not be reminded of the injustices that are part of playing the game. I would like this book to help them become acquainted or reacquainted with many of the older, less well known novels, and I would like to think that gay scholars in particular would be able to use this study as a springboard for parallel projects that still need to be undertaken.

Generally speaking, limitations of talent, time, and space have precluded covering anything more than those male-oriented novels written by Americans before 1965. As a result, the lesbian novel in America, which was covered in Jeannette Foster's 1956 *Sex Variant Women in Literature* and, more briefly, in Jane Rule's 1975 *Lesbian Images,* will not be included in this study. Although several relevant novels by lesbians will be cited, the definitive comparison of gay sensibility as reflected in the fiction of gay women and men in twentieth-century America remains to be written. Also beyond my scope is any sort of systematic "comparative lit" evaluation, although national differences are touched on in my first chapter and in the later discussion of the transplanted Christopher Isherwood. Thus, a counterpart to Foster's book—a comparison of the male homosexual themes in the literature of the United States, England, France, Germany (and Japan, Italy, Russia, Spain, Latin America and everywhere else)—also remains to be written. I have chosen not to discuss post-1965 novels extensively for several reasons: my own lack of perspective, the decreased quality and greatly increased quantity of gay fiction (chiefly paperback pornography) published in the last ten years, and the comparative familiarity with and availability of much of this fiction to the reader of today. It falls to someone else to write a detailed examination of our recent gay fiction and, if it is thought to be necessary or possible, a scholarly study of post-1965 gay male pornography. Further outside the scope of this study is any consideration of minor gay characters in major American novels (e.g., Erik Valborg in *Main Street*), and the reader is asked to remember that discussion of the more important, multifaceted novels will be limited to the admittedly reductive terms of sexual significance and explicitness.

What I have tried to do is to pick out the relevant male fiction—veiled or unveiled—that has appeared in this country over the past hundred years and place it in simple chronological order, adding bits of background on the author and gay life as it seems to have been lived at the time, plus a sprinkling of reviews from both heterosexual and homosexual critics. Generally speaking, I have downplayed both the short story and the "Albertine" novels (e.g., Tennessee Williams' *The Roman Spring of Mrs. Stone*), and I have placed emphasis on historical significance, literary quality, apparent authenticity, and, with respect to plot summaries, a guess of readers' familiarity. With all of these limitations in scope, it would be presumptuous of me to think that *Playing the Game* will or should be accepted as the last word. What I have written is quite clearly a pioneering handbook. Its approach and evaluations may well be regarded as unbearably arbitrary and idiosyncratic; certainly the field is fertile and unexplored enough to warrant any number of other analyses from different points of view, both gay and straight.

Finally, a word on the completeness of my research. Even amid the well-stocked Kinsey Institute for Sex Research Library where she was employed, Dr. Foster felt justified in complaining that "no other class of printed matter except outright pornography has suffered more critical neglect, exclusion from libraries, or omission from collected works than variant belles lettres."[3] This dilemma has recently caused Ian Young to concede, in his preface to *The Male Homosexual in Literature: A Bibliography,* that even with 2,291 titles his coverage is "selective and is not intended to be exhaustive."[4] The difficulties of research in this area have indeed been great, as gay readers must know and straight readers can guess. Until the 1940s such a stigma was attached to the writing and printing of explicitly gay works that much of what did come out in earlier years was obscured by everything from fake names to fly-by-night publishers to later bowdlerized editions with heterosexualized titles. The task of searching out the title of every homosexual novel written by an American and finding a hardback or even paperback copy of it has thus required much literary detective work. The titles cited here can at least be regarded as representative of the fiction written over the last 100 years, and I would of course appreciate being informed of any overlooked novels that should be mentioned in possible future editions of this book.

THE DIM PAST

BEFORE 1920

THE MAIN REASON for the dearth of explicitly gay novels in America from the nineteenth century up to 1920 is that sexual perversion was regarded as hardly a fit subject for fiction—or, for that matter, nonfiction. Almost everything published on homosexuality during these years was confined to the treatises of pioneering doctors, psychiatrists, and sex investigators, but even they betrayed a certain nervousness, uncertainty, or distaste in broaching the subject. In his 1883 *Sexual Impotence of the Male,* Dr. William A. Hammond cited the case of a twenty-eight-year-old man who came to him for treatment of "pederastic tendencies to which he had repeatedly yielded, though always afterward experiencing the most intense feelings of remorse."[5] The doctor prescribed bromide of sodium, the study of mathematics, "cold baths every morning, a liberal diet and plenty of outdoor exercise," with the result that his patient became supposedly "free from all pederastic tendencies; in fact, entertaining the liveliest disgust for it, and thinking seriously of marriage." Rather gloomy glimpses of nineteenth-century gay life emerge from the several American case studies cited in Havelock Ellis' *Sexual Inversion.*[6] While M. O. boasted of having had "about

1

30 homosexual relationships" and H. C. insisted that "inversion is the source of so much good," the other two Americans mentioned by Ellis fall into the more customary tale-of-woe category. One was a teacher who ended up in the Cook (County) Insane Hospital after a tempestuous affair with a letter carrier in Chicago; the other, a 31-year-old virgin of a "naturally religious temperament," explained his sexual renunciation in this way: "The desire to love and be loved is hard to drown, and, when I realized that homosexually it was neither lawful nor possible for me to love in this world, I began to project my longings into the next."

Even by 1918 the attitude of medical "experts" toward homosexuals, as exemplified in *Autobiography of an Androgyne,* shows that American doctors still remained extremely negative and even crackpot in their views. In his wrongheaded foreword to this book, Dr. Alfred Herzog (Ph.B., A.M., M.D., editor of the New York *Medico-Legal Journal,* member of the New York and New Jersey bars) divided gay men into two groups: "The vicious homosexualist acts the part of the male. The unfortunate, insane or congenital homosexualist acts the part of the female."[7] On the basis of this reasoning, Dr. Herzog was begrudgingly sympathetic toward the book's author, "Earl 'Jennie June' Lind," who quite obviously fell into the latter category. Most of the autobiography was written in 1889, but, in Jennie June's words, it was "fated to wait eighteen years for publication, primarily because American medical publishers—on the basis of the attitude of the profession—have had an antipathy against books dealing with abnormal sexual phenomena."[8] At the end of this inadvertently campy book, which details the sexual romps of a "born 'nymphomaniac,' if this word may be used of one who has no nymphae," Dr. Herzog appended a "Questionnaire on Homosexuality." The questionnaire, which includes forty-six questions about heredity, health, interests, sexual proclivities (Latinized), and peculiarities, begins as follows:

The governments of all cultured lands take from time to time censuses of the blind, the deaf, and other defective classes. None has ever taken a census of homosexualists, although the latter are fully as numerous as the two definite classes previously named, and their effect on the social body is even more marked. The Medico-Legal Journal, on the basis of the following questionnaire, makes the first essay, in the history of culture, in lining up the defective class in question. . . .[9]

With gay men tagged as defective, insane, or criminal as late as 1918, it is little wonder that they were hesitant to write fiction about themselves, even if it could be published in this country. Of course, by 1920 other minority groups could already point to an ongoing tradition of their "own kind" of novel. The American Negro novel had begun in 1853, and by World War I first-generation Jewish writers were publishing autobiographical novels in praise of having found the Promised Land. Most homosexuals, however, were obliged to pass for heterosexuals, and what they wrote was obliged to pass as non-gay if it was to be published in the United States.

But passing and playing the game were in some ways surprisingly easy a century ago because of the quaintly paradoxical attitude taken by the genteel tradition toward homegrown homoeroticism. Because of our national prudishness about unabashed heterosexual passion, what emerged by default in many novels was a glorification of male friendship, a point made some years ago by Leslie Fiedler in *Love and Death in the American Novel*. Fiedler traces "innocent" homoeroticism all the way from James Fenimore Cooper to Ernest Hemingway and offers this explanation of "why middle-class readers were not appalled at the implications of the homoerotic fable . . .":

How could Antinous come to preside over the literature of the nineteenth-century United States, which is to say, at a time and in a place where homosexuality was regarded with a horror perhaps unmatched elsewhere and ever. Certainly, in the popular literature of the period, the "sissy," the effeminate boy, nearest thing to a fairy mentionable in polite books, was a target upon which the fury of a self-conscious masculinity vented itself with especial venom. In the long run, however, so violent a disavowal of male inversion fostered an ignorance of its true nature . . . "evil love" could only be conceived of in connection with "evil women," and the relations of males seemed therefore healthy by definition . . ."[10]

However naïve Fiedler may have been regarding the "innocence" of nineteenth-century homoeroticism, he was indeed correct in pointing out that it was Victorian ignorance which prevented our grand-parents from recognizing what are now regarded as quite obviously gay motifs. Still, novelists who were gay hardly had all the freedom they might have desired. Compared with their counterparts in England and Europe, they had to be quite devious, and compared with their countrymen writing poetry, they usually had to contrive to be even more obfuscatory in order to have their fiction published here.

In England homosexuality had been written about rather extensively during the latter part of the nineteenth century, and the subject continued to attract a wide variety of writers on up through 1920. In the 1886 "Terminal Essay" following *The Book of the Thousand Nights and a Night,* Sir Richard Burton had detailed his theory of the gay "Sotadic Zone," which stretched from Mediterranean countries through the Near East to embrace much of the Far East, the South Seas, and all of the New World. A more influential theorist was Edward Carpenter, the sandal-wearing socialist and poet whose lofty thoughts about Noble Uranians were expressed in "The Intermediate Sex" (1896). Carpenter felt those of "homogenic" temperament formed an aristocracy of sensitive souls who were able to excel in art, literature, music, acting, and teaching because of their androgynous qualities. Meanwhile, John Addington Symonds was writing essays and verse in praise of the new universal brotherhood, and at Cambridge University the "Apostles" were caught up in the melioristic notion that the finest moments of Greek civilization could be recaptured if moral progress continued on through the twentieth century. However, the fiction written in England during these years was not always composed in the spirit of the Noble Uranian. Although E. M. Forster was inspired by Carpenter to write his happily-ever-after-in-the-greenwood *Maurice,* other novels set out to titillate rather than to propagandize. In the more lurid category were *The Sins of the Cities of the Plain* (1881), which described the underground world of male prostitutes, and *Teleny* (1893), which was about the torrid love affairs of a concert pianist who was Frenchified and moved to Paris in the second edition to avoid shocking British readers.[11] Other relevant British fiction published before 1920 included the muted presentation of decadence in Wilde's *The Picture of Dorian Gray* (1890); the school novel of Edward Clarke, *Jaspar Tristram* (1899), which detailed the anguish of an unrequited crush; D. H. Lawrence's view of homosexual impulses as being both twisted and tantalizing in "The Prussian Officer" (1914); and a lighthearted view of eccentric people of various sexes on the Mediterranean island of "Nepenthe" in Norman Douglas' *South Wind* (1917). In general, British writers of the turn of the century were not only willing but eager to touch on gay themes, a fact confirmed by all of the fiction, poetry, and essays to be found in Brian Reade's anthology, *Sexual Heretics: Male Homosexuality in English Literature from 1850 to 1900*.[12]

On the continent during these years there was a great burst of literary activity, and it was the pioneering liberation movement in Germany that sparked the publication of more positive books with a gay theme. "It is a salient fact," observed the American author Edward Stevenson ("Xavier Mayne"), who wrote *The Intersexes* (1908), "that in no other language is annually published so much distinctive literature of the similisexual instincts—novels, essays, poems, dramas—as in German." He goes on to say that in "specialistic" German bookshops one could buy the gay fiction of Friedrich Hölderlin, Alexander von Sternberg, Emil Vacano, William Walloth, and Adolf Wilbrandt.[13] (Wilbrandt's *Fridolin's Mystical Marriage,* based on Karl Ulrich's concept of bisexuality, was translated into English in 1884 and is thought to be the first novel of its kind to appear in the United States.) As early as 1912, Magnus Hirschfeld's Scientific-Humanitarian Committee was urging gay writers to declare themselves "freely and openly," and by 1920 German homosexuals were busy petitioning for legislative reform, publishing gay magazines and yearbooks, and even producing a "gay lib" silent movie.

Stevenson mentions (in *The Intersexes*) about a dozen novelists, including Huysmans, Eekhoud, Loti, "Rachilde," and Essebac, among those dealing with gay themes in French. There were two opposing approaches in French fiction, according to Marc Daniels' "La Belle Epoch," which was translated and serialized in *Tangents* some years ago. One was the "decadent monster" tone of such novels as Lorrain's *Monsieur de Phocas* (1901) and Jean Binet de Valmer's *Lucien* (1910); the other was exemplified by idyllic, youth-worshiping pastoral fiction such as Count Jacques Adelsward-Fersen's "Une Jeunesse" and André Gide's *L'Immoraliste*.

Only now coming to light is the fact that gay fiction was getting published even in Czarist Russia. According to Simon Karlinsky's recent article in *Gay Sunshine,* the most telling gay novel to come out during the "period of relative freedom of speech and advocacy (1905–1917)" was Michael Kuzmin's *Wings* (1907).

Just as gay novelists in other countries were relatively successful at getting into print, here in the United States a rather large number of homoerotic poems were being published without much alarm or even notice. In much of Walt Whitman's poetry, of course, there is perfunctory inclusion of feminine pronouns, but even the most homophobic are finally beginning to concede that Whitman's most heartfelt theme was the "adhesive" love between males. By 1900 Whitman was recognized by the cognoscenti as *the* gay American poet. No one else could approach him in "loftiness, directness, and clarity," Stevenson wrote, but he went on to add that there were a few other Americans who were also interjecting "the accent of at least psychic Uranianism in their verses." Much more recently, the author of *Greek Love,* J. Z. Eglinton, has detected a strain of Uranianism in the poems of Bayard Taylor and Henry David Thoreau. Taylor wrote of the voluptuous beauty of a young man in a Smyrna bazaar in "To a Persian Boy," and in "On the Headland" of a loneliness that could be relieved by "the sunburnt sailor," while in Thoreau's "Sympathy" the poet remembers a younger man he might have loved "had I loved him less." In 1905 a Chicago firm published a small volume of verses compiled by Wallace Rice called *The Athlete's Garland,* and while many of the poems (e.g., "Basketball at Bryn Mawr") merely exude what is now known as school spirit, others are more sensuous than sentimental, exalting the athlete's body rather than the game. Muscular legs are admired in Whitman's "The Runner," and the subjects of other poems include a naked diver poised against a purple sky and two lovingly described football players who "cling" to each other and fall, more in a swoon than a tackle. Some of these poems were taking their place in household editions right alongside the "best-loved" volumes of the Fireside Poets, and this ironic set of circumstances prevailed as long as American readers interpreted homoeroticism as synonymous with friendship.

Compared with homosexual novelists abroad, early writers of gay fiction in this country were inhibited for several reasons—puritanism had a more terrifying effect on our writers, publishers, and readers, and in general America lacked an aristocracy of gentlemen loftily above the cares and concerns of the homophobic "lower classes." And as opposed to their compatriots who were writing poetry, the novelists suffered from having to specify who was doing what to whom, a problem that writers of gay verse were often able to circumvent. But in contrast to later American novelists faced with know-it-all Freudians who prided themselves on being able to recognize a "fairy" when they saw one, our earlier gay writers were in a position to get away with a great deal—and some of them did.

NEAR MISSES

It could be argued that all of the books cited in this chapter miss the mark as compared with what will eventually be recognized as the traditional homosexual novel, but two works published in the 1840s must indeed be labeled as false starts.[14]

One was a novel by James Fenimore Cooper called *Jack Tier,* which features the strange and secretive love of a sailor, Jack Tier, for the master of his ship, Stephen Spike. This affection causes some comment on board, and just when it seems that Cooper might have written a *Billy Budd* in reverse, he comes up with a typically nineteenth-century surprise ending: Jack is none other than Spike's first wife, who has chosen to masquerade as a sailor for reasons that are not very important to us here.[15]

The other near miss is Walt Whitman. If he had allowed himself to write novels rather than poetry, the heritage of our gay novelists would be much richer—or at least different. He did, however, write one novel, *Franklin Evans* (1842), which contains the following plea to the reader:

> The pure and virtuous cast scorn upon such as I have been, and as thousands now are. But oh, could they look into the innermost recesses of our hearts, and see what spasms of pain—what impotent attempts to make issue with what appears to be our destiny—what frightful dreams —what ghastly phantoms of worse than hellish imagination—what of all this that resides, time and again, in our miserable bosoms—then I known that scorn would be changed to pity. It is not well to condemn men for their frailties. Let us rather own our common bond of weakness, and endeavor to fortify each other in good conduct and in true righteousness, which is charity for the errors of our kind.[16]

Whitman scholars realize that "our kind" refers not to homosexuals but to alcoholics, as *Franklin Evans* is a temperance novel. No case is going to be made that Whitman was writing a gay novel in disguise, but it is interesting and possible to read parts of this novel from a gay point of view. For example, when the title character first visits a "musical drinking-house" in Manhattan, he finds himself seduced, but not, it seems, by the alcoholic atmosphere alone:

> It was indeed a seductive scene. Most of the inmates were young men; and I noticed no small number quite on the verge of boyhood. They played the same as the rest, and tossed off glasses of liquor, without apparently feeling any evil effects from it. Little as I knew of the world, I felt that there was something wrong here.

Although Franklin marries twice in this badly written novel, his wives soon die, and his strongest relationship is formed with a bachelor in Virginia, with whom he eventually lives. Finally, it is interesting to note that at this early date, a cameo appearance is made by a market-wagon driver who is, not surprisingly, one of the attractive as opposed to the evil characters in the book.

BAYARD TAYLOR'S NOVEL
OF BOSOM FRIENDSHIP

A little noticed nineteenth-century novel that exalted male friendship at the expense of heterosexual hearth and home was *Joseph and His Friend* (1870) by the "Laureate of the Gilded Age," Bayard Taylor. Although some of his poetry conveys homoerotic touches, the details of his life present no conclusive evidence that Taylor was any more overtly homosexual than he should have been. He was born in Kennett Square, Pennsylvania, in 1825, became a sailor, wrote travel books and "household" poems, mixed with the Nathaniel Parker Willis "Bohemian" set in New York, but married twice and died in Germany in 1878. What is clear, though, is that in at least one of his six novels (which include a juvenile, *Boys of Other Countries*), Taylor set out to celebrate "manly love" as boldly as possible within the conventions of genteel fiction.

Joseph and His Friend is prefaced by a dedication to "those . . . who believe in the truth and tenderness of man's love for man, as of man's love for woman . . ." and by two lines from a Shakespeare sonnet: "The better angel is a man right fair;/The worser spirit a woman colour'd ill." The hero is a handsome blue-eyed twenty-two-year-old Pennsylvania farmer, Joseph Asten, who is "different"— he shrinks from "all display of rude manners" and hungers for the taste of "higher things." Joseph broods over the facts that love must be "hidden as if it were a reproach; friendship watched, lest it express its warmth too frankly . . . ," and he wanly concludes that in his search for companionship there is only "one gate . . . free to me,—that leading to the love of woman."[17]

The woman that Taylor provides for Joseph is a dreadful thirty-year-old city girl, ironically named Julia Blessing, who secretly takes arsenic to improve her fading complexion. But just before Joseph marries Julia, he meets his "friend" on a train, a twenty-eight-year-old with "all the charm of early manhood": golden hair, dark gray eyes, and a mouth at once firm and full. Joseph gazes at Philip Held, and Philip answers his gaze with a look implying "We are men, let us know each other!"—with Taylor adding that this sort of look "is, alas! too rare in this world." A convenient train wreck throws Joseph at Philip, who happens to be on his way to Joseph's very neighborhood to inspect a forge and furnace for his company. The night before Joseph's wedding, Philip tells him that "a man's perfect friendship is rarer than a woman's love," and he promises: "I can be nearer than a brother. I know that I am in your heart as you are in mine. There is no faith between us that need be limited, there is no truth too secret to be veiled."

Taylor's novel goes on to belie Philip's final vow, of course. The marriage is disastrous, but even as Joseph drifts away from Julia toward Philip, the author stops short of lifting the veil to show that the men's love for each other is more sexual than brotherly. The nearest that Taylor comes to candor is midway through the novel when Joseph is "ruined" (because of his father-in-law's chicanery) and Philip soothes him with an alternative to suicide. They could both go to a great valley, Philip says, "dotted with groves of orange and olive" and be free from "the distorted laws of men." Joseph suggests they wait, and the author closes the chapter with this set-piece paragraph, significant for its repetition of the word "alas!":

They took each other's hands. The day was fading, the landscape was silent, and only the twitter of nesting birds was heard in the boughs above them. Each gave way to the impulse of his manly love, rarer, alas! but as tender and true as the love of woman, and they drew nearer and kissed each other. As they walked back and parted on the highway, each felt that life was not wholly unkind, and that happiness was not yet impossible.

In the last few chapters of the novel, Taylor sets the stage for what could conceivably be a genuinely gay denouement. With "the worser spirit" dead from an overdose of arsenic, the two men are finally free to go out West together to find that homoerotic happiness for which they seem to yearn. Indeed, Joseph does go out to California on a trip and thinks he recognizes the paradisical valley that Philip had described. The two exchange "manly love" letters, but in the final paragraph we learn that Philip will have to content himself with the role of brother-in-law rather than lover—Joseph returns to take a sudden and almost inexplicable interest in Philip's look-alike sister, Madeline Held.

CHARLES WARREN STODDARD, THE "GAYEST OF THE GAY"

Three years after the appearance of *Joseph and His Friend,* a Boston firm published a more widely read book, *South-Sea Idyls,* by Charles Warren Stoddard, a thirty-year-old bachelor who had grown up in California to become an actor, a bookstore clerk, and a traveling newspaper correspondent. What the following passage from Franklin Walker's *San Francisco's Literary Frontier* (1939) is trying to express—in 1930-ish obliquity—is that Stoddard was gay:

. . . as he had grown older, Stoddard had come to realize that there was a fundamental maladjustment in his nature, an epicene turn to his friendships which made him too dependent on his male companions. Sympathetic acquaintances explained his nature by saying: "He has a woman's soul in all its strange and endless changeableness." He in turn asked why the world made no greater effort to understand the girlish boy, and consigned the bitter moments of his anguish to his many diaries. With marriage out of the question, he would always be the prey of unsatisfactory and frequently unsocial friendships. How was he to escape from the unrest inherent in a body that craved comfort, bound him in lethargy, or drove him onward towards forbidden pleasures?[18]

Through literature, apparently, as, in Walker's words, the emphasis in *South-Sea Idyls* "is not on the customary brown maidens with firm breasts, lithe limbs, and generous impulses, but on the strong-backed youths . . ."

Stoddard's book is prefaced by a wistful poem describing "The Cocoa-Tree" which stands "widowed" and forlorn, waiting for "ships that never come." A characteristic pattern in the tales is a blossoming friendship between the narrator, an American, and a good-looking young native with whom the narrator begins to "chum," live, and sleep. Stoddard gets away with all this by suggesting that the American's interest in these "scamps" and "scape-graces" is that of a kindly avuncular gentleman who is interested in civilizing and Christianizing the noble scalawag. The book was publishable because Stoddard ostensibly focused on the lush, strange beauty of the exotic, much as Melville had done; the author apparently felt satisfied he had muted any hint of the erotic by playing down emotional attachments and playing up the atmosphere of fun-loving farce.[19]

One feature of Stoddard's young men is that they, rather than the narrator, become the aggressors. Here is the description of being in bed with the naked Kana-ana from "Chumming with a Savage":

> I thought how strangely I was situated: alone in a wilderness, among barbarians; my bosom friend, who was hugging me like a young bear, not able to speak one syllable of English. . . . A bit of cliff, also, remote and misty, running far into the sea, was just visible from my pyramid of pillows. I wondered what more I could ask for to delight the eye. Kana-ana was still asleep, but he never let loose his hold on me, as though he feared his pale-faced friend would fade away from him. He lay close by me. His sleek figure, supple and graceful in repose, was the embodiment of free, untrammeled youth. You who are brought up under cover know nothing of its luxuriousness.[20]

The title of one of his tales, "In a Transport," can be interpreted on two levels: it is the story of an American sailing on a Tahiti-bound transport with forty "bold" French sailors, and it is a narrative of almost continuous if never clearly defined ecstasy. From the first page the narrator is embracing Thanaron, his charming young curly-headed French sailor with an incipient mustache, and for whatever reason they seem hardly to let go of each other until they reach Tahiti. On one occasion, their excuse is based on the seductive atmosphere of the South Pacific and, lamely enough, the need to keep in practice:

> There was something in the delicious atmosphere, growing warmer every day, and something in the delicious sea, that was beginning to rock her floating gardens of blooming weed under our bows, and something in the aspect of Monsieur le Capitaine, with his cap off and a shadow of prayer softening his hard, proud face, that unmanned us; so we rushed to our own little cabin and hugged one another, lest we should forget

how when we were restored to our sisters and sweethearts. . . . Who took me in his arms and carried me the length of the cabin in three paces, at the imminent peril of my life? Thanaron! Who admired Thanaron's gush of nature, and nearly squeezed the life out of him in the vain hope of making their joy known to him? Everybody else in the mess! Who looked on in bewilderment, and was half glad and half sorry, though more glad than sorry by half, and wondered all the while what was coming next? Bless you, it was I! And we kept doing that sort of thing until I got very used to it, and by the time we sighted the green summits of Tahiti, my range of experience was so great that nothing could touch me further. It may be that we were not governed by the laws of ordinary seafarers.

Stoddard even sketches a passionate shipboard romance, as the first officer, B—— ("very soft dark eyes . . . long lashes"), is the "happy possessor of a tight little African, known as Nero . . . as handsome a specimen of tangible darkness as you will sight in a summer's cruise." Finally, in the last paragraph of "In a Transport," the excuse for what comes very close to being an orgy with interesting juxtapositions of necks and arms and knees is merely the fact that they have docked at Tahiti:

Twilight, fragrant and cool: a fruity flavor in the air, a flower-like tint in sea and sky, the ship's boat waiting to convey us shoreward. . . . O Thanaron, my Thanaron, with your arms about my neck, and B____'s arms about you, and Nero clinging to his master's knees,—in fact, with everybody felicitating every other body, because it was such an evening as descends only upon the chosen places of the earth, and because, having completed our voyage in safety, we were all literally in a transport!

About thirty years later, Stoddard's *For the Pleasure of His Company: An Affair of the Misty City* repeated the theme of *South-Sea Idyls* in stateside terms. Published by A. M. Robertson in San Francisco in 1903, this little-noted, almost lost autobiographical novel tells the story of Paul Clitheroe's unsuccessful bouts of writing, acting, and love in San Francisco, and it ends with his escaping into the arms of three naked South Sea Islanders.

At the start of the novel, Paul is a struggling and unappreciated poet-traveloguist, already disenchanted with Bay Area "Bohemia" and nervous about his future. Into his life comes Foxlair "the Faithless," a "swarthily handsome" Southern gentleman with the "physique of a trained athlete." Foxlair, who asks Paul to go on a moonlight ride in his buggy ("in Bohemia everything and anything is in season"), is soon not only living with Paul but actually proposing, as in this passage:

"Look here, Paul Clitheroe," cried Foxlair, turning suddenly upon the youth who was seated in his deep, sleepy-hollow chair. "I love you better than any fellow I ever met. You understand me; these brutes about us are incapable of it." He came and sat on the arm of Paul's chair, facing him, his two hands resting on Paul's shoulders, and resumed: "Let's leave this cursed land. Let us sail into the South Seas. You love them and so do I. There we can be princes, or even kings, and have retinues of lovely slaves, and live a life,—oh, such a life as here we can only dream of. Come, will you go to Tahiti, Samoa, Tongatabu?"

Paul is tempted but answers that he has no money, and shortly afterward, Foxlair steals Paul's clothes and leaves town, never to be heard from again. Paul tries acting, discusses with a lesbian why "tomboys" are delightful and "girl-boys" are unpleasant, and through a fairy-godmother, Little Mama, meets a beautiful actor with "melodramatic eyes," named Grattan Field. "And now I leave you: I leave you two together!" says Little Mama to the two young men, her work done. "Follow me not—I vanish into thin air." Surely the first fag hag in American literature, Little Mama is the founder of the Order of Young Knighthood, with headquarters in some "Bower of Beauty" in the nearby valley of Avalon, and she glows as her two "Jewels" begin to regard each other with more than the brotherly love she has urged them to share. For a while Paul loves "that wildly impulsive, strangely contradictory, utterly ungoverned and ungovernable nature" (i.e., Grattan) to whom he extends the "hospitality of his chamber." At the end of the novel their love has soured and Paul is on an ocean cruise, deciding he is weary of "Bohemianizing." It is evening, the ship is anchored, and on board his artistic chums are finding "temporary insensibility" in drink. Suddenly Paul spies a canoe manned by three naked islanders, "pals in the past," and he motions them to approach. He climbs down into their canoe, and, after a "moment of passionate greeting," they whisk him "off into the night" to spend the rest of his life, presumably, in Tahiti, Samoa, or Tongatabu. This novel is almost as gay as Edward Stevenson's *Imre,* which was to be published three years later in Italy; the key difference is that while Stevenson discusses homosexuality per se, Stoddard persists in the use of such euphemisms as "chum" and "pal."

In one of his tales from *South-Sea Idyls,* Stoddard asks the following question with Kahele, a "most promising specimen," in mind: "Who was the gayest of the gay, and the most lawless of the unlawful?" In American literature of the Victorian era, the answer to at least the first question is Charles Warren Stoddard, and, what is more, it seems that toward the end of his life he wanted this fact to be known. At the close of another "bosom-friend" tale in his 1904 *The Island of Tranquil Delights,* Stoddard removed his mask for a moment. In the following confession the code word is "careful":

It does not matter if in my calmer moments reason cautions me to beware—my head and my heart don't hitch—they never did—and so I have written as I have written; and I shall not have written in vain if I, for a few moments only, have afforded interest or pleasure to the careful student of the Unnatural History of Civilization.

THE HOMOSEXUAL AS VILLAIN

As long as the scenario remained outdoors, there was a certain fresh-air freedom for writers of a century ago to tell of the attractiveness of a male as seen through the eyes of another male. It was as if the overwhelming and undeniable "naturalness" of Nature were bestowing a silent benediction on anything that could conceivably take place out in the open in the sunshine under God's great blue sky. And it was also all the more acceptable if the attractive male was a member of one of the more picturesque darker (Polynesian, Indian, Algerian) or more passionate, impulsive (French) races or one of the lower classes (Whitman's workmen).

When, however, a sexual attraction was suggested between two white gentlemen behind the closed doors of a drawing room, fresh air naturalness often gave way to hothouse unnaturalness and produced the decadent atmosphere that characterized Oscar Wilde's *The Picture of Dorian Gray* and Jean Lorrain's *Monsieur de Phocas*, a 1901 novel full of depraved artists, circus acrobats, duchesses addicted to morphine, and pimps.

Perhaps the first novel published in America which sketches homosexuality in the darker colors of evil was *A Marriage Below Zero* by "Alan Dale," published by Dillingham in New York in 1889. Very little is known of the author's life, but it appears that he was really Alfred J. Cohen, a music and drama critic for the New York *Evening World* from 1887 to 1895.[21] It seems unlikely that "Dale" was gay; whatever the case, he certainly wrote a melodramatically anti-gay novel.

The first part of this drawing-room tale is set in England, where Elsie Bouverie meets and marries the "pretty" twenty-five-year-old Arthur Ravener, whose best friend is Captain Jack Dillingham. The two men are known in society as Damon and Pythias, since they are so often together, but it is difficult to imagine what Arthur sees in Jack, who is an unpleasant, ugly man ten years older than he, with a puffy face and beady black eyes. He is, in short, the homosexual as villain.

Even though there is a hint that the marriage is Arthur's way of "borrowing a cloak of respectability," Elsie continues to believe in her kindly husband during the first months of their marriage. Eventually the fact that it is never consummated begins to prey on her mind, and her more worldly mother suggests hiring a private detective to investigate the possibility of another woman. In a melodramatic scene, Elsie journeys into London one night to call at Arthur's townhouse, where she discovers her husband, pale and trembling, in the company of Captain Jack.

The setting shifts to New York, where Arthur has been advised to take a rest cure to recover from the emotional collapse occasioned by his wife's discovery. While in New York, Elsie and Arthur go to hear a famed preacher, whose sermon deals with Sodom and Gomorrah, and Arthur's face becomes white "as death." Arthur deserts his wife and travels incognito to Paris with Jack. When Elsie reads Arthur's note breaking off their marriage, she swoons, but then determines to chase after him in "one more effort to save my husband from a fate which I did not understand." She arrives in Paris as the newspapers are publishing the exposé of a homosexual scandal "that was agitating the never very placid surface of Parisian society," and finally in a hotel room she finds her husband dead from an overdose of laudanum. Staring down at her is a picture frame that contains two portraits, one of her husband and the other of Captain Jack. This is the overwrought conclusion of the novel:

> My grief gave place to a violent, overpowering sense of anger. Tearing the frame from the wall, I threw it roughly to the floor. The glass broke with a crisp, short noise; but with my feet I crushed it into atoms. Then stooping down, I picked up the photographs, and tore them into smallest pieces. In the same frenzied manner, I went to the window, opened it, and gathering up the bits of glass—regardless of the fact that they cut my hand until the blood flowed freely—I flung them with the torn photographs from the window and looked from it until I saw them scatter in all directions. Then turning away, and without another look at the dead form in the chair, I left the room and the hotel.

HERMAN MELVILLE

With the recent publication of Edwin Haviland Miller's *Melville* (1975), the foundation seems to be laid for Herman Melville to emerge as the nineteenth-century godfather of homosexual fiction in this country. Miller carries Richard Chase's 1949 observation that Melville loved men better than women to the specific conclusion that in the 1850s Melville had a profoundly traumatic, unrequited love for Nathaniel Hawthorne. Although Miller's biography is based on a Freudian rather than an unabashedly gay framework, its well-documented thesis reveals how homoeroticism serves as a key not only to *Billy Budd* but to everything from *Typee* to *Clarel*.

As gay scholars begin to reread Melville's loving review of Hawthorne's *Mosses from an Old Manse* ("He [Hawthorne] expands and deepens down . . . and further and further, shoots his strong New England roots into the hot soil in my Southern soul"); or reconsider *Redburn* (Miller mentions the generally unnoticed fact that the setting of chapter 46, Aladdin's Palace in London, is nothing less than a "male brothel," or, more accurately, a house of assignation); or, indeed, as these scholars reexamine all of Melville's writing, other critical analyses will surely build on Miller's foundation to establish Melville as a writer who was fundamentally no less homoerotic than Walt Whitman.[22]

Because Melville was married and a father, many twentieth-century critics have pretended to be puzzled at the gay overtones in his writing, and some of the more misguided have tried to heterosexualize Melville just as they have Whitman. Fiedler thinks of the marriage bed in *Moby Dick* as "innocent," and other leading critics have felt free to reevaluate Melville from a bewildering array of non-gay premises. However, it is interesting that a detached Englishman, the nominally homophobic D. H. Lawrence, couldn't resist commenting, in 1923, on Melville's lifelong search for the "perfect man friend."[23] Of all of Melville's works, it is perhaps *Billy Budd* that has given the heterosexualizing critic the most pause, but since Miller's biography suggests that any number of his other novels, novellas, tales, and long poems are equally homoerotic, the following observations on *Billy Budd* are offered as nothing more than the briefest token while we wait for the definitive gay criticism of Melville's works to be written. A paragraph from Miller's study will help both in introducing and summarizing *Billy Budd* as it relates to the biography's thesis and to the present study:

In the course of the evolution of the tale into its seemingly final form it became a love story, the familiar love story in Melville's books. Now enfeebled in health and by age, and without male heirs after the death of Stanwix in 1886, Melville fell in love with his artifact, or, perhaps more accurately, renewed and restated his love for the icon of the handsome youth. . . . If in the tale Vere and Claggart are in love with Billy, the one as "father" and the other as rival, their love is exceeded by that of the author. Billy is truly Melville's love child, the recipient of pent-up affections and feelings which in life he could, sadly, give to no one, except perhaps to Nathaniel Hawthorne.[24]

Compared with *A Marriage Below Zero,* the homosexual element in *Billy Budd* is portrayed in much more human and believable terms. First of all, Melville gives Claggart every reason to be fascinated with Billy, whose charm and beauty of body and face are described in many glowing phrases. "Dale" conceives of inverted attraction in terms of unaccountable perversity. In *Billy Budd,* Melville views homosexuality as perverse, but for him it was an accountable perversity. In *A Marriage Below Zero,* the point of view is entirely Elsie's, and since the author felt obliged to keep up the pretense that Elsie could never fully grasp what was going on, the feelings of Arthur and Jack and their ilk are hinted at in only the most shadowy fashion. Melville, however, knows exactly what is going on, and although he can be a bit shadowy himself, he is more forthright and compassionate as he allows us to view Billy through Claggart's eyes, "strangely suffused with incipient feverish tears," with "a touch of soft yearning, as if [he] could even have loved Billy, but for fate and ban."[25]

Even though Melville's work is clearly more complex and honest than that of "Dale," the fact remains that because of homophobic nineteenth-century literary standards, Melville was also obliged to cast his (covertly) homosexual character as the villain of the piece. As long as the noble savage was peeped at from behind the pose of feigned bemusement by Melville or by Charles Warren Stoddard, there was no cause to hear off in the distance the condemning thunder of Jehovah. But when the peep becomes a "gaze" and when a traveler's curiosity becomes "depravity," the American writer of the nineteenth century (and, to some extent, of the twentieth) felt the heavy obligation to play the game and end his tale with some sort of retribution. The difference between *Billy Budd* and a number of the earlier gay novels of this century is that while Claggart is "struck dead by an angel of God" as embodied by Billy, the characters in later novels sense the finger-pointing angels of God in their own muddled minds, and the resulting feelings of guilt are so overwhelming that the characters sometimes decide to become the agents of retribution against themselves.

THE REAL THING: *IMRE*

Thus, the situation at the turn of the century was that no American had felt bold enough to publish a work that was both explicitly homosexual and clearly sympathetic. Stephen Crane was tempted to write a counterpart to *Maggie* after seeing a boy with purple-painted eyes on Broadway one night in 1894, but Hamlin Garland found the manuscript—tentatively called *Flowers of Asphalt*—so shocking that Crane abandoned the work.[26] So far as is known, the first American male to write and publish a sympathetic and explicitly gay novel was Edward Prime-Stevenson, and that novel was *Imre: A Memorandum,* published in Naples in 1906, when the author was thirty-eight.

According to the best information available, the author of *Imre* was born in 1868 in Madison, New Jersey, the fifth son of the Reverend Paul Stevenson and the former Cornelia Prime, who had taught at Mt. Pleasant Female Seminary before her marriage.[27] For some of his writings, he was simply E. I. Stevenson; for his two gay works he became "Xavier Mayne"; after he moved to Europe he affected the hyphenated Prime-Stevenson.

After graduating from New Jersey's Freehold Institute and passing the state bar exam, he began writing books instead of practicing law. Several of his earlier novels touch on a gay theme, but since male friendship was universally accepted as innocuous in the nineteenth century, this fact would have remained buried had Stevenson himself not pointed it out in his 1908 apologia, *The Intersexes.* Writing as "Mayne," he mentions that in Stevenson's boys' book about Bonnie Prince Charlie, *White Cockades* (1887), there is a "half-hinted" erotic relationship between a rustic youth and the Prince, and that there is an even more distinguishable sentiment of "Uranian adolescence" in another Stevenson adventure book for boys, *Left to Themselves, Being the Ordeal of Philip and Gerald* (1891).[28] The latter novel ends with "Philip and Gerald walking forward, calmly and joyfully, and in an unlessened affection and clearer mutual understanding, into their endless lives," but it caused little alarm, as that was exactly what boyhood chums were supposed to do during the heyday of Horatio Alger.[29]

The Intersexes is also of interest because of the author's theories about the gay novelist in general and about gay literature in North America. Of "The Uranian in Belles-lettres," Mayne writes:

> The most expressive outlet for the Uranian's temperament is that of belles-lettres. He cannot always be philosophic nor an analyst in the colder forms of literature. He is likely to lack courage to preach to the uncomprehending public. But his capacity for feeling, his faculty for romance, find vivid expression in elegant literature. Often his pen and paper have been his only confidants: and sometimes in fiction or verse of genius he has taken the world into his secret. . . . It is very largely a serious, deeply emotional literature. Humourous modern literature owes less to the Uranian than does any other class of writings. The Uranian's temperament and his problematic social life have checked his mirth. His gayety tends to irony, or is of that artificial good-humour often characteristic of him. . . . "Look into thy heart and write!" is a long-heard counsel. The Uranian has obeyed it with clarity and courage. His page has mirrored his soul. But he has not always been allowed such liberty. Not only does prejudice in society and religion obstruct his press. Exasperating are the comments of critics, editors, translators and so on to conceal or to ignore altogether the personal homosexuality of such or such a writer and of his literary intentions. The conventional modern biographer avoids recognizing the homosexual nature in his subject. The editor is equally timid. The publisher not less so.[30]

Mayne, who surveyed gay writers of all countries and of all times, had this to say about "American Philarrhenic Literature":

> The North-American (by such term indicating particularly the United States) with his nervosity, his impressionability, his complex fusion of bloods and of racial traits, even when of directly British stocks, is usually far more "temperamental" than the English. He has offered interesting excursions at least towards, if not always into, the homosexual library. His novels, verses and essays have pointed out a racial uranianism. In the United States and adjacent British possessions, the prejudices and

restrictions as to literature philarrhenic in accent are quite as positive as in Great Britain. . . . Nevertheless, similisexualism is far from being an unknown note in American belles-lettres, and has even achieved its classics.[31]

The author goes on to discuss Whitman as the "classic" writer, with brief mention made of other poets believed to be "hellenic"— W. E. Davenport, Professor George E. Woodberry of Columbia University, and the Canadian-American Bliss Carman. Mayne quotes from *South-Sea Idyls,* cites *A Marriage Below Zero,* and finds "echoes of the Uranian strain" in "certain sketches of the late H. C. Bunner" and in *The Spirit of Old West Point,* "a charming series of reminiscences of cadet-days, by General Morris Schaff."[32] *Imre* was not included as an American work, because both in the novel and in *The Intersexes,* "Mayne" did everything he could to disguise the fact that he was really New Jersey–born Edward Stevenson.

Some of the games Stevenson played in regard to *Imre* were no doubt necessary—this is not a novel that American publishers would touch, and the author probably felt he was forced to rely on non-English speaking (Neapolitan) typesetters and private publication (125 copies) in a foreign country. In the preface he states that he is not really the author but merely the editor of a manuscript sent to him by a British friend named Oswald. This fact, coupled with his expatriate status—he moved to Europe in 1901 and died there in 1942—suggests that the game-playing was motivated by more than just caution: Stevenson had a healthy dislike for homophobic America. In *Imre* all the allusions to the United States are negative—there is an American specialist in "nervous diseases" whose invariable advice to urnings is marriage, and a whole paragraph is devoted to the comparatively benighted aspects of Yankee civilization:

Fortunately, Imre had not been born and brought up in an Anglo-Saxon civilization; where is still met, at every side, so dense a blending of popular ignorances; of century-old and century-blind religious and ethical misconceptions, of unscientific professional conservatism in psychiatric circles, and of juristic barbarisms; all, of course, accompanied with the full measure of . . . Yankee social hypocrisy toward the daily actualities of homosexualism. By comparison, indeed, any other lands and races—even those yet hesitant in their social toleration or legal protection of the Uranian—seem educative and kindly; not to distinguish peoples whose attitude is distinctively one of national common-sense and humanity. But in this sort of knowledge, as in many another, the world is feeling its way forward (should one say *back?*) to intelligence, to justice and to sympathy, so spirally, so unwillingly! It is not yet in the common air.[33]

A rather obvious result of this feeling was Stevenson's decision to set his gay love story with a happy ending in a faraway land. While he probably would have conceded that some homosexuals were indeed falling in love with each other in America at this time, the setting of this uplift tale in Boston or Philadelphia would have been at variance to the secondary motif of anti-Americanism in the novel.

Imre is written from the gentlemanly point of view of thirty-year-old Oswald, who is spending a leisurely summer of language study in Hungary, and Stevenson has created a simple plot to serve as the framework for his apologia. In the first chapter, "Masks," Oswald meets Imre, a twenty-five-year-old Hungarian army officer, at an outdoor café and falls in love with him. During the long evening walk which comprises most of the middle chapter, "Masks and—a Face," Oswald confesses and defends his urningism to Imre but receives no definite response in return. This talky chapter is dominated by Stevenson, who argues the case for homosexuality with the well-organized thoroughness one might expect from a former law student. In the last chapter, "Faces—Hearts—Souls," Imre finally makes a similar confession to Oswald, and the novel ends with them in each other's arms and on the verge of going to bed together for the first time.

In this novel of idealized love, it comes as no surprise to find that Imre is quite as beautiful as Billy Budd. Here is part of an early description of Imre:

He was called "Handsome N . . . ," right and left; and he deserved the sobriquet. Of middle height, he possessed a slender figure, faultless in proportions, a wonder of muscular development, of strength, lightness and elegance. His athletic powers were renowned in his regiment. He was among crack gymnasts, vaulters and swimmers. . . . Yet all this force, this muscular address, was concealed by the symmetry of his graceful, elastic frame. Not till he was nude, and one could trace the ripple of muscle and sinew under the fine, hairless skin, did one realize the machinery of such strength. I have never seen any other man—unless Magyar, Italian or Arab—walk with such elasticity and dignity. It was a pleasure simply to see Imre cross the street.[34]

In the middle chapter are two turn-of-the-century responses to urningism. The first reaction is recalled by Oswald as he tells Imre of having made a confession of love in England to a perfect "Man-Type" who was straight. According to Oswald, this "Man-Type" responded, with "curled lip," by saying:

I have heard that such creatures as you describe yourself are to be found among mankind. I do not know, nor do I care to know, whether they are a sex by themselves, a justified, because helpless, ploy of Nature; or even a kind of *logically* essential link, a between-step . . . as you seem to have persuaded yourself. Let all that be as it may be. I am not a man of science nor keen to such new notions! From this moment, you and I are strangers! I took you for my friend because I believed you to be a . . . man. You chose me for your friend because you believed me . . . stay, I will not say *that!* . . . because you wished me to be . . . a something else, a something more or less like to yourself, whatever you *are!* I loathe you! . . . I loathe you! When I think that I have touched your hand, have sat in the same room with you, have respected you! . . . Farewell! . . . . I will keep your hideous secret. Only remember never to speak to me! . . . never to look my way again! Never!

The second response comes from Imre after Oswald has introduced the subject of male relationships:

You seem to forget sometimes that I am a man, and that you too are a man. Not either of us a—woman. . . . You often suggest a . . . a . . . regard . . . so . . . what shall I call it? . . . so romantic, . . . heroic . . . passionate—a love indeed (and here his voice was suddenly broken) —something that I cannot accept from anybody without warning him back . . . back! I mean back coming to me from any other *man*. . . . Our friendship must be friendship as the world of today accepts friendship! Yes—as the world of *our* day does. God! What else could it be to-day . . . friendship? What else—to-day?

Oswald, however, is interested in defining and defending "the friendship which is love, the love which is friendship," and in the quiet of the night, in the course of his confession, he makes it clear to Imre that many homosexuals do not measure up to his standards of acceptable behavior:

> . . . ignoble, trivial, loathesome, feeble-souled and feeble-bodied creatures! . . . the very weaklings and rubbish of humanity! . . . Ah, those patently depraved, noxious, flaccid, gross, womanish beings! perverted and imperfect in moral nature and in even their bodily tissues! . . . A Heliogabalus, a Gilles de Rais, a Henri Trois, a Marquis de Sade; the painted male-prostitutes of the boulevards and twilight-glooming squares! The effeminate artists, the sugary and fibreless musicians! The Lady Nancyish, rich young men of higher or lower society; twaddling aesthetic sophistries; stinking with perfume like cocottes! The second-rate poets and the neurasthenic, *precieux* poetasters who rhyme forth their forged literary passports out of their mere human decadence . . . the cynical debauchees of little boys; the pederastic perverters of clean-minded lads in their teens; the white-haired satyrs of clubs and latrines!

It is clear, of course, that Oswald is thinking of himself and Imre as Uranians of quite a higher sort, and Oswald is quick to follow up with a roll call of the dead and glorious gay.

> What a contrast are these to the great Oriental princes and to the heroes and heroic intellects of Greece and Rome! To a Themistocles, an Agesilaus, an Aristides and a Kleomenes; to Socrates and Plato, and Saint Augustine, to Servetus and Beza; to Alexander, Julius Caesar, Augustus and Hadrian; to Prince Eugene of Savoy, to Sweden's Charles the Twelfth, to Frederick the Great, to indomitable Tilly, to the fiery Skobeleff, the austere Gordon, the ill-starred Macdonald; to the brightest lyrists and dramatists of old Hellas and Italia; to Shakespeare (to Marlowe also, we can well believe), Platen, Grillparzer, Hölderlin, Byron, Whitman; to an Isaac Newton, a Justus Liebig—to Michel-Angelo and Sodoma; to the masterly Jerome Duquesnoy, the classic-souled Winckelmann; to Mirabeau, Beethoven, Bavaria's unhappy King Ludwig;—to an endless procession of exceptional men, from epoch to epoch . . . [who] belonged to Us.

At the end of the middle chapter, Oswald reluctantly concludes that Imre must be heterosexual because his long confession has not moved Imre to make a corresponding commitment. In the last chapter, though, Imre's notes from summer camp become increasingly affectionate and in the climactic scene which ends the novel, Imre comes to join Oswald on a warm afternoon. He is tired from his journey from the country, and Oswald urges him to nap on the sofa. Soon Oswald begins changing for dinner and, while he is "scarce half dressed," is magnetically drawn to his sleeping guest and sits down beside him. Imre awakes, puts an arm around Oswald and starts to talk, but Oswald, excited by the nearness of Imre's body, is visited by the "Sex Demon" who brings his "storm upon my traitorous nature, in fire and lava!" (i.e., Oswald has an erection).[35] After staggering to another chair, he apologizes to Imre, who smiles and says, "Dear Oswald! Brother indeed of my soul and body! Why does thou ask me to forgive thee? . . . For—oh, Oswald, Oswald! I am just as art thou. . . . I am just as art thou!" Later that night, after dinner and a moonlight walk, the two are back in Oswald's room, and Imre delivers an unnecessarily long and flowery invitation for Oswald to go to bed with him:

> My quest, like thine, is over! . . . I wish no one save thee, dear Oswald, no one else, even as I feel thou wishest none save me, henceforth . . . Alike have we two been sad because of our lonely hearts, our long restlessness of soul and body, our vain dreams, our worship of this or that hope—vision—which has been kept far from us. . . . Come then, O friend! O brother, to our rest! Thy heart on mine, thy soul on mine! For us two it surely is . . . Rest!

Physical demonstrativeness in this scene is limited to Imre's putting his arm around Oswald and holding him "to his heart." For the modern reader, *Imre* must seem fastidiously genteel and etherealized. It is, after all, up to us to interpret the climactic "Rest" as the men going to bed, even though it *could* be interpreted as merely the end of restlessness, and the fleeting mention of Imre in the nude is couched not so much in terms of sexual interest as from the viewpoint of a dispassionate physical culturist examining Eugene Sandow. Nonetheless, this novel is a landmark in American gay fiction. *Imre* is the first, the best, the brightest and in a sense the only novel of its time written by a male American which reflects the same spirit of exaltation that moved Carpenter to write so positively about "the Noble Uranian" in England. *Imre* is the felicitous result of Stevenson finding himself at the right place at the right time—away from the killjoy culture of Middle America and before the shadow of Freud darkened the consciousness of the gay novelist and gay novel. Stevenson's glorying in the gay men of the past and his insistence on being allowed to love in the present add up to what has only in the last few years been called "gay pride." As gay fiction returns to an American setting and moves on into the defensive twenties and thirties, *Imre* stands in sharper and sharper relief; it is not until the 1933 publication of *The Young and Evil* that Stevenson's tender story of the love for a beautiful young Hungarian army officer finds its equal.

BACK IN THE CLOSET: *BERTRAM COPE'S YEAR*

Henry Blake Fuller's 1919 *Bertram Cope's Year* not only replaces the mid-European summer mellowness of *Imre* with the harsher atmosphere of America, but takes us back in time as well. Instead of being a modern postwar novel, *Bertram Cope's Year* is a bittersweet backward look into Fuller's own prep school days in the 1870s, and therefore the veil momentarily removed by Stevenson is carefully readjusted by Fuller in an attempt to again mask the unmentionable.

Fuller, aged sixty-two when this novel was published, was by 1919 nearing the end of a writing career that had begun in the 1880s with his romances detailing the charm of Italy and Switzerland. Fuller could never forgive his parents for letting him be born and raised in Chicago instead of New England, the home of his more illustrious relatives. Instead of relishing the rawboned virility of Chicago, he found himself more at home within the gentlemanly tradition of New England and the psychological remove of Henry James.

"The happiest year" of his life, the school term 1873–74, was spent at the Allison Classical Academy at Oconomowoc, Wisconsin, where he lived in a small cottage with five other teen-aged boys.[36] Four of them were members of the "Jolly Quartette," and although Fuller was never fully accepted by this group of cigar-smoking, poker-playing "regular fellows," his living with them in the cottage was the closest he came in his life to belonging. Thus, even though in later years he could recall his "sufferings" at having to study in the midst of "unwashed stewpans," the joy of being an honorary Quartette member gave the academy a special place in his memory for many of the same reasons that Alexander Woollcott was so attached to Hamilton College.

One of the most attractive of the Quartette was Frank Donaldson, a sophisticated older student from Brooklyn who kept a horse and T-cart and was in many ways everything that the studious Fuller was not. They did have a bond, though, in music, and their duets became "justly celebrated" on campus. In *Bertram Cope's Year,* much of Bertram seems to be based on Donaldson, but rather than writing himself into the novel as a fellow student, Fuller views life in a college town through the eyes of a middle-aged bachelor, Basil Randolph.

The setting of the novel is Churchton, near Chicago, where Randolph is "a haunter of academic shades, an intermittent dabbler in their charms." Randolph first meets Bertram, an attractive young English instructor, when he attends a college tea at the home of Medora Phillips, a widow who also collects people and who becomes Randolph's rival as they embark on their separate campaigns to nab Bertram. Medora's excuse is that she views bachelorhood as an amusing challenge, and she has three marriageable young ladies boarding with her who she hopes will prove to be irresistible snares. Randolph's excuse is never fully spelled out, and Fuller tries in the Charles Warren Stoddard style to preserve the illusion that the older man's interest in Bertram is merely avuncular.

Fuller's chapter titles indicate the flavor of the novel and some of the events: "Cope at a College Tea," "Cope Goes A-Sailing," "Cope at the Call of Duty," "Cope Shall Be Rescued," "Cope Gets New Light on His Chum." Randolph and Bertram are strolling on the beach one Sunday morning from the train to Medora's summer house, where they have been invited to spend the day. At Randolph's suggestion, they disrobe and go swimming in the lake, but Fuller is circumspect enough to limit himself to describing Bertram's "young legs and arms" as no more than "lithe." In no way does Fuller intimate that, when the two naked men are lying down on the beach and talking and drying off in the sun, Randolph is enjoying the experience any more than he should.[37]

As if Medora, Hortense, Amy, and Carolyn were not enough competition for Randolph—and, perversely enough, they are not —Fuller brings in one more rival for the affection of Bertram in the thoroughly dislikeable character of Arthur Lemoyne. Just as Randolph has moved into a lovingly described larger apartment so that he can better entertain Bertram overnight ("Think of not being able to put a man up, on occasion!"), Arthur arrives to foil everyone's plans. And, what is worse, Arthur is about as gay as one could be in respectable fiction: he had "dark, limpid eyes, a good deal of dark wavy hair and limbs almost too plumply well turned . . . the fingers (especially the little fingers) displayed certain graceful, slightly affected movements. . . ."

Randolph is totally "dashed" and begins to suspect why Bertram backed out of spending what was going to be a glorious weekend together downstate at Indian Rock. The reader finds out that in the privacy of their rooms Arthur actually presses his hand "on Cope's own," but after taking a drag role in the school play, Arthur goes too far. He makes a seductive gesture to an attractive male cast member and so is asked to leave both campus and town. At the end of the term, Bertram also leaves to join Arthur somewhere in the East without saying good-bye to Randolph who, when asked in the last chapter whether he will "cultivate some other young chap next year," replies that he will not.

Critic John Pilkington comments that "Fuller's choice of homosexuality as his subject matter was an experiment that amounted almost to a sensation . . . in view of Fuller's long-standing aversion to the slightest hint of indelicacy in fiction—an aversion which colored his distaste for naturalistic fiction—his choice of the homosexual theme becomes very remarkable." Pilkington feels the novel is a failure:

Its fatal weakness lies not so much in Fuller's choice of homosexuality for his subject matter as in his failure to deal adequately with the impact of sexual abnormality upon the lives of his characters. Although he supplied abundant evidence of the homosexual tendencies of all the major male characters, he never once indicated the tension or the emotional conflicts which accompany or result from their sexual deviations. To have probed the inner psychological problems of his characters would, of course, have violated Fuller's sense of delicacy. . . .

More importantly, to have probed these problems with understanding and incisive candor would have violated Fuller's pose that all of these gay or semi-gay relationships were something that he himself knew nothing about. Actually, *Bertram Cope's Year* is written more guardedly than Taylor's and Stoddard's tales, so that Fuller could have argued that the essential conflict was based on the fact that Bertram and Randolph were of different ages rather than of the same sex. In a rather peculiar way, viewing the conflict as one of age is actually quite satisfactory for both the naïve heterosexual and the aware homosexual who read the novel. The average straight reader of 1919 would not have been able to fathom that the decorous and prissy Randolph was lusting to get Bertram into bed, and thus such a reader could accept the conflict in terms of the benevolent kindliness of a gentleman versus the ingratitude of a fickle youth. The average gay reader, recognizing the latent gayness of both Randolph and Bertram, can perceive that while Arthur Lemoyne is not as sexually electrifying as he might be, he is still more attractive than the middle-aged Randolph.

In spite of the delicacy with which the subject was handled, no New York firm wanted to publish *Bertram Cope's Year,* but finally Ralph Seymour, publisher of *Poetry,* brought out the novel as a personal favor. It was generally ignored by the critics, few copies were sold, and eventually Fuller collected the unbound sheets from Seymour and destroyed them. Although he was to live ten more years following the publication of this novel, Fuller's literary output dwindled during the twenties, and the last years of his life illustrated the point underscored in *Bertram Cope's Year* and stated in one of his poems—"it's sad to be old and alone."[38]

REPRESENTATIVE SHORTER WORKS

Henry James' "The Pupil"

Based on the several intense relationships that James had with younger men as revealed in Leon Edel's biography, *The Life of*

Henry James, one might expect to find any number of homoerotic allusions in the works of the master. Graduate students in English have no doubt written many term papers on the strange relationships in *The Turn of the Screw,* but James' ambiguity has kept the novella from being highly regarded or even well known among gay readers. The one story that has been anthologized with other gay works is "The Pupil," written in 1890 and first published in a British magazine in 1891. If anyone could be circumambient in defining interpersonal relations, it was James, and the feelings between Pemberton, the tutor, and Morgan Moreen, the pupil, are certainly sketched in terms of love more than lust. The story revolves around the question of whether the precocious Morgan will leave his down-at-the-heel American family and go off to live with Pemberton. At the end of the story, Mrs. Moreen says her fifteen-year-old son may indeed leave; Pemberton wavers momentarily, and the sense of being abandoned by both for these seconds proves to be too much for the weak heart of Morgan, who promptly dies. Just as Fuller was able to evade the sticky problem of having to define the male relationship that would have resulted from Bertram living with Randolph, James sidesteps this delicate situation by never allowing a union to take place. "The Pupil" was the first of James' stories to be rejected by the *Atlantic Monthly,* but Edel does not think it was necessarily rejected because of the hint of homosexuality. "Friendship and affection between tutors and their charges were regarded as normal in the Victorian age," he says. "A more plausible theory is that the prosaic Scudder (*Atlantic* editor) was worried that the *Atlantic*'s readers would resent a story about an American family which jumped its hotel bills. . . ."[39]

Two Stories by Willa Cather

At first glance it appears that "Paul's Case" and "The Sculptor's Funeral" (both 1905) have no connection with overt homosexuality, but on closer reading both stories provide an unflinching look at the stifling conditions that sent sensitive young men from the smaller towns and cities of mid-America into the havens of the big cities at the turn of the century. While not all of these young men were gay, some of them undoubtedly were, and Cather has shown with photographic realism the drab ugliness that must have been beyond endurance for the homosexual adolescents who were unlucky enough to have been born and raised in a provincial environment.[40] Although there is a hint of the shame that Harvey Merrick had to "hide in his heart from his very boyhood," the main point of "The Sculptor's Funeral" is that Harvey was, for whatever reason, different from everyone else as he grew up on a Kansas farm. When the coffin is brought back from the East to be placed in the parlor adorned with "a Rogers group of John Alden and Priscilla, wreathed with smilax," the mourners crack sly small-town jokes and mutter such comments as "Harve never could have handled stock none." The comment from the crying father is thematic: "He was ez gentle ez a child and the kindest of 'em all—only we didn't none of us ever onderstand him."[41] In "Paul's Case," the young high school dropout escapes from Cordelia Street in Pittsburgh, but the effect on Paul is as deadly as that which Sand City, Kansas, must have had on Harvey Merrick. Paul loathed going home from the glamour and excitement of Carnegie Hall, where he was an usher, to Cordelia Street:

> . . . his father in his nightclothes at the top of the stairs, explanations that did not explain, hastily improvised fictions that were forever tripping him up, his upstairs room and its horrible yellow wall-paper, the creaking bureau with the greasy plush collar-box, and over his painted wooden bed the pictures of George Washington and John Calvin, and the framed motto, "Feed My Lambs." . . . The moment he turned into Cordelia Street he felt the waters close above his head. After each of these orgies of living, he experienced all the physical depression which follows a debauch; the loathing of respectable beds, of common food, of a household permeated by kitchen odors . . . a morbid desire for cool things and soft lights and fresh flowers.[42]

Cather explains that "because, in Paul's world, the natural always wore the guise of ugliness . . . a certain element of artificiality seemed to him necessary in beauty," and this incisive comment helps to explain Paul's absconding with some money to spend a few precious days in New York City, where he buys new silk underwear, orders violets and jonquils for his room at the Waldorf, drinks champagne in the dining room and goes out on the town with a "wild San Francisco boy, a freshman at Yale." At the end of the story Paul, who wore a defiant red carnation when called to account for himself before a meeting of the high school faculty, decides that rather than return to the overwhelming dreariness of Cordelia Street, he will throw himself in front of a train.

Sherwood Anderson's "Hands"

While technically a part of *Winesburg, Ohio* (1919), the story of Wing Biddlebaum in "Hands" is complete in itself and has appeared in gay anthologies. In a few pages, Anderson is able to convey the cruelty of small-town Americans toward a suspected homosexual and the sharp loneliness and helplessness of someone who must constantly be on guard against reaching out and touching another human being. The significance of the title is that when Biddlebaum was a teacher in Pennsylvania, he taught—and occasionally touched—his pupils with his expressive hands. When a half-witted pupil began imagining aloud "unspeakable things," a shiver went through the villagers as "hidden, shadowy doubts that had been in men's minds . . . were galvanized into beliefs," and Biddlebaum was run out of town.

With lanterns in their hands a dozen men came to the door of the house where he lived alone and commanded that he dress and come forth. It was raining and one of the men had a rope in his hands. They had intended to hang the schoolmaster, but something in his figure, so small, white, and pitiful, touched their hearts and they let him escape. As he ran away into the darkness they repented of their weakness and ran after him, swearing and throwing sticks and great balls of soft mud at the figure that screamed and ran faster and faster into the darkness.[43]

What Wing likes to describe for George Willard, the young newspaper reporter who is the continuing character throughout the novel, is a kind of "pastoral golden age" when clean-limbed young men come across a green open country to listen to an old man talk.

When his hands touch George's shoulder, however, Wing is horrified and rushes off to his little house, where he fixes himself some bread and honey and goes to bed.

The vision of Wing Biddlebaum being hounded out of town at night by his indignant Christian neighbors marks an appropriate end for this section. For those writers who were daring enough to allude to the existence of the gay man in this country, the patterns of alienation, furtiveness, flight, and death were used to spell out the plight of outcasts otherwise unmentionable in fiction. Most of the glimpses of unambiguous joy—Stoddard's American embracing a young native or Stevenson's Oswald being kissed by the love-starved Hungarian officer—are, significantly enough, set elsewhere. The more characteristic gay fiction, which comes closer to the tone of the biographies in Ellis and of Lind, presents characters being overwhelmed by their awareness of depravity, their insistent desire to escape from their loneliness by reaching out and touching another man, their fear of both the God who destroyed Sodom and Gomorrah and the Middle-American vigilantes who regard themselves as the self-anointed deputies of this God. By 1920, the United States seemed ready to recognize and even welcome all sorts of new postwar ideas and theories and approaches in literature, but the line had to be drawn somewhere even during the twenties, and when that line was drawn, what remained forbidden was the freedom of American homosexuals to write and publish candid novels about themselves.

THE TWENTIES

American literary historians devote separate chapters or books to the 1920s because this decade was, as Carl Van Doren has noted, "the liveliest in the history of American fiction."[44] Not only were our modern giants emerging in mainstream literature, but some of our minority writers were also gaining national recognition: the twenties witnessed the "Harlem Renaissance" and an increasingly rich and diverse body of Jewish fiction. The devil-may-care amorality now associated with the "Roaring Twenties" would lead one to expect that this decade would have triggered a burst of homosexual fiction in the United States, but it did not. American sophisticates knew all about Freud, and some of them were even reading Marcel Proust,[45] André Gide, Ronald Firbank, D. H. Lawrence, T. E. Lawrence, Virginia Woolf, Compton MacKenzie, and Radclyffe Hall with varying degrees of appreciation. But a middle class that was voting the straight Republican ticket and conferring best-seller stardom on Mary Roberts Rinehart and Gene Stratton Porter was not quite ready for an American counterpart to *The Well of Loneliness*. Even at the Algonquin Round Table, it was "smart" to affect a wisecracking rather than sympathetic attitude toward the subject, and this is the sort of thing our leading wits used to titter about:

> There are so many featherbeds
> So many little maidenheads
> There's practically no excuse
> For sodomy or self-abuse.[46]

In short, the American mentality was so wised-up that the camouflaged approach of *Joseph and His Friend* and *South-Sea Idyls* would no longer work, but at the same time it remained so homophobic that *The Well of Loneliness* was judged to be obscene.

As a result, gay writers of the twenties had to remain officially in the closet and still had to play some sort of game if they wanted to be published. We now know, for instance, that the poet Hart Crane was gay—John Unterecker's recent biography includes touching letters about his cruising Cleveland parks at night in 1923—but *The Bridge* had to be written from an ostensibly non-gay point of view. It is also apparent from Jonathan Root's biography of Richard Halliburton that this dashing author of best-selling travel books was gay—he had a special fondness for YMCAs, spent the night with Rod La Rocque, went flying with Ramon Navarro, and settled down with another bachelor in Laguna Beach. But in *The Royal Road to Romance* (1925) and *New Worlds to Conquer* (1929), Halliburton was obliged to weave in pretty "Kashmiri maidens, Parisian ballerinas, Castillian countesses . . . thus adding," as Allen Churchill has noted, "a soupçon of sex to his rhapsodic prose."[47]

And in the little relevant fiction published during the decade, games had to be played as well. Carl Van Vechten hid behind the pose of urbane wickedness, Robert McAlmon pretended to be "just visiting," and even the heterosexual Waldo Frank seems to have been playing—and losing—some type of unrecognizable game in his strange novel of 1920, *The Dark Mother*.

THE DARK MOTHER:
VEILED VILLAIN AS A BIG BROTHER

Waldo Frank, now a generally forgotten man of American letters, went to Yale and to Europe, fell under the influence of Freud, Marx, and Spinoza, had three wives and five children, and wrote such other books as *Down in Russia* (1932), *The Jew in Our Day* (1944) and *Cuba: Prophetic Island* (1961). *The Dark Mother*, which was completed after Frank had some mystical experiences, is the story of young David Markand's struggle to become a Person by relying on some never clearly defined mystical vision. The gay angle in this novel of the McKinley era is provided by Thomas Rennard, who first meets David while vacationing near the upstate New York village where the boy lives with his widowed mother.

The early scenes are Horatio Algerish in their simplicity, and if there is any sex at all between Thomas and David (which, given the tone of the novel, seems improbable) it occurs in the idyllic evening darkness at the very outset. In one scene David is out of doors, remembering "last night" and "brief strained words within the trees," and then, putting a strand of grass into his mouth, he watches as Thomas comes toward him. Thomas introduces himself, says he comes from New York City, and asks if David is going there.

"Yes." David wanted to say: "How did you know?"

"We hadn't much to say—last night—to each other, did we?" Thomas Rennard laughed. They looked at each other.[48]

After this odd scene, the rest of the novel is all downhill as far as intimacy between David and Thomas goes. After David's mother dies, the boy does go to the city to seek his fortune, and after staying awhile with his rich uncle's family, he shares bachelor's hall with Thomas, apparently as merely a roommate. The other main character in the novel is Tom's sculptress sister Cornelia, who, suspicious of her brother's interest in David, warns Tom not to corrupt the boy. The novel ends with Cornelia jumping out of a window and David leaving Tom to go to bed with a girl.

In his book on Waldo Frank, Paul Carter made this criticism of *The Dark Mother:* "The reader . . . who has been led to expect a definite resolution of the problems posed by the conflict between Tom and David is left unsatisfied by the ending of the novel, which by its irresoluteness reduces the psychological conflict to the level of a case study."[49] A definite resolution seems impossible if no definite basis for conflict has been established, and throughout the novel Frank shies away from giving any clear-cut evidence that Thomas is indeed a practicing homosexual or that David is a latent bisexual. Nonetheless, there are enough veiled hints to enable Stark Young to claim in his review in the *New Republic:* ". . . one thing Mr. Frank does do: he brings home to us anew in this book the very valuable reminder that there are vast areas of life that our literature has not yet known how to include."[50]

CARL VAN VECHTEN AS GAY NOVELIST

In addition to homophobia, there is another reason why the serious, anguished novel depicting a gay character as the victim of society was not written and published here during the twenties. Very simply, the prevailing spirit of the decade called for having as much fun as everyone else rather than engaging in social criticism and protest. This philosophy is summed up by Frederick Hoffman in his literary study, *The Twenties:*

It is of the utmost importance to be amusing . . . the worst sin is to be serious, which is the equivalent of being stupid. . . . If you would stay alive and continue living graciously, avoid Theodore Dreiser like the plague. If you cannot be witty yourself, at least appreciate the wit of others. The worst enemies of society are those who try to reform it or who too soberly and pessimistically make literature out of its obvious but amusing inequities.[51]

While Hoffman is specifically describing the spirit of the Van Vechten novels, the attitude he describes is characteristic of much of the more popular fiction of the decade. Van Vechten managed to write gay novels that were rather "gay": in one sense of the word, they were spirited, irreverent and bubbly, and in the other they were the closest thing to homosexual fiction that was published here during the twenties.

Although Van Vechten married twice and died (in 1964) before it was permissible to come out, it would seem that a man who knew the key to *Bertram Cope's Year,* thought Freud dull, was a pal of Gertrude and Alice, dressed up for parties like a berserk dowager Chinese empress, got lavender letters from Ronald Firbank, judged drag balls at the Rockland Palace Casino, served as a fleshpot guide for Somerset Maugham, became a fan of Jean Genêt and James Purdy, and had a large collection of self-taken photographs of male nudes must surely have been capable of the bisexual response. In fact, his great interest in and correspondence with servicemen (for three years during World War II, he never missed a night of duty as captain of the Stage Door Canteen) seem to have been prompted by feelings that went beyond those of simple patriotism, and an examination of his novels will reveal instances when Van Vechten was quite clearly winking at the closeted gay reader of the 1920s.

One night when the teen-aged Carl was sitting on the front porch of the other free spirit in Cedar Rapids, Iowa, Mrs. Mahala Dutton Benedict Douglas, he announced, "I'm so damned bored with this town. I'd like to put on a bath towel and run through the streets naked."[52] In a sense, running through the streets naked to shock that Middle West mentality is what Van Vechten did in the novels written in New York during the twenties—although in every novel there was some sort of literary bath towel to hide the more private parts. In *Peter Whiffle* (1922), a slightly veiled autobiographical roman à clef, there are decadent overtones that recall Huysmans' *A Rebours* and Wilde's *The Picture of Dorian Gray,* although Van

Vechten's treatment of diabolic perversity is more satiric than serious. In *The Tattooed Countess* (1924) the author characterizes the stultifying Midwestern town of Maple Valley as "inverted," as a place where people worried about surfaces but bore hidden scars and where they had love affairs behind closed doors and made clothes for the orphans out in the open. The only thing for sensitive young Gareth Johns to do is leave the town, and as he does so, gum-chewing Mrs. Bierbauer says from her front-porch rocking chair, "Good riddance to bad rubbidge." In *Firecrackers* (1925), set in Manhattan, a good-looking young acrobat-florist, Gunnar O'Grady, is told by an older, worldlier, sexually sophisticated character:

> I believe . . . that we are born what we are, some one way, some another, that we cannot change, no matter how hard we strive to. All we can do, with whatever amount of effort, is to drag an unsuspected quality out of its hiding place in the unconscious. If it is there, *in us,* it can neither be virtue nor vice. It can only be ourselves.[53]

Although there are subtly secretive gay overtones in *Nigger Heaven* and *Spider Boy,* probably the most homosexual of Van Vechten's novels is *The Blind Bow-Boy* (1923). The title of the novel indicates its theme (the allusion is to Cupid) of the irrationality of love, and a plot summary would lead one to expect a bona fide gay novel: Harold Prewitt is raised by female relatives in a small town, is called a sissy by neighborhood roughs, goes to New York in search of love, finds women and marriage unsatisfactory, and ends by going off to Europe with another man who is known by everyone to be gay.

What distinguishes *The Blind Bow-Boy* from the novels Carson McCullers was to write on the same theme is its frothy tone: as he was writing this novel, Van Vechten told a friend, "My formula at present consists in treating extremely serious themes as frivolously as possible." Thus, for instance, the gay man who lures Harold off to Europe is the notoriously promiscuous Duke of Middlebottom, who affects sailor uniforms and whose stationery is imprinted with "A thing of beauty is a boy forever." When someone suggests that the Duke invite his friends to be in the audience for his all-nude original summer opera, *L'Apres-midi Byzantine,* he quips, "I have

no friends, only people that amuse me, and people I sleep with . . .
the people that amuse me are all in the play . . . the theatre isn't
big enough to hold the others." Another campy character in this
novel is the grand dame Campaspe Lorillard, who appears in several
other works almost like Van Vechten in drag. Campaspe finds
Waldo Frank's *The Dark Mother* unreadable and feels that his
taking everything so seriously reduces him to the level of Gene
Stratton Porter.

Since *The Blind Bow-Boy* was written in a sense of high-spirited
fun and since the Duke was satirized rather than being presented
as was the marriage-breaking villain in *A Marriage Below Zero,* few
critics were shocked by the novel and most felt it was more
naughty than nasty. Ernest Boyd compared Van Vechten with
Beardsley, Burton Rascoe thought the novel "roguish," and Edmund Wilson called it "iridescent." While Heywood Broun earnestly
praised Van Vechten for propagandizing "for all those brave beings
who seek, in spite of tyranny, to follow their own inclinations," a
more whimsical note was sounded by Ronald Firbank, who wrote
the author to tell him how wonderful it was "to have attracted
another butterfly like myself." After this novel came out, Henry
Blake Fuller wrote to say he felt quite left behind by Van Vechten's
headlong dash into the world of forbidden delights. "Each of your
books is like a nail on my coffin," Fuller wrote. "After so much
youth, spirit, invention, I find myself intoning a Whitmanian Miser-
ere: 'Goodbye, My Fancy.' "[54]

The other Van Vechten book of special relevance is *Excavations,
a Book of Advocacies,* which was published in 1926 to "provoke
the reader to share my own enthusiasm for certain . . . more or less
obscure figures in the literary and musical world." Among the
writers were the almost forgotten Edgar Saltus, an American friend
of Oscar Wilde whose works were more purple than lavender and,
of course, Firbank: "Ronald in Lesbosland . . . Sacher-Masoch
in Mayfair . . . The Oxford tradition with steam from the Paris
bains de vapeur . . ."[55] Of particular interest is what Van Vechten
has to say about *Bertram Cope's Year.* After quoting George Moore
in praise of "the abnormal" in Balzac (". . . the final achievement of
genius is the introduction and artistic use of the abnormal"), Van

Vechten devotes a paragraph to the Fuller novel. Aside from *The Turn of the Screw,* he says, "I cannot recall a single English or American novel of the first rank that deals with [homosexuality] save in a perfunctory or passing way," and he goes on to characterize Fuller's treatment of the theme as "skillful" and "studiedly restrained." He adds that to "one who had no key to its meaning," *Bertram Cope's Year* "would probably prove unreadable," but he explains that any more forthright treatment would result in suppression of both book and author.[56]

In the final analysis, Carl Van Vechten's giddy "fun" approach to his novels and private life during the twenties might be viewed as a compensatory mask to hide the darker sufferings encountered when one fails to fit into an alien world. One biographer has insisted that, whatever Van Vechten's life may have been, it was not a tragedy.[57] This may well be, but the point here is that the camp game-playing of fifty years ago was not a very convincing denial of tragedy; rather, it was a valiant but brittle attempt to make everyone think that being a homosexual was really loads of fun. Dorothy Parker once said that during the twenties Manhattanites felt that they *had* to be smarty, and the smartiness of Van Vechten's novels, which seemed to grow more forced as the decade wore on, may well have been motivated by the author's desire to deny the fear that he might after all have much in common with the wistful Henry Blake Fuller. In a letter to Mabel Dodge Luhan, Van Vechten pointed out that it was the image of a lonely man rather than sex which was central to his novels: "I don't think I ever think of sex at all. It plays around here and there, but that's not what my books are about. They seem to me to be books about a man who is alone in the world and is very sad."[58]

THE "UN-GAY" BOHEMIANS OF NEW YORK AND EUROPE

In 1930 Carl Van Vechten was living grandly amid Victorian elegance on West Fifty-fifth Street, with candle sconces on the walls, figurines on the piano, and calla lilies on the table. At the same time, downtown in Greenwich Village, there were surely many relatively creative and talented gay people living a more bohemian existence, but they have been generally ignored by our chroniclers of the Village. (About the only relevant comment that Albert Parry has in *Garrets and Pretenders, a History of Bohemianism in America* is that during the twenties "lesbian harems were open to the knowing" and "lady-like men were at the service of other secret sinners.")[59] Whatever candid gay literature was written and perhaps even privately published in the Village during this time is generally out of circulation today, as are many of those creative gay people who left this country during the twenties to take up residence in Europe.

Even in Europe, though—or perhaps especially in Europe—the spirit of the times was not conducive to the serious novel of social protest, even from some gay people who must surely have had cause to be bitter. As Kay Boyle remembers the twenties, most of the gay writers she knew formed an almost immune elite and were able to live their lives free of police harassment and arrest in Manhattan as well as in France. And straight writers, Miss Boyle adds, felt no need to write novels pleading for understanding of and sympathy for homosexuals. "We had no feeling it was necessary," she has said. "They were accepted in our circle and were accepted everywhere. We just accepted them without having to champion them."[60] One of Miss Boyle's close friends, Robert McAlmon, did write fiction about gay people in Europe during the twenties, but he usually struck a tone that revealed more dismay than acceptance and certainly more detachment than identification.

ROBERT McALMON AND THE
HOMOSEXUALLY-HELPLESSLY "LOST"

Born in Clifton, Kansas, McAlmon was a model for painters and sculptors in New York before he married a rich British lesbian, Bryher, who was more interested in Hilda Doolittle than in him. He received enough money from the divorce settlement to establish Contacts Edition Press in Paris, where he published Hemingway, Stein, William Carlos Williams and his own work. The precise basis for McAlmon's interest and involvement in the gay millieu does not emerge from the reminiscences of people who knew him at this time. In *That Summer in Paris,* Morley Callahan comments: ". . . it had been a very nice thing for him to marry a rich girl and get a handsome divorce settlement, but I had always believed his story that he hadn't been aware it was to be a marriage in name only; he had insisted he was willing to be interested in women."[61] Kay Boyle remembers him as a desperate, lonely man who, although always intrigued by the theatrical and bizarre, "was certainly not interested for a moment in the homosexuals who went to see Gertrude Stein."[62] McAlmon's own comments on *Distinguished Air,* the collection of his gay stories which he subtitled *Grim Fairy Tales,* suggests a definite personal remove from the homosexual world that characterizes the point of view in the stories themselves. McAlmon insists that he is presenting "variant types with complete objectivity, not intent on their 'souls,' and not distressed by their 'morals.' "[63]

While none of the expatriates was interested in the soul of anyone else during the twenties, the tone of both "Distinguished Air" and "Miss Knight" does indeed reveal some authorial distress at the morals of the gay set in Europe, and what McAlmon called "complete objectivity" seems today more like a peculiar double-standardized homophobia as he portrays the various lost characters. In fact, McAlmon's attitude toward fags is very similar to the he-man disdain of Jake Barnes in Hemingway's 1925 novel, *The Sun Also Rises:* "I was very angry. Somehow they always made me angry. I know they are supposed to be amusing, and you should be tolerant, but I wanted to swing on one, any one, anything to shatter that superior, simpering composure."[64]

In the more positive of the two stories, "Miss Knight," McAlmon focuses on Charlie Knight, a thirty-year-old cocaine-sniffing drag queen from Illinois who camps it up in a "Berlin bitchery that many travellers slummed in through the two years after the great war." Miss Knight says:

I was talkin' to a guy—one of these here highbrows, you get me, just scientifically interested and all that, you know—and he sez to me, "did you get queer in the army?" and I sez to him, "my god Mary, I've been queer since before you wore diddies." I wuz on to that guy too; trying to pass off as a real man. He's one of them kind that tell you they're real men until they get into bed with you, and then they sez, "Oh dearie, I forgot, I'm queer." Whoops, dearie! What us bitches will do when we draw the veil. Just lift up our skirts and scream. . . .[65]

During the story Miss Knight calls everybody "Mary," says "Whoops, my dear!" rather often, falls for a beautiful blond policeman who is "real rough trade" (a "war-made queer one"), serves Thanksgiving dinner in drag, recalls being arrested in the Portland, Oregon, YMCA, almost loses her policeman to a lesbian at a drag ball, and finally becomes depressed and disappears. While some people suspect suicide, Kate Matthews, his lesbian friend, believes otherwise. "No sir, believe me," she says, "you can trust the bitches to take care of themselves. He's probably alive and eating better than any of us by now. Luck changes quick for them." Six weeks later, Kate gets a letter from Miss Knight, postmarked New York, which contains a payment of a loan and a promise to return to Paris on February 1, 1922. The story ends with Kate commenting: "That one! If she was run over by a truck or a steam roller, she'd turn up, about to appear in Paris, or London, or Madrid, or Singapore. She's just that international."

With the presence of the apparently straight McAlmon persona in "Distinguished Air," the attitude toward gay people switches from a grudging admiration of their pluckiness to an implicit indictment of their comparatively silly, empty, desperate lives. The setting is the same—Berlin in the early twenties—and the narrator is a restless American who is invigorated by a brilliant, crisp autumn day. The first gay person who comes along the street is chichi Foster Graham, who once *had* a distinguished air, and Foster begins camping, hands on hips, cruising the passing men. The narrator cheerfully suggests that Foster might get picked up—but by a policeman, to which Foster replies: "Tut, tut, this isn't New York. It's a shame for me to make an effort to get off with anybody here, because they're all on their heels to start things themselves." The other gay American the narrator bumps into is Carrol Timmons, who has an "elderly auntlike visage" and who thinks Foster is a "tiresome boy."

That night the narrator comes across cartoonist Rudge Kepler and his pretty English girlfriend Goldie, who want to have a night on the town and see some "swell places." So with the perfectly legitimate rationale of slumming, the three go to a queer bar to see the outlandish sights, which eventually include Foster Graham and Carrol Timmons.

During the evening at the Palast, Kepler gets drunk and dances good-naturedly with Foster, Goldie goes back to the hotel, and the All-American "Western soul" of the narrator begins to rebel at the sordidness of the scene. He notices "Foster getting increasingly maudlin with a soldier, and Carrol Timmons, down the room . . . being sloppily affectionate with the boy at his side." With a line out of Hemingway, the narrator says to Kepler, "Hell, let's get out of here." From the Palast, the two men go to a straight dance hall, where the people look more "sensible," and leave at 4 A.M. to go elsewhere to dance, where the narrator becomes headachy, light-headed, and drunk on cognac. By 8 A.M. they join up with a raffish crowd to go to the O-la-la for more dancing and breakfast, and the bleary-eyed narrator has to go to the water closet to vomit. At the end of the story, on "the tide of a hangover gloom," Kepler and the narrator agree to have "no more nights like this—at least until the next time. It was really too depressing to see so much of a kind of life that one had not consciously helped to cause, and could not do much to alter."

The double standard that operates especially in "Distinguished Air" allows McAlmon to view straight and gay members of the Lost Generation in different terms. A close textual reading of "Distinguished Air" gives no clues that McAlmon wrote it with conscious irony to suggest that the narrator and Kepler are, after all, as lost as Graham and Timmons. Although one could argue that the sight of a heterosexual vomiting at 8 A.M. is as disquieting as the sight of a gay man getting sloppily affectionate, McAlmon insists on the implicit equation that heteros are only temporarily/deliberately "lost" while the homos are permanently/helplessly lost. Becoming a member of the jaded "lost generation" was an evening game to be played by "normal" thrill-seekers who wanted to go slumming, but McAlmon's homosexuals are not just visiting the Palast—they actually *belong* there in that grim outpost of decadence and depravity, and they can never aspire to qualify as the "good sort" who go to the straight dance halls. To a certain extent, then, the Midwestern mentality that Van Vechten mocked in his New York novels tinged McAlmon's views toward the Sodom and Gomorrah of the Berlin bitcheries. In Van Vechten's novels, both gay and straight characters "find" themselves in New York, while Mc-Almon implies that the gay characters are irretrievably lost even before coming to Berlin, and wherever they go they will remain lost. In his *Grim Fairy Tales,* much of the grimness was provided by McAlmon himself.

Other Works, Published or Not

The gamut of other relevant fiction written during the twenties runs from comparatively respectable novels with exaggerated or veiled homosexuals, to privately printed novels, to works that were never published at all.

An example of the first category is Charles Brackett's 1929 *American Colony,* which is set on the French Riviera. Sydney, stifled by the "curiosity and malice and crowding intimacy" of gay life in Paris, comes to stay with some straight friends, who are the major characters. Although Sydney is allowed an experience (with "some French sailor or local gangster, probably," his host guesses) that makes him "believe in the existence of a personal god,"[66] he doesn't fit in very well, and the novel ends with his host resolving to kick the "goddamned pervert" out of the villa the next morning. (Of incidental interest is the fact that although the novel is dedicated to Alexander Woollcott, Brackett caricatures him as a boring raconteur who makes a cameo appearance at a cocktail party.) Veiled homosexuality is to be found in Clarkson Crane's 1925 *The Western Shore,* in which a Berkeley English instructor becomes fond of young men.[67]

An example of a privately printed novel (750 copies, J. A. Norcross, 1928) is the anonymously written *The Strange Confession of Monsieur Mountcairn,* which is so badly written that it may have been the inferior quality as much as the subject matter that prevented it from being commercially published.[68] The French-sounding title was apparently designed to suggest the wicked and forbidden rather than to indicate the locale, as the story takes place in an American city and concerns the unhappy love affairs of "Win" Baldwin. Win's problem is that all he wants to do in bed is kiss and hug; he is shocked when his friend Paul suggests further experimentation. In one chapter there is a dream of Gabriel conducting a "celestial museum" tour where the female body is compared with a cottage and the male with a castle. The novel ends with Win wondering why he is crucified by his own heart, but he is comforted to think, after considering the "miserable overcrowding" of China and India, that homosexuality is perhaps Nature telling us, "It is my way."

The sort of fiction that was neither published nor publishable is typified by a curious typewritten manuscript, "Boys, Men, and Love," by "J. P. Starr," dated 1925, and donated by Manuel boyFrank to the One, Inc. library in Los Angeles some twenty years ago.[69] This 600-page work includes some semi-erotic short stories in the form of personal narratives, all with Western rural settings and with such titles as "Lessons Learned in a Barn" and "Cowboys and French Horns." Interspersed among the stories are nonfiction guides to gay courting. "Going on the Prowl" starts with "Finding a doric without help is for the inexperienced man hazardous and wasteful of time," and the first sentence of "Manly Congress in the Nest" reads: "When you get your captive into a threatless lair, start fondling him, equivocally at first if you be still doubtful, but more freely as you sense approbation." The story behind "Boys, Men, and Love" is as fascinating as the work itself; boyFrank, who is now writing a novel of his 1909 cowboy days with an emphasis on "pairing off," says that the manuscript resulted from a sharing of true confessions among soldiers stationed at Rockwell Field in San Diego during World War I. Since he could take shorthand, boyFrank was asked to preserve these narratives, which stemmed from a bull session on personal hygiene. He lugged his notes all over Europe during the war, he says, and finally retyped everything during the twenties. Although boyFrank claims to be only the compiler and not the author of any of the pieces, the style of at least the nonfiction guides is very close to that which characterizes boyFrank's own in his letterwriting today.

Since the homosexual novel as we have come to know it did not emerge here until the 1930s, it is difficult to point to any sort of pattern or trend that characterized the few gay works that managed to get published during the twenties. However, in comparing the novels of the twenties with what came before and what followed, one adjective that might be applied equally to the works of Van Vechten and McAlmon is "outlandish."

The xenophobic view of homosexuality as being outlandish in the sense of foreign was neither new nor uniquely American. As far back as the Middle Ages, semantic confusion among churchmen resulted in the indictment of Bulgarians as sodomists, and during the nineteenth century the Love That Dared Not Speak Its Name was often referred to as a euphemism bearing a foreign accent. For centuries the British liked to think that homosexuality was a product of Italy and arrived in England via France, while during the nineteenth century the Italians referred to it as *"il vizio Inglese"* and the French blamed the Arabs or, depending on political winds or the latest scandal, liked to think of it in terms of *"le vice anglais"* or *"le vice allemand."*[70] In nineteenth-century America, it was almost unthinkable to regard Sodom and Gomorrah in homegrown terms, and, as has been pointed out, the most plausible settings for sketches of homoeroticism were those of faraway, exotic foreign lands. Using this connotation of "outlandish," one can cite examples from both Van Vechten and McAlmon. Van Vechten's most blatant homosexual is the Duke of Middlebottom, who brings the recognizably British brand of Oscar Wilde wickedness with him across the Atlantic, and there is in McAlmon a hint that Illinois-born "bitches" really don't belong in America so much as they do to an international set that is more comfortably at home in the relative decadence of Berlin or Paris or London.

More important, both Van Vechten and McAlmon felt obliged

to portray their gay men as outlandish in the sense of being bizarre, flamboyant, and fey. Their neurotic birds of paradise, the Duke of Middlebottom and Miss Knight, cannot be regarded as representative of the average gay person living in America, and for a more accurate glimpse of what it was like to be gay in this country during the twenties, we must rely on bits of information now surfacing in such books as Unterecker's *Voyager.*[71] There is more truth about what it meant to be gay packed into one of Hart Crane's letters about the "kindness" of a twenty-year-old Bohemian athlete in a Cleveland park than can be found in all the fiction published during the decade, and this more accurate picture of gay life became characteristic of at least some of the novels written and published here during the 1930s.

NOTES

1. Ray Lewis White, *Gore Vidal* (New York: Twayne, 1968), p. 139. As this manuscript was in the final stages of editing, news was received that a Parisian publisher, Flammarion, had just brought out *Comme Un Frère, Comme Un Amant: L'homosexualité masculine dans le roman et le théâtre americains de Herman Melville à James Baldwin* by Dr. Georges-Michel Sarotte, a professor at the University of Paris. Given the combination of xenophobia-homophobia that has characterized our attitude toward gay literature, it is entirely appropriate that the first person to recognize in print what Americans have always preferred not to recognize is a foreigner.

2. Louie Crew and Rictor Norton, "The Homophobic Imagination," *College English* (November 1974), p. 274.

3. Jeannette Foster, *Sex Variant Women in Literature* (New York: Vantage, 1956), p. 15.

4. Ian Young, *The Male Homosexual in Literature: A Bibliography* (Metuchen, N.J.: Scarecrow Press, 1975), p. vii.

5. Hammond discusses this case in *Sexual Impotence in the Male* (New York: Birmingham, 1883), p. 64 ff. Hammond also wrote about the "Mujerados" among the Pueblo Indians in New Mexico Territory in the *American Journal of Neurology and Psychiatry* for August 1882.

6. Havelock Ellis, *Studies in the Psychology of Sex* (New York: Random House, 1936). Ellis cites M.O., 186 ff., H.C., 173 ff., the teacher, 169 ff., and the virgin, 111 ff. H.C., who gave up medicine to "follow literature,"

describes an incident with the overblown style that might have characterized gay fiction had it been published here seventy years ago; "One evening, in Broadway, I conceived suddenly a full-fledged desire for a youth issuing from an hotel as I passed. Our glances met and dwelled together. At a shop window he first accosted me. He was an invert. With him, in his room at the hotel whence I had seen him emerge, I passed an apocalyptic night. Thereafter commerce with boys only in the spirit ceased to be an end; the images were carnalized, stepped from their frameworks into the street. That boy, that god out of the machine, I see him clearly . . . the dimples in his knees, the slenderness of his ankles, the softness of his little feet, with insteps pink like the inside of a shell. How I gloated over his ample roundness, his rich undulations!"

7. Alfred Herzog, introduction to *Autobiography of an Androgyne, The Medico-Legal Journal* (1918), p. viii. With this categorization, Herzog believes he is making the definitive "distinction between those in whom homosexual practices are a vice and in whom they are a misfortune."

8. *Ibid.*, p. 1. A typical escapade of Jennie June on the loose, from pp. 133-34:

> One evening at the close of about eighteen months of my avocation as a Fourteenth Street "street-walker," I was promenading up and down. Now and then some habitue of the district would recognize me, stop, and flirt for a few minutes. Finally I encountered a party of six adolescents. Four had never met me previously, yet all talked in a most free and unrestrained, as well as indecent manner. After a while, one proposed that I accompany him to his room.
> "I am afraid those other fellows will follow us and hurt me."
> "They are all friends of yours."
> "I am not so sure about that. You know some fellows hate a fairie, and some of those boys appear very heartless. You saw how rough they were to me right on the street! If they should try to hurt me, would you fight for me?"
> "Of course."
> "How could you alone fight against five fellows?"
> "Well, I would do the best I could, and depend on you to help me."
> "Don't think of depending on me. You know a girl can't fight. All a girl can do when fellows fight is to look on."
> "You could at least scream, couldn't you?"
> "Yes, I could scream."
> "Well, you do the screaming, and I'll do the fighting."
> A few minutes after we arrived in the young man's quarters in a furnished room house, the other five burst in. They proved to be as heartless a gang as I had ever met, although belonging to the prosperous class of society. Micturiverunt super meis vestibus atque me coegerunt facere rem mihi horribilissimam (balneum ani cum lingua), etc.

9. This questionnaire was pasted in between pages 258 and 259 at the end of an appendixed article in which Lind discusses "The Case of Oscar Wilde."

10. The quotes on this page come from Fiedler's analysis of this situation

in *Love and Death in the American Novel* (New York: Criterion Books, 1960), pp. 345-46. However much he tries in this book, Fiedler can "never shake off the nagging awareness that there is at the sentimental center of our novels . . . nothing but the love of males!" (p. 365) In a September 22, 1976, letter to the author, Fiedler concludes by saying he should not be thought of as having taken an "adversary position" toward gay literature in America, yet at the same time he clings to the insistence that it has not been "useful" to recognize the homosexual novel as a "special sub-category" of American fiction.

11. The following passage from *Teleny* will help explain why British readers might prefer to think that this sort of thing was going on in Paris rather than in London: "Another push, and half the phallus was in his body. I pulled it out half an inch, though it seemed to me a yard by the prolonged pleasure I felt. I pressed forward again, and the whole of it, down to its very root, was all swallowed up. Thus wedged, I vainly endeavored to drive it higher up—an impossible feat, and, clasped as I was, I felt it wriggling in its sheath like a baby in its mother's womb, giving myself and him an unutterable and delightful titillation. . . . Surely the rain-awakened flowers must be conscious of such a sensation during a shower, after they have been parched by the scorching rays of an estival sun."

12. The years immediately following 1900 were gloomy ones for many British gay writers because of the arrest and imprisonment of Oscar Wilde in the late 1890s. In 1906 Lytton Strachey was pessimistic when he wrote the following to John Maynard Keynes: "It's madness of us to dream of making dowagers understand that feelings are good, when we say in the same breath that the best ones are sodomitical. If we were crafty and careful, I dare say we'd pull it off. But why should we take the trouble? On the whole I believe that our time will come about a hundred years hence, when preparations will have been made, and compromises come to, so that, at the publication of our letters, everyone will be, finally, converted."

13. "Mayne" was really New Jersey–born Edward Stevenson, whose further views on early gay literature are discussed later in this chapter in conjunction with his novel *Imre*. Additional background information on the emergence of gay culture elsewhere can be found in two recently published books, James Steakley's *The Homosexual Emancipation Movement in Germany* (Arno Press) and John Lauritsen and David Thorstad's *The Early Homosexual Rights Movement* (Times Change Press).

14. While most readers may feel that going back to Cooper is stretching a point, authorities on the early American novel might argue that this section should instead begin with Charles Brockden Brown. It is conceded that a glance at Harry Warfel's biography of Brown is not unrewarding (there are letters to dear male friends alluding to his "self-loathing" and "depravity" and his hero in *Arthur Mervyn* is infinitely obliging to older men), and it could be that a separate study of our minor novelists from the period 1750–1850 is warranted.

15. In *Love and Death in the American Novel,* Fiedler terms this surprise ending a "last minute" loss of nerve in what should have otherwise been a homoerotic novel. Regarding loss of nerve, it might be noted that throughout his book Fiedler perversely argues that the truly unacknowledged minority influence in American literature is not homosexual but rather that of those "dusky, non-Aryan" members of the tribe of Israel who wander in and out of our novels so disguised that only he is able to recognize them.

16. Walt Whitman, *Franklin Evans; or The Inebriate* reprinted as a part of *The Collected Writings of Walt Whitman: The Early Poems and the Fiction* (New York: New York University Press, 1963), p. 180. The other quote is from p. 156. For an extremely naïve sketch of Whitman and the "frolicsome lads" at Pfaff's, see Albert Parry's *Garrets and Pretenders.*

17. Bayard Taylor, *Joseph and His Friend* (New York: G. P. Putnam and Sons, 1870), pp. 23 ff., 51. Other quotes are from pp. 90-91, 112, 216-17.

18. Franklin Walker, *San Francisco's Literary Frontier* (Seattle: University of Washington, 1970), p. 273. Buried in a footnote in the back of this book (p. 390), is Walker's somewhat more forthright statement that, based on his reading of Stoddard's diaries, there is the "most compelling evidence" that Stoddard had an "epicene nature."

19. The "safety of farce" to disguise intense emotional attachment of two males was exactly the ploy that Melville used, according to his recent biographer, Edwin Haviland Miller. Miller cites a passage from *Omoo* in which a "retrograde lover" falls out of love with the narrator and in love with a "smart" sailor who has just stepped ashore flush from a lucky whaling cruise, and the nineteenth-century reader was supposed to smile at the thought that it was only the sailor's money that interested Kooloo. Stoddard possibly adapted his strategy from Melville.

20. Charles Warren Stoddard, *South-Sea Idyls* (Boston: James R. Osgood and Company, 1873), pp. 32-33. Edward "Xavier Mayne" Stevenson commented in 1908 that "in a book so light-heartedly fantastic it is difficult to say where the personal and absolutely reminiscent are to be understood," and the book appears to fall into that twilight zone between nonfiction and wish-fulfillment fiction. Other Stoddard extracts come from pp. 308-9, 322-23 of *South-Sea Idyls;* p. 39 of *For the Pleasure of His Company;* and p. 276 of *The Island of Tranquil Delights.*

21. This information about "Dale" is given in Noel I. Garde's *"A Marriage Below Zero:* The Very First One?" in the July 1958 issue of *Mattachine Review,* p. 23. For a further discussion of *A Marriage Below Zero* and an overview of underground life in America during the nineteenth century, see Vern Bullough's *Sexual Variance in Society and History* (New York: John Wiley and Sons, 1976), chapters 18-20.

22. One such critic has already emerged: Robert Martin of Montreal, who gave a paper on Melville and Hawthorne at the annual MLA meeting in San Francisco in 1975 and who has written a gay response to Miller's biography in the *Nation* (February 14, 1976). Martin's paper concluded by noting that

all of the white men in *Billy Budd* were prevented from saying "I love you" to each other, something that Melville could put in the mouth of only "poor, ignorant Queequeg, who did not know any better." In his *Nation* review, Martin criticizes Miller for his blinding fidelity to orthodox Freudianism, which denigrates homoeroticism to the level of adolescent experimentation.

23. "Couldn't find him," Lawrence adds in *Studies in Classic American Literature* (New York: Viking, 1971), p. 142.

24. Edwin Miller, *Melville* (New York: Braziller, 1975), p. 358.

25. For a further discussion of *Billy Budd* as it embodies the motif of the military villain and victim, see the author's article, "But for Fate and Ban" in the November 1974 issue of *College English*, pp. 352-59.

26. John Berryman, *Stephen Crane* (New York: William Sloane Associates, 1950), p. 86.

27. Information on Stevenson's background and early works is found in Noel I. Garde's "The Mysterious Father of American Homophile Literature" in the *One Institute Quarterly* (Fall 1958), pp. 94-98, and "The First Native American 'Gay' Novel" in the *One Institute Quarterly* (Spring 1960), pp. 185-90.

28. "Mayne" discusses *White Cockcades* and *Left to Themselves* in *The Intersexes: A History of Similisexualism as a Problem in Social Life,* privately published with preface dated 1908, and reprinted in 1975 by Arno Press, New York, pp. 367-68.

29. The final paragraph of *Left to Themselves* is quoted by Garde on page 95 of the *One Institute Quarterly* (Fall 1958). A good case could probably also be made for veiled homoeroticism in all of the Alger novels, focusing as they do on the warm relationships that blossom between a young man and his chum/or an older male benefactor.

30. Xavier Mayne, *The Intersexes,* pp. 279-80.

31. *Ibid.,* p. 376.

32. Mayne mentions Bunner and Schaff on page 383.

33. Xavier Mayne, *Imre: A Memorandum* (Naples: The English Book Press, 1906), pp. 187-88.

34. *Ibid.,* pp. 42-43. Imre was so attractive, in fact, that not only street children but dogs and cats would look at him "with friendly interest." Other quotes are from pp. 141-42, 102, 115-18, 180, 204-5.

35. Turn-of-the-century erections had to be described obliquely, even in gay novels. On page 177, Oswald adds, "I struggled in shame and despair to keep down the hateful physical passion which was making nothing of all my psychic loyalty, asserting myself against my angriest will. In vain!"

36. Information about Fuller's school life and friends is contained in John Pilkington's *Henry Blake Fuller* (New York: Twayne, 1970), pp. 23-24.

37. The swimming scene in *Bertram Cope's Year* (Chicago: The Alderbrink Press, 1919) starts on page 85. A rather different swimming scene appears in Jack London's 1913 *The Valley of the Moon.* Ex-prizefighter Billy Roberts admires the near naked "Sandow"-like physique of former football coach Jim Hazard as the latter swims near Carmel. Roberts and Hazard

become good friends—they swim and shower together and rub each other down in "training camp style"—but London's interest in perfect physiques is more eugenic than homoerotic. Billy is happily married, and a major motif of the novel is the magnificent racial superiority of untainted Anglo-Saxon stock. The final Pilkington quotes are from pp. 150-51.

38. In 1917 Fuller published twenty-five free-verse experimental biographies under the influence of *Spoon River Anthology* in a volume entitled *Lines Long and Short,* which began with "Tobias Holt, Bachelor," who was old, sad, and lonely. Pilkington quotes Hamlin Garland as saying that Fuller lived in a series of dingy roominghouses and that no one ever called on him at home, as they could never be sure of a welcome.

39. Leon Edel, *The Life of Henry James: The Treacherous Years* (Philadelphia: Lippincott, 1969), p. 100.

40. The theme of the "village sissy" growing up in the Midwest is one that would not be out of place among the epitaphs in Edgar Lee Masters' *Spoon River Anthology* (1917), but his main treatment of homoeroticism (female/innocent) seems to be confined to *The Domesday Book* (1920).

41. Willa Cather, "The Sculptor's Funeral," as reprinted in *Willa Cather's Collected Short Fiction* (Lincoln: University of Nebraska Press, 1965), p. 177.

42. Cather, "Paul's Case," as reprinted in *Willa Cather's Collected Short Fiction,* pp. 247-48.

43. Sherwood Anderson, *Winesburg, Ohio* (New York: Viking, 1960), p. 32.

44. Carl Van Doren, *The American Novel* (New York: Macmillan, 1940), p. 322.

45. Proust's concept of "men-women" (as it appears in the 1932 Random House edition of *Remembrance of Things Past*) (Vol. 2, p. 13) is one that unfortunately held sway among many heterosexual readers and homosexuals as well for over a generation. Their "ideal is manly simply because their temperament is feminine . . . lovers from whom is always precluded the possibility of that love the hope of which gives them the strength to endure so many risks and so much loneliness, since they fall in love with precisely that type of man who has nothing feminine about him, who is not an invert and consequently cannot love them in return. . . ."

46. As quoted by Allen Churchill in *The Literary Decade* (Englewood Cliffs, N.J.: Prentice-Hall, 1971), p. 134. The smart-aleck approach of our leading wits toward homosexuals is even more embarrassing when contrasted with the views of homosexuality and androgyny taken by the Bloomsbury circle in England during the decade. The immense differences between the two cultures can be seen when one compares the way homosexuality is handled by our biographers of Alexander Woollcott (from Samuel Hopkins Adams through Howard Teichmann) and by Michael Holroyd in *Lytton Strachey.*

47. Churchill, *The Literary Decade,* p. 266. Root's noncommittal biography of Halliburton is *The Magnificent Myth* (New York: Coward-McCann,

1965), and Unterecker's much more grown-up biography of Crane is *Voyager* (New York: Farrar, Straus and Giroux, 1969).

48. Waldo Frank, *The Dark Mother* (New York: Boni and Liveright, 1920), p. 11.

49. Paul Carter, *Waldo Frank* (New York: Twayne, 1967), pp. 41-42.

50. Stark Young, *New Republic* (December 29, 1920), p. 148.

51. Frederick Hoffman, *The Twenties* (New York: The Free Press, 1962), p. 121.

52. Edward Lueders, *Carl Van Vechten* (New York: Twayne, 1965), p. 22.

53. Carl Van Vechten, *Firecrackers* (New York: Alfred Knopf, 1925), pp. 99-100. His formula is quoted in Lueders, p. 74.

54. Bruce Kellner covers these reactions to the novel in *Carl Van Vechten and the Irreverent Decades* (Norman: University of Oklahoma Press, 1968). On page 187, Kellner quotes an interesting 1925 letter from Firbank, who was "pitching a parasol" on the Libyan desert: "I am a spinster, Sir, & by God's grace, intend to stay so." He did, dying the following year.

55. Van Vechten, *Excavations* (New York: Knopf, 1926), pp. 172-73.

56. "Abnormality" and *Bertram Cope's Year* are discussed in *Excavations,* pp. 138-40.

57. Lueders, *Carl Van Vechten,* p. 20.

58. Kellner, *Carl Van Vechten and the Irreverent Decades,* pp. 166-67. For an example of a more serious novelist's treatment of Van Vechten's "frivolous" themes (e.g., the gay angle of Harlem's speakeasies), see John Dos Passos' handling of Dick Savage at the end of *The Big Money.*

59. Albert Parry, *Garrets and Pretenders* (New York: Dover, 1960), p. 327. As late as 1959, about the only relevant thing that Allen Churchill had to say in *The Improper Bohemians* was that the Village remained the best place for young homosexuals to find a "haven." Both Parry and Churchill insist on presenting bohemianism as an essentially heterosexual sport.

60. Conversation with the author, San Francisco, January 1975.

61. Callahan discusses McAlmon in *That Summer in Paris* (New York: Dell, 1964), pp. 76-77.

62. Conversation with the author, San Francisco, January 1975.

63. McAlmon as quoted in Boyle's *Being Geniuses Together* (Garden City: Doubleday, 1968), p. 148.

64. Hemingway, *The Sun Also Rises* (New York: Scribner's, 1954), p. 20.

65. McAlmon, "Miss Knight," as reprinted in a paperback collection of four of his stories under the misleading title, *There Was a Rustle of Black Silk Stockings* (New York: Belmont Tower Books, 1963), p. 50. No mention is made in this reprint that a limited edition of *Distinguished Air* had been privately published in Paris during the twenties, and the front-page blurb announces, "Discovered! The scandalous 'lost novel' by the master of the Hemingway–F. Scott Fitzgerald circle." In addition to "Miss Knight" and "Distinguished Air," the book includes "The Lodging House" and "The

Highly Prized Pajamas," which focus on lesbian themes. The other quotes from McAlmon's stories come from pp. 68-69, 10, 25, and 44.

66. Charles Brackett, *American Colony* (New York: Liveright, 1929), p. 123. A more famous novel about the Riviera milieu that includes some gay characters is Fitzgerald's *Tender Is the Night* (1934).

67. Published by Harcourt Brace, Crane's novel seems extremely veiled today, but according to an old friend who knew Crane in Berkeley, *The Western Shore* was regarded as daring for its time. For the next few decades Crane continued to write novels, all of which are tinged with homoeroticism.

68. The city of publication as well as the author's name is missing from the title page, but one educated guess is that the author was the Poet Laureate of New Jersey, Benjamin Musser.

69. Parts of "Boys, Men, and Love" were printed in the *One Institute Quarterly* in the early sixties, and another copy of the manuscript is owned by the Homosexual Information Center in Los Angeles. It would be interesting to trace the metamorphosis of "Lessons Learned in a Barn" down through the decades as softcore typescripts turned into hardcore paperbacks. In 1971, for instance, a paperback titled *3 Big Underground Classics* (Guild Press, Washington, D.C.) included an updated version of the "barn story" called "7 in a Barn," in which all the nominally straight young men service one another.

Mentioned in the text is the letter from boyFrank to the author, December 1974.

70. This same pattern governed past references to syphilis, with the Italians calling it "Mal Francese," the French calling it "Mal de Naples," and so on. It is interesting but saddening to note that the concept of Sodom being elsewhere still prevails as the official party line in China and Russia. Viewing gayness as bourgeois decadence, Chinese officials claim there are no homosexuals among their teeming millions, and the official Russian view is almost as severe. One of the results of the Russian attitude is that gay officers in the Red Army must wait until they get a furlough in Vienna before they can safely climb into bed with each other.

71. A seamy view of Manhattan gay life in the twenties can be found in the 1975 Arno reprint of *The Female Impersonators* (1922), the sequel to "Jennie June" Lind's *Autobiography of an Androgyne*, which had also been published by the *Medico-Legal Journal* in New York. In this book, the author writes of his career as a "Fairie" among the "Hermaphroditoi" and the pugs and thugs down on the Bowery.

THE THIRTIES

"TODAY THERE IS SCARCELY a schoolboy who doesn't know what a 'pansy' is," Dr. La Forrest Potter, Associate Professor of the New York School of Clinical Medicine, observed in his *Strange Loves: A Study in Sexual Abnormalities*.[1] "Before the War we used to consider homosexuality as more or less a foreign importation. We regarded ourselves as true exponents of the sane and uncompromising traditions of our pioneer ancestors. All those foreigners who were fortunate enough to have been permitted entrance to our shores, so we thought, were leavened by our practical matter-of-factness. Their dross of abnormal desire—assuming that they may have been thus infested when they landed in this country—was burned away in the melting pot of our staunch masculine or commendably feminine characteristics. This is what we thought. . . . And yet today there are homosexual 'joints,' 'queer' clubs, pervert 'drags,' or homosexual plays in practically every considerable American city." By the 1930s, a superficial knowledgeability toward homosexuals was emerging in America, and this new attitude seemed almost invariably to be expressed in scandalized gasps.[2] In 1934 there were "ten million male and female 'queers' in this country," wrote Dr. James Segall, who found "something terribly sinister in this decadence—in this repulsive suggestion of senility and impotence. It is so out of keeping with the lusty traditions, the he-man virility of our young country."[3] The perception of many heterosexuals was so distorted that they viewed the gay male as a weird combination of preying bogeyman and carnival freak: "hardened inverts" were inflicting "invisible scars" on the youth of America in hobo jungles, according to William Manchester's *The Glory and the Dream,* and Dr. Potter's book was being promoted with all the ballyhoo of a sideshow barker, as witness an advertisement in a 1938 science-fiction magazine.[4] "THE THIRD SEX! *Man or Woman?* THE TRUTH REVEALED! Must These Subjects Be Clothed in Silence Forever?" were some of the headlines from this ad, which included the following body copy:

Do you know what really goes on among the men and women of the Shadow World? Do you know that their number is constantly increasing? The strange power they wield over normal people is almost unbelievable. . . . Fearlessly, openly, the real meaning of many misunderstood subjects is daringly revealed. Sadism—Necrophilia—Phallic Worship —Sodomy—Pederasty—Tribadism—Sapphism—Uranism—the normal man and woman will refuse to believe that such abnormalities exist and are practiced.[5]

This advertisement and these comments are indicative of the attitudes of middlebrow Americans when homegrown gay fiction made its debut in this country. The "age of innocence" for variant literature was finally over, according to Jeannette Foster, who noted that following the customs clearance of *The Well of Loneliness* there sprang up the "wave of mediocre work which always follows profitable publication of better material in any field."[6] Most gay fiction of the decade was not mediocre only because it tended to be derivative and polemic, however. Since most of the gifted gay writers and major publishers were afraid to come out with frankly pro-homosexual novels, the field was left to hacks willing to tailor their books to the "cheap thrills" formulae of pulp magazines. While the rules for playing the game were slightly different from what they had been, the options for gay novelists were still limited: they could write an honest novel and put it in a drawer, camouflage the gayness through the Albertine strategy, write a sensationalized exposé and send it off to Godwin or Castle, or arrange to have a candid novel published privately or abroad. The last-named option was chosen by the authors of the best gay novel written here during the thirties, Charles Henri Ford and Parker Tyler, but it carried with it a severe penalty. When copies of *The Young and Evil* were sent here in 1933 by the Obelisk Press in Paris, customs officials declared the novel obscene, and it has remained generally unread on this side of the Atlantic.

THE YOUNG AND EVIL

Ford and Tyler were born in the South and were in their twenties when their novel was published. Ford was living in Mississippi when he started the novel, and at the same time he was in "very close correspondence" with "the beautiful Parker Tyler," who was living in Greenwich Village.[7] Ford has explained that Tyler's "letters were so witty and campy and I used so much of his extracts in the dialog that I just decided I should give him credit as co-author. And I did in my chapter outline give him entire chapters to write, too." Both men later became poets, and Tyler went on to write film criticism that included a 1972 study of homosexuality in the movies called *Screening the Sexes*.

In 1965 an excerpt from the novel was finally printed in this country in Maurice Girodias' anthology, *The Olympia Reader,* and in an afterword to this excerpt Tyler commented:

. . . in 1933, our book was duly attacked and defended in the columns of the *Herald Tribune*'s Paris Edition, consigned to burning and banning by the customs authorities of other countries, and then left to the loving, lingering care of collectors. . . . A grand silence on the book, like a dark age, was interrupted . . . only by strange, if gratifying, queries like this: "Dear Mr. Tyler, I have heard of your novel, *The Young and Evil,* and wonder if you can tell me where I might be able to obtain a copy." I would point vaguely in the direction of some esoteric bookshop.[8]

Quotes from three early commentators on *The Young and Evil*— Gertrude Stein, Djuna Barnes, and Louis Kronenberger—are cited inside the front cover of the 1960 Olympia Press reprint.[9] Stein wrote that the novel "creates this generation as *This Side of Paradise* by Fitzgerald created his generation," whereas Barnes was equivocal in her praise. "Never, to my knowledge," Barnes said, "has a certain type of homosexual been so 'fixed' on paper. Their utter lack of emotional values—so entire that it is frightening; their loss of all Victorian victories: manners, customs, remorse, taste, dignity; their unresolved acceptance of any happening, is both evil and 'pure' in the sense that it is unconscious. No one but a genius, or Mr. Ford and Mr. Tyler, could have written it." Ford has commented that the only review in America, in the *New Republic,* was written by Kronenberger, who termed the novel "the first candid, gloves-off account of more or less professional young homosexuals . . . both authentic and alive." (The photo of Tyler inside the cover of the 1960 edition was taken by Van Vechten, who switched from novels to photography in the thirties.)

The distinction of *The Young and Evil* does not rest on its slice-of-life plot, but even in this regard it stands out in contrast to the "apprenticeship novel" pattern that began to typify much gay fiction. The authors begin their story in Greenwich Village, take the gayness of their characters for granted, and detail the adventures of Karel and Julian, who live on West Third Street, bump into friends at "coffeepots," give parties, go to bars, pick up "the kind that makes homosexuality worthwhile," fall in love, get arrested, and, more than anything else, talk.

They talk about how they look:

Why *do* you hold your lips that way?
Because I think it looks adorable.

. . . and about love:

You don't know what love is. You've never wanted me so that every line of me made you ache.
What does my love mean then?
It may be some minor pathology.

. . . and to rude ladies who stare at them on subways because they are wearing mascara:

. . . why, how do you do, you look *so* much worse since your accident.

. . . and they listen to others talk at a drag ball:

. . . I'd rather be Spanish than mannish. . . .
. . . Did you see that basket?. . . .
. . . says he wears a flower in his buttonhole because it simply won't stay in his hair. . . .
. . . has a fish hooves?

The milieu presented in *The Young and Evil* is, of course, a rather specialized one—the literary/artsy set in the Village. They smoke marijuana or Benson & Hedges or black cigarettes with gold tips, write poetry, play "A Good Man Is Hard to Find," wear makeup, and ask one another "*Little Review* questions." Everyone in the novel is quite poor—Julian says he would have sex with President Hoover for the price of a suit, overcoat and hat—but then so is everyone else in the Village, and poverty does not turn the gay characters into Socialists or Communists. Karel is asked to give a talk at a political meeting, and his theme is that "the secret of political freedom does not lie in the removal of our economic difficulties." To the artist, Karel says, "absent meals, bedless nights and overcoatless cold are merely incidental," and he insists he can think as sharply and rapidly in a cold doorway as he can "in a steamheated room after a heavy meal." He concedes, however, that he is a "slightly above average person." Julian is also skeptical about Communists, and he thinks they eschew anything definite as they are all so "hazy."

There is nowhere in the novel the sense of being overwhelmingly oppressed in a homophobic society, because everyone in madcap Greenwich Village has about as much sex as he can handle. Indeed, Karel and Julian are more wary of carloads of gangsters who might rape them than of police who might arrest them, and it is not surprising that the brush Karel and a friend have with the law is depicted as more amusing than shattering. In the chapter called "Cruise," Karel and Frederick go up to Riverside Drive one night for the sailors, some of whom are walking around in the darkness with their flies still open. When a melee breaks out, Karel and

Frederick shriek, "Save us from these sailors!" and are rescued by, of all people, plainclothesmen. Everyone is taken to jail, where Karel and Frederick are charged with being disorderly. Karel is searched, has to yield up his makeup pencil, and thinks that one of the sailors being questioned is still "cute-looking with a sweet mouth. Anyway, he's not so hoity-toity by this time, the concupiscent bugger." Karel tries to write a poem that night in jail, and the next morning he tells the judge that his writing has appeared in all the best places (*Bookman, Sun, Post*). The judge winks at Karel and Frederick, dismisses the case, and tells them to be more careful next time. "There's at least one judge in the world," Karel says, "with a sense of civilization," and the two rush off to a drugstore to celebrate: Karel has a chocolate ice-cream soda and Frederick has a Coca-Cola with vanilla ice cream in it.

Gore Vidal has said that *The Young and Evil* "reads surprisingly well today,"[10] and the reason this novel towers over everything else written in the thirties is that Ford and Tyler were primarily inventive poets and only incidentally gay novelists. On nearly every page the reader comes across sparkling poetry and wit that is, unfortunately, rarely found in the more traditional gay tales. Thus, *The Young and Evil* has aged well not only because the authors captured the gay scene authentically but also because they had the ingenuity to match their subject matter to a style that was as spirited and amusing and free-floating as any of their characters. Of the three critical quotes cited on the front of the Olympia reprint, Kronenberger's evaluation seems to be the most accurate and perceptive: after over forty years, *The Young and Evil* is still "alive."

THE WAVE OF MEDIOCRITY

Six other novels containing a major gay theme came out during the early thirties, and with the exception of Mrs. Niles' *Strange Brother*, these books were published by pulp-paper presses. Generally out of print and hard to find, these novels are worth mentioning because of their historical interest rather than their literary merit.

A SCARLET PANSY: The Many Loves of Fay Etrange

Some of these early novels might well have been written during the twenties but had to wait until the favorable rulings on the *Ulysses* and *The Well of Loneliness* cases to be published. If this is the case, Robert Scully's *A Scarlet Pansy* may have been written before the others, as the time period in this novel is about 1910–1917. (The edition quoted here will be the undated Royal revised; the novel was perhaps first published by Faro in 1933.)[11]

If any of these early novelists were writing tongue in cheek, Robert Scully was. His story of the brief life and loves of Fay Etrange appears to have been written expressly to amuse other gay people, who would have recognized his mock Goody-Two-Shoes style for what it was. *A Scarlet Pansy* reads as if Scully had found a copy of *Autobiography of an Androgyne* and had yielded to the temptation to parody the adventures of "Jennie June" Lind as she roamed the big city, New Testament in one hand, trick-towel-sponge in the other, in search of sexual adventure. Scully knew that his readers would remember the insufferably virtuous Elsie Dinsmore types from their childhood reading and would be delighted with this inverted spoof about a country innocent turning into a flaming sexpot.

One distinctive characteristic of this novel is that, perhaps to ease its publication somewhat, Scully has used the feminine pronoun throughout in reference to Fay, but the knowing reader senses immediately that Fay is a gay male. Fay was born in a "quaint little white cottage" in Huntsville, Pennsylvania, leaves the farm for the big city (Baltimore), gets a job as a coal hauler, takes shorthand courses at the Y, is seduced right and left by dirty old men, gets a job in New York as a steno, and, in a chapter called "Love Always Finds Her in Church" (she accepted no part of the tenets but reveled in the "pageantry and music"), she falls in love with a church worker named Teddy. With Teddy she experiences a "new fall from grace," but she breaks off their relationship when his sexual demands become too great.

Scully's chapters detail a variety of sexual experiences, all told from the "conscience-stricken" point of view of the refined young "lady" who ever professes to be shocked at the bold advances of males. In one chapter Fay takes the day boat to West Point, recalls a lecture on the hermaphroditism of earthworms, and cruises the polo team. In another she goes to a costume party, meets Miss Bull-Mawgan and Elsie Dike, and makes out in the back stairway with an Irish cop whose opening line is "Do yuh like me, kid?" Several chapters are devoted to a cross-country tour with Henri Voyeur and Percy Chichi: they attend the famous Iceman's Drag Ball in Atlantic City, cruise marines on Market Street in Philadelphia ("Want to join our party, soldier of the sea?" "Sure! Whither away?"),[12] "do" Lafayette Park in Washington and the bathing resorts in Chicago, and in San Francisco are house guests at the Beach-Butsch home, where everyone is dreaming of a utopian gay island. The novel ends with Fay in Europe, where, after medical school, she has gone to work on a cure for gonorrhea. When World War I breaks out, she joins the Red Cross and falls in love with an American lieutenant, and in the last chapter they are both wounded at the front. Fay gives up her tourniquet for the lieutenant, in whose arms she dies.

A Scarlet Pansy had a good sale, according to Miss Toto le Grand, who wrote a recent series of articles called "The Golden Age of Queens" for a San Francisco bar magazine.[13] Miss le Grand went on to say that the novel was available "most often 'under the counter.' Try to buy one now! It cleverly and humorously depicts the life and loves of a pre-war . . . queen. It's wildly amusing, very camp, very gay." Scully's novel should not be criticized, then, because it falls short of reality with its superficial plotting, total caricatures, and improbable conversations. Altogether, there is a Van Vechtenish breezy delight in the bizarre and outrageous that makes *A Scarlet Pansy* seem to belong far more to the twenties than to the thirties.

STRANGE BROTHER: Strange Novel

The most "respectable" of these six early novels was *Strange Brother,* written by Mrs. Blair Niles and published by Horace Liveright in 1931. During the twenties Mrs. Niles wrote such books as

Casual Wanderings in Ecuador and *Condemned to Devil's Island,* and her publishers promised that if you were to visit her in her Park Avenue apartment, she would come to the door "dressed in vivid silks (preferably pajamas)." The book was respectable because it was written by a published author who was simply describing another exotic milieu with as much insight and understanding as she could. Thus, unlike the five other novels, *Strange Brother* was reviewable, and this is what *The Saturday Review of Literature* had to say:

> . . . This is less a novel than a piece of special pleading . . . a panorama of abnormality is unrolled with the utmost tolerance and sympathy, though never with approval.
>
> Such subject matter is, even today, on the borderland of the unmentionable, and it partakes inevitably of the bizarre and the sensational. We are, therefore, often confused in our judgment of the merits of the novel by the (in this day and age) faintly disreputable exoticism of the novel. When the book settles itself in our minds, however, there is a definite critical residuum; a weak narrative, structurally unsatisfying, manipulated to the necessities of the all-important didacticism . . . and . . . her statement, "Look, these are our strange brothers," and her plea, "Be kind and understanding to them, for their sorrow is great." Altogether, *Strange Brother* is interesting and informative, though not particularly meritorious as a novel.[14]

Strange Brother is written through the eyes of a Big Sister, June Westbrook, an attractive heterosexual young lady who becomes the confidante of young, gay, troubled Mark Thornton after meeting him in a Harlem nightclub. Mark had grown up in a small town, discovered "pain as an emotion" while swimming with a male friend out at the pond, and was urged by the kindly town queer to go to New York, "where he could fight the battle with himself, unhandicapped by small-town talk."[15] Mark has a job teaching drawing at a settlement house, and in spite of his reading *Leaves of Grass* and *Love's Coming of Age* and his taking an interest in local court cases, he is afraid to come out.

What happens to Mark is not altogether improbable for those guilt-ridden days. Because he is embarrassed by drag balls and dismayed by the "sordid tragedy of men's lavatories—underground in the subway" and seems to have more pity than desire for men who sit in the gallery of a moving-picture house with "eyes of hungry animals," he falls for straight Phil Crane. A handsome, muscular naturalist, Phil is a member of June's social set who midway through the novel deserts Mark by marrying and going off on an expedition. At the end of the novel, a neighborhood fruit peddler threatens blackmail when he tells Mark of having noticed a gay ex-convict slipping out of Mark's room late at night. Although Mark truthfully insists that "Lilly-Marie" is no more than just a friend, later that night he puts a pistol to his head. "Remember—it will free you," he whispers to himself. "No more lonely nights—no more prowling— walking the streets hour after hour, hoping at last to sleep . . . no more fear . . ." Mark shoots himself, and, with a vision of Phil Crane rowing toward him in a boat, he dies.

Strange Brother has two main weaknesses. One, as pointed out by the *Saturday Review* critic, is the "special pleading" aspect, which manipulates everything to portray Mark as consistently vir-tuous, bewildered, and pathetic. The other weakness is that since Mrs. Niles was writing from a secondhand remove, she was unable to capture the immediacy of the gay experience. For instance, when she ventures to re-create gay party chitchat, she comes up with nothing more authentic than:

> So glad you came, dearie.
> Darling, where've you been keeping yourself?
> Another drink, dear?[16]

Another example is the passage about the sexually electric atmos-phere of a subway lavatory. This description is given through the eyes of a vaguely embarrassed matron rather than from the view-point of a flesh-and-blood gay male, who might be expected to re-spond with more than mere sympathy in such an atmosphere. In a genuinely gay novel, Mark would be allowed to have sex once in a while, but Mrs. Niles allows no cruising—Mark just wanders around at night, feeling sorry for himself and other "outcasts." If the author had allowed Mark to climb into bed a few times with "the kind that makes homosexuality worthwhile," he probably would not have committed suicide, which he was apparently obliged to do to move the hearts of her straight readers to pity.

TWILIGHT MEN: Ersatz Proust

While *Twilight Men,* written by André Tellier and published by Greenberg in 1931, might possibly be the work of a gay male, its presentation of the gay world is almost as wooden as that of Mrs. Niles. There is none of the immediacy and ironic humor found in *The Young and Evil* and certainly none of the campiness that characterizes Scully's novel. The tone is more that of an updated *fin de siècle* decadence, and the focus is on the desperate and even sordid aspects of gay life in Manhattan.

The opening tries to suggest if not the influence of Proust at least simulation of the continental sensibility of the previous generation. The setting is France; the main character is a willowy, wealthy youth named Armand; and among the aristocratic characters in the background is the mysterious Comte de Rasbon, who is disappointed that his natural son is turning into a dreamy, effeminate poet. The first part of the novel ends with Armand falling in love with two young men, one of whom dies a natural death, the other jumping out of a window after confessing his love.

The rest of the novel is set in New York, where Armand has come to find a new life. He gets picked up in the park and goes to live with Stephen Kent in Greenwich Village, where he writes poetry, takes morphine, goes to parties, falls in love, but never bumps into anyone as alive as Julian and Karel. The melodramatic ending of the novel is signaled by the appearance of the Comte de Rasbon, who summons his son for an interview at his midtown hotel. Armand is told that because of his gayness and his drug addiction, he is going to be committed to an institution:

> Confinement, Armand. No more drug. That hurts, doesn't it? But if you weren't such a vile, perverted little animal, it wouldn't be necessary to lock you up.[17]

Armand kills his father with a candlestick, wanders around in a daze, takes a taxi uptown, rents a room and, despondent over his current unfaithful lover, takes a lethal dose of morphine in an attempt to get to sleep. *Twilight Men* was sold for seventy-five cents, with the back cover of the dust jacket explaining that the "great success of this novel . . . makes possible this reprint at a popular price." Other novels being published by Greenberg at the time included *The Outcast*, a lesbian novel by Anna Weirauch, and *Ladies of the Evening* by Milton Herbert Gropper (a racy tale that gives the reader an amazing inside picture of call houses).

BETTER ANGEL: "Better" Ending

In 1933 Greenberg brought out Richard Meeker's much less melodramatic *Better Angel,* a novel distinctive in that it transcended the pulp formula by ending on a carefully contrived note of uplift. Even though it offered no cheap thrills, *Better Angel* was probably accepted by Greenberg simply because the subject matter itself was regarded as sufficiently *outré* to tantalize the sensation-seeking reader of the Depression years.

The most convincing part of this idealized novel is the first third, which shows Kurt Gray growing up in Barton, Michigan, where he reads a lot and plays the piano, as all "sissies" were supposed to do, but Meeker adds a few details that help to create an atmosphere of comparative realism. One of them has to do with Kurt's response to those little ads that used to start out, "YOUNG MEN, Are you losing your Manly Vigor?" and which used to confuse masturbating middle-class boys of two generations ago. The other detail that has a touch of Dreiser realism is the town revival service where they sing "Just As I Am" and where Kurt goes forward to be "saved."

The middle chapter is set at the university in Ann Arbor, and Kurt discovers ("as if he had been initiated into some secret fraternity") Plato, Cellini, Michelangelo, Shakespeare, Shelley, plus Ellis, Carpenter and Wedekind. "From them he learned that his sin . . . was not the unique sport he had believed it to be."[18] Kurt's "sin" was having fallen in love with another student, Derry, who in a "matter-of-fact" way has sex with him occasionally. Before he graduates, Kurt is also seduced by the clever David, who has marcelled hair and gleaming, manicured fingernails. The novel ends with Kurt going to Europe and returning to suburban New York, where he teaches music at a boys' prep school, writes orchestral suites, and chooses David over Derry as his lover. The last scene is set in his comfortable apartment at twilight, and it shows Kurt reading about Herakles and Hylas, just as he used to back home in Barton. He closes the book in a mood of great serenity and near exaltation:

Strange that life should smooth to the calm of a summer pool—a pool so pregnant with quiet strength that all the fears and distrusts sank into it and out of sight. Strength here against laughter and derision, strength here for the spectral years ahead, strength, and joy in strength.[19]

Herbert, the school porter, comes in with a load of firewood and asks if he may not turn on the lights. Kurt smiles in the darkness and says, "All right, Herbert. Put them on."

GOLDIE: He Dyed for Beauty

Goldie and *Butterfly Man,* the last two of these novels, revert to the sensationalism that characterized the last half of *Twilight Men.* Written by "Kennilworth Bruce," *Goldie* was published in 1933 by William Godwin, Inc., which was also advertising Gerald Foster's *Lust* ("A book for harassed men and curious women"). The inside blurb on the *Goldie* dust jacket reads, inaccurately enough, "Not since 'The Well of Loneliness' has the delicate theme of sexual inversion been handled so artistically."

Goldie details the busy life of Paul Kameron, a Midwestern honor student and athlete who, after becoming a squadron ace with the Royal Flying Corps in World War I, bails out over Germany, is brought out in a POW camp, and returns to New York after the war as the lover of a furrier whom he met in Europe. Paul is somewhat comforted about having entered "Limbo" when he discovers there are "more than four million others in the United States who dwelt in that twilight realm of sex" and that other homosexuals included "Diocles, Achilles, Homer, Alexander the Great, Pythagoras, Demosthenes, Julius Caesar, Virgil, Benvenuto Cellini,

Michelangelo, Leonardo da Vinci, Shakespeare, Marlowe, Francis Bacon, Leo X, Francis I, Henry IV, Louis XIV, Louis XV, the Marquis de Sade, scions of the House of Orleans, Oscar Wilde, William II, James I, and many others of the world's great geniuses."[20]

Paul becomes "Goldie" when he starts dyeing his hair, and his downward slide begins when his furrier-lover catches him with the shop janitor. Goldie begins to hustle on Broadway after an auntie shows him the ropes, has an affair with a gangster, meets a shoe fetishist, and gets a job in a gay restaurant in the Village. He soon meets Jack Shaw, who writes "catchy" ad copy and has come up with the inspiration to form a gay liberation club. At the first meeting, held in a restaurant and attended by six people, Shaw begins by saying:

"We want security. We want the same protection that the law gives everyone else but us. Just because the law can't pigeonhole us as either male or female, we are not protected. On the contrary, we are actually persecuted by the law itself. . . . I'm telling you here and now, fairies have just as much right to live as everyone and everything else. . . ."

Then a man named Loomis has his say:

"It's just as Shaw says, the law owes us something. Let's organize. Let us begin with the legislature of the State of New York. They should pass a law protecting us. Or at least they should abolish the old law making us criminals. It's the church people that stir up all this stuff against us. We must be organized to fight them. . . . The Nudists are facing the same problem and they are conquering it by organization. I know because I've been interested in Nudism for a long time. Why, I remember reading of the Spartans who first abandoned their loincloths for running, wrestling and gymnastics. The Y.M.C.A. and other athletic clubs have abandoned trunks in their swimming pools and gymnasiums. There will come a day when—"

Loomis is asked to yield by the Professor, who wears "antiquated spectacles":

"I don't like to interrupt the learned gentleman's decalogue . . . but I have done some research into the origin of inversion, and a brief dissertation will not be amiss here. Herodotus claims that the Persians were taught the habit by the Greeks, but if we go back further than that, we find in the Bible that it started with Cain and Abel. I interpret the Scriptures that way . . ."

The dissertation is, of course, amiss, but they finally agree on a resolution that Shaw has drawn up. Shaw reads it aloud:

"Whereas sexual inversion is inherited and ineradicable in a majority of instances; and whereas so-called abnormal intercourse between male and female is tolerated just as much as normal intercourse; and whereas France and Italy have ceased for a century to make inversion a crime and haven't suffered by it; Now, therefore, be it resolved that we do hereby organize under this Constitution in order to advocate a change in the laws of the State of New York, of the several states of the United States, to permit adults to dispose of their persons as they wish, providing that they do not disturb the public peace or give scandal to the young or the public at large while doing so."

Loomis suggested the name "Knights of Freedom" for the new organization.

"Too masculine," reasoned Shaw. "We've got to let the Lesbians in. We can't advocate freedom for men and not for women. Not since the Suffrage Act, anyway."

"I have it," interjected Paddy, "let's call it 'The Twilight League.' "

"Excellent!" responded Loomis.

The future of The Twilight League darkens when Goldie discovers that it cannot raise twenty-five dollars bail for Shaw, and that several members are planning to exploit the league by compiling a gay anthology all members would have to buy and by starting a course on "inverted love" all members would be coerced into taking. Strangely enough, the last straw is one of the members planning "to establish an agency where wolves could obtain fairies when they wanted them" through an "elaborate card system and a photograph gallery." Goldie then analyzes why the organization was doomed:

The fact that The Twilight League could never function smote Goldie grimly. It would be impossible to organize the adherents of Limbo. They were born to be alone. They had renounced the companionship of women, the prospect of home and comfort in old age, just to be alone. They were essentially selfish; hadn't they given up everything to gratify that Self? They must continue sneaking about, apprehensive of the law, having contempt for one another. That was the real tragedy of their existence.

The ending of *Goldie* is complicated and morbid. After The Twilight League fails, Goldie gets a letter from Constance, a woman who thirteen years earlier bore him a son and who now is dying in New Orleans. Goldie rushes down South to see Junior, who, he discovers one night when they are sharing a bed, has been turned into a "pansy." Goldie shrieks, "I would rather see him dead!" strangles his son, and on the last page is himself executed for murder —"the noose jerked a grim period to his reflections and Paul Kameron was with the Squadron in another world." Precisely which of the other worlds Kennilworth Bruce has in mind is not exactly clear, however. On the one hand, the inside information in the novel suggests that Bruce must have been gay himself, but on the other hand, there are a number of homophobic passages (such as The Twilight League analysis) which sound more as if they were written by a straight outsider. A possible explanation is that Bruce was indeed gay but was occasionally viewing the gay scene with alarm in order to make his novel appeal, here and there, to both gay and straight readers.

BUTTERFLY MAN: A Straight Lad Victimized

More than any of the rest of these novels, *Butterfly Man* by Lew Levenson (originally published by Macauley in 1934) must have struck the gay reader as monstrously homophobic: gay life is shown as totally damned and damnable, and the only ray of hope is the salvation offered by a heterosexual woman. The novel is so transparently hateful, though, that even those gay readers blinded by self-loathing must have quickly recognized it as anti-faggot trash.

Levenson's thesis is that perfectly wholesome, normal heterosexual males are seduced by sinister "half-men" and are helplessly swallowed up by an alluring but evil atmosphere from which there is usually no escape. Levenson's victim is young Ken Gracey, a star basketball player from Selma, Texas, who is taken to California to live in a Malibu villa by a mysterious man who holds a mortgage on the Gracey home. This man has designs on Ken but, after putting him into a Hollywood dancing school, kicks him out of the villa when he discovers Ken is interested in girls. Ken then goes on the road with Anita, an alcoholic dancing partner, and he is discovered in Tía Juana by a lecherous New York producer, Howard Vee, who whisks him away to his apartment in Manhattan. Wishing to free himself from the strings Howard has attached, Ken has this conversation with another chorus boy (chubby, pink cheeks, "peppier than seventeen wildcats," gay) while they are on tour in *Sweeter Than Sweet.*

> "I'm glad he's on his way to Europe," Ken said. "I'm glad I didn't go with him."
> "You have the conscience of a saint," Frankie replied. "Suppose you had gone along, what then?"
> "I am selfish. I wanted to be free. Frankie, I'm through eating my heart out. . . ."
> "Meaning what?"
> "I'm going gay."
> Frankie took a flask from his pocket. "Have one, buddy?"
> "No, sistie."[21]

By the time the cast gets to Boston and Ken is getting ready to enter a drag contest, he has started to talk in what Levenson believes to be fag language:

> "Have you got a swig o' something on your hip, dearie?" he heard his neighbor at the dressing table on the right ask.
> "No, I haven't," Ken replied. He looked curiously at the half-nude adolisque [*sic*] who sat there. "Ray Leech, or I'm a so and so! Are you a lush or aren't you?"
> "Be refined, Ken Gracey," Ray said. "I hear you're in."
> "Meaning what?"
> "You'll win the grand prize."
> "Tish and tush, Ella," Ken said. "Who wants a diamond bracelet?"
> "Pawnbrokers—at one third value, baby darling."

During the last third of the novel, Ken slides deeper and deeper into depravity: he has an affair with one of the Al Capone gang, becomes an alcoholic, catches pneumonia and a venereal disease, is sent to jail, and finally meets a nance-hating girl named Constance, who tries to nurse him back to health and heterosexuality. In spite of her ministrations, Ken prefers to lose himself in gin, and at the end of the novel, he rushes out in a drunken stupor to get some air, and, convinced that he is walking "home to Texas," he steps off the pier into the East River and drowns.

SECONDARY THEMES

Another variation of playing the game during the 1930s was the inclusion of gay motifs in novels that were principally concerned with other themes. Of course, heterosexuals as well as homosexuals began including minor gay or near-gay characters, and it should be quickly added that an author's sexual orientation cannot be deduced from the degree of sympathy with which these characters were drawn. It is entirely conceivable that self-assured straight writers felt secure enough to sketch homosexuals in a positive light while less secure or latently gay authors felt obliged to hide behind the smokescreen of homophobia. At any rate, respectable publishing firms seemed willing to bring these novels out, so long as the gay angle was sufficiently subordinated to grander themes, allowing all to escape the stigma already being attached to the gay novel.

THIS MAN IS MY BROTHER: Strange Brother in Montana

One of the comparatively sympathetic treatments occurs with *This Man Is My Brother*, a 1932 novel by Myron Brinig, who is best remembered as a chronicler of Jewish family life in small-town America. Silver Bow, Montana, is a surprising place to find both a fictional Jewish family and a homosexual, but it provides the setting for most of Brinig's novel, which details the conflicts among the members of the mercantile Singermann family. It is true that Brinig turns the gay brother, Harry, into somewhat of a stereotyped closet queen—his novelist brother/narrator thinks he is "too flushed and effeminate," and Harry suffers from "bad nights which are usually bad for men of his peculiar, inverted type. He lay awake in fear of those who might reveal and expose his weakness."[22]

At the same time, Brinig is relatively sympathetic in his handling of Harry's unfortunate attraction to Richard, the bright, athletic young gentile who has been adopted by one of his brothers. Richard is flattered and pleased by Harry's warm concern until, in one of the last chapters, which is set in Miami, his uncle stops by to see him. Richard is spending his spring vacation at a beach hotel with college friends, and on Harry's last night in Miami, a "Death in Venice" mood of longing, sadness, and desperation begins to set in. Richard is collegiately smoking a pipe in his uncle's room; both are in pajamas, as the evening is sultry, and Harry, overwhelmed and bewildered by Richard's sexiness, melts in this overblown paragraph:

> All he saw was that image of beauty before him, and he moved close to it and held it in his arms, close to his heart, and felt an answering beat. Words rose to his lips, but they were too grotesque and suggestive for utterance. He simply held Richard and then moved his head closer to the other, until he seemed to be within the bottomless gray depths of Richard's eyes. The tumult of his restlessness died; he thought that he had never been so happy; it seemed as though all the painful yearnings of his life were at last assuaged. Again he heard the soft strains of music, like flowers expanding, throwing off petals of tone, fluttering petals of color singing with melody.

In a 1932 Farrar and Rinehart novel, Brinig could not allow Richard to respond with a whispered "Gosh, Uncle Harry." The nephew should push Harry away, stare at him with angry eyes that turn to disgust, and rush out of the room—which is exactly what he does. Next morning Harry goes to the beach to tell Richard that it was all a "joke," but Richard scorns him with "hard bitter laughter" and escapes by swimming out into the ocean. "Alone and forsaken," Harry peers "tragically through the curtain of rain after the swimming youth. . . . But what had he done? He had simply revealed his love of beauty in a person of the same sex. Was it such a sin?" In search of "beauty," Harry feels compelled to swim out after his nephew, but rather than getting Richard, he gets drowned. To his credit, Richard does display some touching emotion—however wasted—when the body of his uncle is recovered. He weeps "fiercely."

BEYOND THE STREET: Unrequited Love in High School

Homosexuality is again treated sympathetically—even quite sensitively—in Edgar Calmer's *Beyond the Street*. This novel is something of a *Winesburg, Ohio* set in Starrett High in New York City: most of the students and teachers are vaguely frustrated, and most of this frustration derives from unresolved sexual desires.

One of the subplots concerns the unrequited love within a triangle that consists of English teacher Lloyd Quent, star athlete John West, and history teacher Miss Stewart Cassall. Quent is attracted to West, who has a crush on Miss Cassall, who is always contriving ways to bump into Quent. Although Quent gets to know the star athlete well enough to take him out to dinner, by the end of the novel the boy becomes suspicious, and one day after school he goes into Quent's room to repeat gossip he has heard about the teacher's being gay. Surprisingly enough for a 1930s novel, Quent does not deny the charge, and of course West is obliged to flee the room in a huff. Calmer was also daring enough to include a few scenes of Quent in a gay setting, and his description of the teacher picking up a sailor within the shadows of Riverside Drive is convincing until he has Quent say, "Let's leave here at once."[23]

There is a consistent ring of truth as Calmer depicts the other gay situation in the novel, a crush that brilliant, clever Alex Sadowsky has on a fellow student, good-looking Vincente Fabriques. Again and again, Alex writes little notes to, and has little talks with, Vincente, trying to make sense of a relationship that baffles them both. In the following after-school scene in which Alex is trying once more to explain one of his notes—and his love—Calmer captures the confusion, the pathetic and losing try for decisiveness, and the ultimate frustration that thousands of adolescents have suffered —and are suffering today—in similar situations:

"I remember what I wrote, even if you don't," he said. "Every word, kid . . . do you remember at all? 'Why struggle uselessly,' I said. I can't make you understand it, what it is, our friendship, what I feel . . . only now I"—he drew a deep breath—"I just wanted to tell you that you don't have to worry about me, kid, anymore; you have no more obligations to me." He wanted to hold him close to his body, he wanted to kiss him; he knew it then. But fighting: "I've decided, kid, listen. You don't have to call me up anymore, see? You don't have to wait for me after school. But I mean, I'll just—from now on, I'll just be there if you want to see me about anything, if I can help you or anything. You know. Anyway, I've decided . . ."

Vincente said nothing . . . he glanced about him, awkward; he shifted the books in his arm. "Well," he said. "Well, I'll go now, I guess."

In the postscript to the novel, Calmer writes that Alex, "who was not graduated from Starrett, is employed as an usher in a concert hall in midtown," while Lloyd Quent "is teaching at a high school in Queens, living much the same life."

CRYPTIC, SHADOWY NOVELS

In the nineteenth century Bayard Taylor had written that the reader who did not feel the "cryptic forces" at play in *Joseph and His Friend* would hardly be interested in the external movement of his novel, and sixty years later some American novelists still felt obliged to describe these forces in terms of almost impenetrable enigma. Two exasperatingly shadowy novels of the thirties were John Evans' *Shadows Flying* (Knopf, 1936) and Murrell Edmunds' *Sojourn Among Shadows* (Caxton, 1936).[24]

Since gay people must surely have been a part of the literary salon of his mother, Mabel Dodge Luhan, John Evans was no doubt sufficiently knowing to have been able to write a realistic novel set in Manhattan. *Shadows Flying,* however, is something of a dim allegory set in an unspecified gothic corner of the American landscape where two young men spend a peculiar working vacation. One of them is Jacob, a genteel gayish poet who owns a house in the city; the other is a darkly mysterious Heathcliff type, David Runyon, who shares Jacob's house. They walk a hundred miles to the Runyon farmhouse, where they meet David's adoring mother and sister. While it is never clear that Jacob and David have had sex, it is clear that David's mother wants to creep into David's bedroom at night, and at the end of this slow-moving novel, Evans finally defines the relationship David has with his sister. Jacob spies the "inosculated bodies" of David and his sister as they are having sex out in a little recessed hiding place, and the novel ends with Jacob fleeing the farmhouse in horror. Had the novel ended with David and Jacob having sex in the "teacup," it would have been tagged as a gay novel and, as such, quite probably been regarded as unpublishable by the Knopf editors, who apparently felt that heterosexual incest was perfectly all right.

The book jacket of *Sojourn Among Shadows* mentions that Edmunds had worked as a teacher, basketball referee, lawyer, and shoe store clerk in New Orleans, and that the theme of his book will disturb no one but the "parochially respectable." It is difficult to determine what the theme is, because *Sojourn Among Shadows* is even more peculiar and evasive than *Shadows Flying*. Briefly, the novel is set in the South, and the plot concerns an old tramp telling a weird story to a stranger about his Uncle Tom helping him to run away to a cottage in the woods when he was a boy. In the cottage live an old couple who have an effeminate grandson named David, who makes a pass at the nephew, who grows up to be the tramp. The novel ends with Uncle Tom and David falling over a cliff, the tramp asking the stranger whether he understands, and the stranger, remarkably enough, answering, "Yes."

Among other novels of the decade in which homosexuality pales from the shadowy treatment were Daphne Greenwood's *Apollo Sleeps* (Messner, 1937), George Davis' *The Opening of a Door* (Harper, 1931), and Rex Stout's *Forest Fire* (Farrar-Rinehart, 1933). Greenwood's gay character is a male dancer who charms a bored American wife living in Japan in the early thirties, while the hero of *The Opening of a Door* has a gay uncle in San Francisco and may even be gay himself. Stout's novel is a Western mystery whose hero, a married macho forest ranger, insists that he is not a "cross-eyed bull" (i.e., bisexual), even though he feels strangely drawn to his handsome young assistant.[25]

THE SHADOWY WORLDS OF FREDERIC PROKOSCH

Also in the shadowy category but forming another class by themselves are the exotic and erotic novels of Frederic Prokosch, whose first picaresque, *The Asiatics,* was published in 1935. In that year the Wisconsin-born bachelor was twenty-seven—he had just received his doctorate from Yale and was described at the time as a "vigorously handsome man, with aggressive nose and chin and dark determined eyes," who was the squash racquets champion of France.[26]

Observing the convention that homosexuality was more acceptable if observed elsewhere, Prokosch emerged during the decade as a less effusive, more sophisticated Charles Warren Stoddard, writing lyric tales of a handsome bachelor made up of three parts Richard Halliburton and one part Lawrence of Arabia. This main character typically finds himself in extreme circumstances in places like Aden or Turkey or Iraq, where the natives are *supposed* to be pansexual —and they are. Prokosch plays some very shadowy games when alluding to gay attraction or activities, because his hero, designed for mass appeal and the Carnegie public libraries, is ostensibly straight. However, when the hero is placed in a situation that is either overwhelmingly menacing (e.g., becoming the prisoner of lusty Arabs) or seductive (bathing naked at sunset with an attractive young guide), Prokosch does allow homoerotic thoughts and acts to take place very briefly. At the same time, these lapses are always veiled with enough Middle East mysteriousness to make them appear to be not only quite natural but, given the out-of-this-world landscape and climate, almost inevitable. Throughout these novels, homosexuality is never presented in terms of American aggressiveness. The American bachelor yields to homoeroticism passively, languorously, helplessly—simply because he is disarmed by a fierce sensuality to which any Westerner would apparently have to succumb.

Following *The Asiatics,* Prokosch wrote *The Seven Who Fled* (1937), which features a strange love-hate relationship between Anthony Layeville and the barbaric, tantalizing Tansang, both of

whom die in the Tibetan snow. In *Night of the Poor* (1939), Prokosch switched to an American setting to detail the adventures of
a boy who hitchhikes from Wisconsin to Mississippi, encountering
lust, poverty, murder, wicked boys, a gangster, and a good prosti-
tute. According to critic Radcliffe Squires, *Night of the Poor* reads
as if Prokosch were trying to bring *"Huckleberry Finn* up to date
by adding a drop of Whitman and a soupçon of D. H. Lawrence."[27]

Since the 1930s, Prokosch has continued to write a number of
novels, including the typically exotic *Nine Days to Mukalla,* which
one Midwest reviewer called as "intoxicating as the wine of sin,"
and the somewhat less typical *Idols of the Cave,* which was set in
Manhattan during World War II. To the reading public in general,
Prokosch's novels have turned out to be "casualties of World War
II," according to Squires, who explains that "the daring spiritual
search which characterized literature in the second and third
decades of this century became irrelevant in 1945 to a generation
that was looking primarily for a secure foothold in a corporation
or in suburbia." For the gay reader in particular, the average Prokosch novel has been of only marginal interest, as the rewards to
be gained never seem to be worth the effort of peering through all
of those numerous veils.

LESS SHADOWY NOVELS SET IN EUROPE

Prokosch seemed to be invoking the spirit with which Richard
Burton had written of the "Sotadic Zone" in the nineteenth century:
pansexuality is endemic to the Middle East, and even if Western
moral judgments were pronounced, they could hardly prevail. The
strategy of the geographical remove, then, was unblinkingly accepted during the thirties by our middle-class novel readers, who to
this day find it a satisfactory explanation for scenes of bizarre and
thus "un-American" sexuality.[28] The "lost generation" in Europe
was another group from which American readers expected outrageous goings-on, but in this case many must have felt that
Western moral judgments were indeed applicable: one could over-

look a homosexual Iraqi who didn't know any better, but one could hardly show the same charity to an Anglo-Saxon haunter of Parisian pissoirs, who most certainly should have. Among the American writers who wrote homosexual novels set in Europe during this decade, Kay Boyle and Elliot Paul depicted their gay characters as scamps or monsters, quite in keeping with the expectations of the average American reader. However, Djuna Barnes' gay American male in *Nightwood* probably confounded a number of these people because he was not paying what they would have regarded as a suitable penalty for leading a life of depravity.

GENTLEMEN, I ADDRESS YOU PRIVATELY:
But What Has She Said?

While she was living in France in the early thirties, Kay Boyle used to hear stories from a gay friend of hers about the unpredictable, amoral sailors of Toulon and Marseilles.[29] With one of these sailors in mind she wrote *Gentlemen, I Address You Privately* (1933). Set on the Brittany coast, the novel focuses on the effect that a sly, charming Irish sailor named Ayton has on some of the villagers. Ayton charms a strange, brooding man named Munday into loving him, but their relationship is never very happy, and the novel ends with the discovery that Ayton has sold Munday's piano in order to leave the country with three whores and has left a married woman pregnant with his child.

Other than recalling that Ayton was based on a "certain type of homosexual scoundrel," Miss Boyle has recently remarked, "I'm not quite sure what I was trying to say in that book." From a gay perspective, the novel is weakened by the prevailing sense of secondhandedness that prevents Ayton and Munday from becoming believable, red-blooded lovers; their conversations reflect more what a straight woman might imagine than what two gay men would actually say to each other. Altogether, the novel is fuzzy, as pointed out by the reviewer in the *Nation:* "Miss Boyle is afflicted with metaphorical spots on the eye which consistently get in the way of the object and her proper perception of the object. But Miss Boyle had perhaps best be addressed privately on these matters."[30]

CONCERT PITCH: Falsetto in France

In Elliot Paul's *Concert Pitch* (1938), the gay character is a bit more monstrous than mischievous. This novel concerns Ernest Hallowell, a music critic living in Paris, but it is not he who is gay, since this is a Random House novel, and Hallowell is the main character. The gay character is another music critic, Lucien Piot, who pencils his eyebrows and who is called a "fag" and "pansy" by Ernest's friends.

Piot soon proves these allegations to be all too true by falling in love with a handsome young American pianist whom he contrives to whisk off to an American concert tour. It turns out that the young pianist does not want to be gay, takes a mistress old enough to be his mother, but is finally reconciled with Piot in a melodramatic "deathbed" scene. Meanwhile, Ernest has an affair with the pianist's mother, who is strongly attached to her son, and the novel ends unhappily for all.

NIGHTWOOD: Brooding Women, Plucky Men

The best known, most deeply felt, and generally best written expatriate novel of the thirties dealing with gay themes was Djuna Barnes' *Nightwood,* first published here in 1937 by Harcourt, Brace with an introduction by T. S. Eliot. For one who professed to be frightened at the "loss of all Victorian victories" and "lack of emotional values" in *The Young and Evil,* Barnes succeeded in creating a gothic Parisian world which more than matched Tyler and Ford in amoral abandon. However, there is a significant difference between *Nightwood* and *The Young and Evil:* Tyler and Ford were essentially flip and put love in quotation marks where it seemed to them to belong, while Barnes, brooding over a hopeless lesbian romance that would not let her go, implied that love was the one Victorian victory worth winning, if one only could.

Nonetheless, the gay male in *Nightwood* who serves as counterpoint to, and commentator on, the unhappy Nora-Robin-Jenny triangle finally emerges as a rather positive character. His name is Matthew O'Connor, he is a doctor of sorts from San Francisco who frequents the public lavatories, and he would like to be married to some good man, boil his potatoes and have his baby "every nine months by the calendar." ("Is it my fault," he asks, "that my only fireside is the outhouse?") While Nora whimpers inconsolably over Robin's going off to America with Jenny, Matthew is able to be far more philosophical about the coming and going of "love." His comments on the death of a former bed-companion and perhaps lover, an Arabian "Kabyle," are typical:

> Do a bit for a Kabyle, back or front, and they back up on you with a camel or a bag of dates. . . . He was the only one I ever knew who offered me five francs before I could reach for my own. I had it framed in orange blossoms and hung it over the whatnot.[31]

O'Connor, who would rather talk than listen, finally becomes exasperated at Nora's perpetual grieving over the absent Robin:

> "Oh," he cried, "a broken heart have you! I have falling arches, flying dandruff, a floating kidney, shattered nerves *and* a broken heart! . . . Are you the only person with a bare foot pressed down on a rake? Oh, you poor blind cow! Keep out of my feathers: you ruffle me . . ."

In *Lesbian Images,* Jane Rule goes so far as to say that O'Connor is the main character of *Nightwood,* his "ironic cynicism and self-pity" setting the tone of the book. However, she adds, he is saved by "both his wit and his silliness. Unfortunately the women characters are not so redeemed."[32] What also saves O'Connor is the fact that he never allows himself to be devastated by love in the way that less cynical women tend to be, especially when they love each other, and Djuna Barnes pinpoints this difference through Nora's comparison:

> There's nothing to go by, Matthew. You do not know which way to go. A man is another person—a woman is yourself, caught as you turn in panic; on her mouth you kiss your own. If she is taken you cry that you have been robbed of yourself.

Because of this equation—that lesbian love is more intense than love for or between men—O'Connor emerges in *Nightwood* as relatively plucky and fortunate, if never especially heroic.

Altogether, *Nightwood* seems to have more in common with *Distinguished Air* than with *Concert Pitch* or *Gentlemen, I Address*

You Privately: both Barnes and McAlmon were able to capture the haunted eyes and desperate gestures of the decadent in Berlin and Paris. A crucial difference between the two works is the authors' vision of the suffering that comes from being lost and alone—in Barnes it is personal and palpable, whereas in McAlmon we are supposed to believe that suffering is something other people do.

RELATIONSHIPS TO THE MAINSTREAM

As long as homosexuality was muted in our fiction, gay motifs could be deftly tucked into the more romantic, exuberant types of writing without creating much alarm or even notice. The works of Stoddard, Taylor, Melville, and Fuller could pass under the colors of tales of the sea, of idealized friendship, or of picaresque adventures, and during the twenties nearly everyone assumed that Van Vechten's novels were merely naughty. Once homosexuality surfaced as such, the old masquerades had to be discarded in favor of a new fictional form, and the one that began to develop was a rather peculiar hybridization of the apprenticeship novel and the problem novel. The difference between *Look Homeward, Angel* and *Better Angel,* for instance, is the hero's pubescence: after Kurt Gray discovers he is "different," Meeker's innocuous *Bildungsroman* turns into a problem novel in a way that must have been unsettling for heterosexual readers of the thirties. For any number of valid and invalid reasons, then, the gay novel at this time was regarded as an embarrassing genre, and during the last half of the decade it almost completely disappeared for a period that would last about ten years. At the same time, there were two other types of novel that were gaining national attention and have since become closely identified with the spirit of the thirties—"tough guy" and "proletarian" fiction.

The Relevance of the "Tough Guy" Novel

Since the hero in this sort of novel descended from the hairy-chested he-man that Hemingway had made famous during the twenties, an attitude of revulsion toward "pansies" in the Jake Barnes style was *de rigueur* for the private eyes, soldiers of fortune, and gangsters who served as tough-guy characters in the thirties. As in Hemingway's "The Mother of a Queen" (1938), gay males were useful as weak-sister antitheses to the macho heroes—rather than being hard-boiled, they were laughably easy-over—but at the same time these weak sisters had to be presented as villians rather than victims. The problem of how to shape a pansy with "no iron in his bones" into a menacing force was solved in *The Big Sleep* and *Serenade* in a way that must have been most satisfying for readers during the Depression: the gay characters were extremely wealthy and powerful and thus more oppressive than oppressed.

In Raymond Chandler's *The Big Sleep* the "pansy" that Phillip Marlowe deals with is the kept boy of a wealthy but "very" dead bisexual pornographer. To his credit, this sullen young man (named Carol Lundgren) persists in telling Marlowe "to go —— himself" in a scene that inevitably leads to a showdown. The tough guy's knowledgeability about the "third sex" is displayed during this front-porch tiff between Marlowe and Lundgren:

"All right," I said. "You have a key. Let's go on in."
"Who said I had a key?"
"Don't kid me, son. The fag gave you one. . . . He was like Caesar, a husband to women and a wife to men. Think I can't figure people like him and you out?"
I still held his automatic more or less pointed at him, but he swung on me just the same. It caught me flush on the chin. I backstepped fast to keep from falling, but I took plenty of the punch. It was meant to be a hard one, but a pansy has no iron in his bones, whatever he looks like.[33]

In James Cain's *Serenade* (1937), the menacing "pixie" is wealthy Winston Hawes, a famous orchestra leader who conspires to appropriate hero John Sharp for his own evil ends. Titillatingly enough, we learn that Sharp, a hard-boiled opera singer, has not always been as impenetrably heterosexual as tough guys are supposed to be. "Every man has got five per cent of that in him," Sharp confesses to his motherly Mexican girlfriend Juana, "if he meets

the one person that'll bring it out, and I did, that's all."[34] Before
Juana has a chance to grunt in bovine dismay, Sharp quickly adds
that Hawes has been the "curse" of his life: "I hate it! I've been
ashamed of it, I've tried to shake it off, I hoped you would never
find out, and now it's over!" Juana responds to this change of heart
by slipping down her brassiere and, later, slipping a Mexican sword
into Hawes. Sharp's reaction to seeing the "blood foaming out of
Winston's mouth" is "I wanted to laugh and cheer and yell *Olé!* I
knew I was looking at the most magnificent thing I had ever seen
in my life."

(One of the interesting developments in straight tough-guy novels
is that in recent years the hero has become more humane to gay
characters, and Charles Alva Hoyt explains that by the 1950s a
good tough guy was emerging in contrast to a bad tough guy.[35] In
John D. MacDonald's *The Damned,* the bad one beats up a couple
of "fairies," but the good one comes to their defense, saying, "They
aren't doing you any harm. They're just different from you, man."
Of greater interest, though, is the fact that the tough-guy novel has
in the last decade been turned into a gay novel—lock, stock, and
barrel. During the sixties, a rash of paperbacks with a gay James
Bond theme appeared, but more notably, Harper and Row have
published, as part of their mystery series, Joseph Hansen's *Fadeout*
(1970) and *Death Claims* (1973), novels which feature an in-
surance investigator who is both quite tough and quite gay.

Indeed, the tough guy has emerged in various forms as a great
favorite and even a stock character in all sorts of gay novels over
the last forty years. The main characters in the gay novels of the
thirties—even those presented most favorably, such as Mark Thornton and Kurt Gray—are essentially gentle souls, and it is important
that they remain somewhat weak and bewildered, or at least vulnerable, so as to elicit the sympathy or empathy of the reader. However,
by the mid-fifties, William Talsman was creating gay characters
that were as ferociously rough and tough and ungrammatical as
anyone in the Cain or Chandler novels. In Talsman's *The Gaudy
Image,* two holdup men hide out in a seedy roominghouse and have
sex not only with each other but also with the wrestler and the boxer

down the hall. During the last twenty years, as the emphasis in much gay fiction has shifted from sympathetic realism to sexual wish-fulfillment, the tough guy is a character that readers have almost come to take for granted. Even in the essentially nonpornographic novels of recent years, it is likely that a main character will be some form of toughie, such as John Rechy's macho hustler or William Carney's sadistic master. In pornographic fiction, it is essential that all the main characters create an outwardly tough image because toughness is equated with butchness and sexual attractiveness; gay readers will respond to a sexual scene between a professional half-back and a Marine lieutenant (or lifeguard, lumberjack, fur trapper, cowboy, policeman, sailor, truck driver, high school coach, thug, father of three, etc.) in a way they never would if it were just a hairdresser and a librarian going to bed. Thus, the tough guy has been appropriated to serve the special ends of gay fiction, and Ernest Hemingway would turn over in his grave if he knew that the indirect descendants of his literary prototype were fucking the day-lights out of each other.)

The Irrelevance of Proletarian Fiction

Some younger readers may wonder why gay men, as members of what we think of today as an oppressed minority, did not express feelings of indignation and rage in the form of proletarian novels during the thirties. This genre was, after all, serving as an appropri-ate outlet for literary spokesmen of other persecuted minorities; from Michael Gold's *Jews Without Money* to Richard Wright's *Uncle Tom's Children* and *Native Son,* Jewish and black writers were indicting America for its heartless mistreatment of the down-trodden. Sympathetic gay novels such as Niles' *Strange Brother,* on the other hand, were written more in sadness than anger, reflecting the fact that during the thirties there was very little of that political feistiness that gay men have displayed in recent years.

The obvious explanation of why Twilight Leagues fizzled, "adherents of Limbo" were unorganizable, and gay protest fiction didn't appear is that, unlike members of other minority groups, homosexuals were obliged to pass as heterosexuals and remain invisible. During this time most gay men had to keep up a day-to-day camouflage to convince everyone from mothers to employers to policemen and sometimes even themselves that they were not what they were, and this general invisibility kept them from sharing any sense of political solidarity. While they knew they could go from coast to coast and recognize each other, in the thirties the "gay community" was thought of in terms of sexual rather than political comrades-in-arms.

But the need to remain invisible was not the only reason gay men hesitated to write proletarian novels. Forty years ago gay males told themselves that rather than being downtrodden (read *déclassé*), they were all, like Karel in *The Young and Evil*, at least "slightly above average" and actually formed a marvelous elite in the best traditions of the Noble Uranian. Many fancied their secret brotherhood to be superior to the Masons and just a little lower than the angels, whom they resembled in beauty, grace, mystery, and ability to take flight at a moment's notice. Were they not, after all, as plucky as Miss Knight and as fastidiously "smart" as anyone in Van Vechten's novels? Did they not, in fact, affect a Noël Coward elegance with their cultivated palates, their dramatically decorated apartments with copies of *The New Yorker* and chic cigarette boxes on the cocktail tables, and their color-coordinated wardrobes complete with scarves for all occasions? Yes, says a gay man who remembers the thirties. "We all felt different, a cut above the dull heteros. We were better, more intelligent, different in the best of all possible ways.[36] In this context, it can be understood that when these gay males felt tempted to reach out toward the blue-collar laborer, their motivation was *not* political. At the time it was more rewarding to play games with rough trade in a city park than with editors and publishers in the world of American letters, and to a considerable extent it is for this reason that we have so few gay novels to tell us what it was like to be in the "shadow world" of the 1930s.

NOTES

1. *Strange Loves: A Study in Sexual Abnormalities* (New York: Padell, 1933), pp. 2-3. In a section titled "America 'Gone Pansy,' " Dr. Potter goes on to concede that there are thousands of "abnormals who can no more be held accountable for their queerness than they could be held accountable for their astigmatism, or clubfeet, or gallstones. They are no more to blame for their abnormally wide hips, feminine buttocks, hairless chests and mincing walk than they are to blame for a sinus infection, malaria, pyorrhea or hemorrhoids." (p. 45.)

2. This information is based on Arno Karlen's explanation of why serious research was not being done at the time in his *Sexuality and Homosexuality* (New York: Norton, 1971), p. 305: "Two forces worked against a study of the homosexual world being made in the thirties and forties. One was the moderate increase in permissive attitudes and the new knowing manner; flip knowledgeability always makes research seem unnecessary. Second, traditional attitudes still underlay this seeming liberation, distorting most writings on deviance."

3. Dr. Segall discusses "Inversions and Perversions" in *Sex Life in America* (New York: Bernard Marks, 1934), pp. 154-56.

4. In his account of homosexual hobos in *The Glory and the Dream* (Boston: Little, Brown, 1974), Manchester mentions on page 22 that the young Eric Sevareid was scarred when a strapping invert tried to seduce him for twenty-five cents. In Sevareid's 1946 memoir, *Not So Wild a Dream,* the broadcaster said he felt that abnormality was confined to British schoolboys and Paris bohemians, and he insists that during the unsuccessful seduction, he had no idea what was going on.

5. A copy of this advertisement, taken from a 1938 issue of *Tales of Wonder,* was used to illustrate an article on gay science fiction in the Pittsburgh *Gay News* for March 6, 1976, p. B10.

6. Foster, p. 241. Speaking of lesbian novels of the thirties, Foster adds: "Some of these inferior tales were censorious, some defensive, but all were so unrestrained that in this country, at least, certain pressure groups, notably the Catholic League for Decency, were roused to crusade for wholesale suppression." *The Well of Loneliness,* with an afterword by Barbara Grier, was republished in paperback in 1975 by Diana Press, Baltimore.

7. Ford's comments on the novel come from "Conversations in Kathmandu," an interview that appeared in *Gay Sunshine* (Spring 1975, pp. 20-26).

8. Parker Tyler as quoted by Maurice Girodias in his *The Olympia Reader* (New York: Grove Press, 1965), pp. 211-12.

9. Copies of this cardboard-back edition, reissued as one of the "Travellers Companion Series" by Olympia in Paris, were apparently allowed inside this country, as various university libraries own copies. *The Young and Evil* quotes come from pp. 56, 174-75, 117, 155-65, 118 ff., 183-91.

10. Vidal terms the novel a "pioneer work" of interest to "devotees of camp" in his 1966 essay "On Pornography," originally published in the *New York Review of Books* and quoted here from the reprint in *Sex, Death and Money* (New York: Bantam, 1968), p. 7.

11. According to Noel I. Garde's bibliography, *The Homosexual in Literature,* Scully's novel was also published by Nesor in 1937 and the later Royal edition (perhaps published in the late forties or early fifties) showed an improvement in vocabulary and style. It might also be added that among Garde's listings for the 1930s is *Secrets of a Society Doctor,* which was supposedly copyrighted by Harold S. Kahm in 1935 but seems not to have been published until after the war, as a Designs Publishing Corporation "Intimate Novel," with Jerry Cole listed as the author. One of the subplots concerns a fake psychiatrist befriending a distraught young gay man and then, a jump behind the reader, introducing him to another lonely gay man at the end of the novel.

12. Scully, *A Scarlet Pansy* (New York: Royal, n.d.), p. 126. This unlikely question and the even more unlikely response is no more fey than most of the chitchat in the novel.

13. The novel was discussed in the September 5, 1974, issue of the *Bay Area Reporter.*

14. This unsigned review appeared in *The Saturday Review of Literature* (October 31, 1931, p. 251). The publisher's quote about Mrs. Niles' pajamas is cited on page 1027 of the 1942 edition of Kunitz and Haycroft's *Twentieth Century Authors.* In a pioneering piece of gay literary criticism, Henry Gerber termed both *Strange Brother* and *Twilight Men* "anti-homosexual propaganda." A founding member of Chicago's Society for Human Rights, Gerber discussed these novels in "Recent Homosexual Literature," an article in the February 1934 issue of *Chanticleer,* a mimeographed literary magazine. This article is quoted by Jonathan Katz on page 394 of his *Gay American History* (New York: Crowell, 1976).

15. Niles, *Strange Brother* (New York: Harris, 1949), p. 135.

16. *Ibid.,* p. 312. It might be added that Mrs. Niles' literary weaknesses have more recently characterized Laura Z. Hobson's *Consenting Adult* and, to a lesser extent, Patricia Warren's *The Front Runner* and *The Fancy Dancer.*

17. Tellier, *Twilight Men* (New York: Pyramid Books, 1957), p. 209. This paperback features a quaint blurb promising that the story "dares to expose the most intimate experiences of the so-called 'third sex,' " plus updated illustrations that are inadvertently amusing.

18. Meeker, *Better Angel* (New York: Greenberg, 1933), pp. 84-85. The listing of famous gay people (all safely dead, of course) was almost a stock feature of sympathetic gay writing. Another list occurs in *Strange Brother* when Mark Thornton thinks of everyone he will include in his "manly love" anthology.

19. The final quotes are from page 284. The ending of *Better Angel* refutes the cliché that all early gay novels ended in suicide. Of the other six "major" novels in this chapter, the only clear-cut suicide is in *Strange Brother*. There is none in *The Young and Evil* or *Goldie;* the hero's death is clouded by mental confusion in *Twilight Men* and *Butterfly Man;* and of course we cannot take seriously Fay's giving up her tourniquet at the end of *A Scarlet Pansy*.

20. Bruce, *Goldie* (New York: William Godwin, Inc., 1933), p. 95. Many of the names on these lists are unknown to the apparently less well-educated American gay men of more recent generations: if you ask them to name illustrious homosexuals, most will begin—and end—with movie stars. Additional *Goldie* quotes are from pp. 241, 242-43, 244, 248, 253-54, 273, and 275.

21. Levenson, *Butterfly Man* (New York: Castle, n.d.), p. 181. The other quote is from pp. 200-1.

22. Brinig, *This Man Is My Brother* (New York: Farrar and Rinehart, 1932). Harry is described as effeminate on page 13, as sleepless on page 44. Other quotes are from pp. 301, 304-7.

23. Calmer, *Beyond the Street* (New York: Harcourt, Brace, 1934), p. 236. Other quotes are from pp. 289-90, 303-4.

24. Even what we now regard as the more obviously gay novels were not always recognizable to the readers of the thirties, Dr. Potter complained in *Strange Loves*. On page 3 he says "it is extremely doubtful if one person out of a thousand can read, for instance, 'The Well of Loneliness,' . . . 'Twilight Men,' . . . or 'Strange Brothers,' [sic] and then make a clear-cut statement as to just what the authors are attempting to describe." Based on his perceptiveness in *Strange Loves,* the doctor is no doubt speaking for himself.

25. Stout discusses bisexuality on page 119 of *Forest Fire;* in a personal note to me, Noel I. Garde has theorized that Stout may well have originally planned to have the assistant seduce the ranger, but decided against it at the last minute. It should be added that some of the "bisexual fiction" written during the thirties was not regarded as publishable until its author became a respectable man of letters in later decades. See, for instance, Paul Goodman's novelette, *Johnson,* written in 1932-33, published in *New Letters* (Winter–Spring 1976), pp. 15-81.

26. Prokosch is pictured (shirtless) and described in *Twentieth Century Authors* (New York: H. W. Wilson, 1942), p. 1132.

27. Radcliffe Squires, *Frederic Prokosch* (New York: Twayne, 1964), p. 103. Squires discusses the post–1945 mood on p. 7.

28. Another variation of this game—the historical remove *plus* the geographical—has been successfully played by the popular American paperback novelists Kyle Onstott and Lance Horner. The historical remove has also been used to great advantage, of course, by the British/South African

Mary Renault, who in addition has quite probably used the Double Albert Strategy (i.e., transforming two lesbians into two male characters) in some of her novels.

For a further example of the significance of the geographical remove, see Thomas Wolfe's 1935 *Of Time and the River*. Francis Starwick is necessarily mysterious at Harvard, but when he and Eugene Gant are in freewheeling Paris, the truth dawns and the mystery is penetrated: Starwick is nothing but a "fairy."

29. All of the information here about the writing of *Gentlemen, I Address You Privately* is based on an interview with Miss Boyle in San Francisco, January 1975.

30. *Nation*, November 29, 1933, p. 630.

31. Djuna Barnes, *Nightwood* (New York: New Directions, 1961), pp. 91, 110. Other quotes are from pp. 154-55 and 143.

32. Jane Rule, *Lesbian Images* (Garden City: Doubleday, 1975), p. 186. Earlier commentators, most notably T. S. Eliot and Jeannette Foster, felt that no one in *Nightwood* was "saved" but rather that all were helplessly lost and doomed. Eliot said the novel had a quality of horror close to Elizabethan tragedy, and Foster termed it a tragic prose poem of misfits and outcasts.

It is interesting to note, in passing, that some European gay writers were just as nervous and frustrated as their American counterparts, with a case in point being Julian Green, the son of American parents who was born and raised in France. Writing in his diary in 1930, Green lamented: "Thought this morning about the story I am writing at present. I stand with my back to the wall. In hesitating to talk about the hero's love for a young man, I falsify truth and seemingly conform to accepted morality. I act with a prudence that will make me lose all respect. It is behaving thus that one finally becomes a man of letters." This entry is found on page 12 of Green's *Diary 1928–1957* (New York: Harcourt, Brace and World, 1964).

33. Raymond Chandler, *The Big Sleep* (New York: Knopf, 1939), p. 120.

34. James Cain, *Serenade* (Baltimore: Penguin, 1948), pp. 139, 151.

35. Hoyt discusses this new slant on pp. 228-29 of his essay "The Tough Guy as Hero and Villain," in David Madden's collection, *Tough Guy Writers of the Thirties* (Carbondale: Southern Illinois University Press, 1968).

36. From background notes especially written for this study by "Phil Andros," Berkeley, California, 1975.

THE FORTIES

A T THE END of his revised version of *The City and the Pillar,*
Gore Vidal explained that he wrote the novel because he was
"bored with playing it safe. I wanted to take risks, to try something
no American had done before."[1] In the late forties, with *The Young
and Evil* still generally unheard of and the gay pulps of the thirties
gradually going out of print and mind, the postwar burst of novels
with gay themes was regarded by many as *the* breakthrough for
homosexual fiction in America. From today's standpoint, of course,
the authors of most of these novels seem to have been playing it
very safe indeed, by providing an array of multiple-choice interpretations to camouflage the gayness of their main characters and, not
incidentally, of the writers themselves. But from the standpoint of
the forties, such authors as Vidal, Truman Capote, Tennessee Williams, John Horne Burns, and Ward Thomas were regarded as quite
daring for using a theme that had been almost entirely unmentionable in the prewar and pre-Kinsey era.

World War II helped to liberate gay novelists in their personal
lives and to nudge Americans to question—if only halfheartedly
and briefly—some of their cherished opinions about absolute right

and wrong. As Ray Lewis White observes in his study of Vidal, "Only after World War II did many Americans have the courage to write seriously and to read understandingly about the one area of life seldom before explored—the world of the homosexual. Perhaps the experience of World War II did indeed lead to a reassessment of individual and national values; or perhaps the war taught Americans that only the relative morality of the individual—in the extreme, the homosexual—could be valid and important."[2] But the appearance of Alfred Kinsey's *Sexual Behavior in the Human Male* in 1948 was a clincher: the notion that homosexual acts were performed only by bogeymen-freaks was questioned by the statistic that one male out of every three had performed or would be performing such acts at least once during his lifetime. In some cases merely confirming what gay men had been telling one another for years, the Kinsey report went on to claim that on a continuum chart 13 percent of the male population was more homosexual than heterosexual. Such startling statistics helped to make the book a best-seller and forced major publishers to admit that there was both a curiosity about male homosexuality and an audience for novels with gay themes. It was after the war, and particularly during 1948 and 1949, that most of the gay fiction of the forties was published— so much of it, in fact, that by the end of the decade a *New York Times* reviewer complained that it was getting to be a "groaning shelf."

TWO "ALMOST GAY" NOVELISTS

The war years were much more significant for the fiction that was ultimately produced after 1945 than for the appearance of very much during the duration itself. For the first half of the forties, the trend that had begun in the mid-thirties continued, with the appearance of additional minor gay characters and themes in major fiction. A typical example of this sort of novel in the early forties was Henry Bellamann's 1940 *King's Row,* a sort of *Our Town* with epic sweep, in which the too beautiful Jamie Wakefield tries to kiss his high school friend at the end of a twilight walk. Eugene O'Brien included a case of mistaken homosexuality in the Navy in *One Way Ticket* (1940); Frederic Prokosch continued to write his veiled stories; and there were homosexual overtones in Paul Goodman's *The Grand Piano* (1942), Charles Jackson's *The Lost Weekend* (1944), and Fitzroy Davis' book about a rather gay theatrical troupe, *Quicksilver* (1942). Generally speaking, though, Americans were reading Marquand and Steinbeck and the Bible during the war years, and the only "almost gay" novels to appear before 1945 were those written by Harlan McIntosh and Carson McCullers.

THIS FINER SHADOW as Gay Novel

One of the most peculiar, uncertain and uneven gay novels ever published was Harlan McIntosh's *This Finer Shadow,* which was brought out by Lorac Books in 1941 and copyrighted by the author's widow. According to the publisher's blurb, McIntosh was born in John Day, Oregon, in 1908, as a youngster tried to defend a "queer" boy whom other schoolchildren were tormenting, was a state insane asylum attendant, ran away to sea, and in 1933 returned to this country to marry and to write his novel. The manuscript was repeatedly rejected, withdrawn, and rewritten; finally it was rewritten with the encouragement of John Cowper Powys, but was rejected again. "In despair," the blurb concludes, "McIntosh committed suicide on August 9, 1940, by plunging from the roof of the apartment house where he and his wife were living. This is his testament."

Although the blurb is careful to insist that McIntosh "himself was not homosexual," *This Finer Shadow* appears to have more than an assumed, vicarious interest in the problems of bisexuality. It seems likely, however, that the manuscript was not rejected solely because of its gay overtones; a number of valid aesthetic objections could have been raised as well. Even in its final draft, what emerges is a weird cross-breeding of the gay novel, the tough-guy genre and the exotic picaresque—quite as if, neatly enough, McIntosh had decided to write a work interweaving the gay literary strands of the thirties. Although Powys called it a work of "genius," *This Finer Shadow* never quite coheres, and both McIntosh and his novel have been forgotten, even by gay readers.

The three strands from the thirties are interwoven in the character of former seaman Martin Devaud, a twenty-eight-year-old semi-toughie whose bisexual experiences in exotic ports of call are remembered in veiled flashbacks. At the outset he and his shipmate buddy, Rio, are staying in the Bowery in New York City, and Martin gets a job through the strings-attached kindness of Mr. Roberts, a middle-aged employment counselor. Roberts falls in love; the love is not returned, and he then makes the mistake of introducing Martin to Deane Idara. Martin falls in love with Deane, who returns his love, but Deane is a woman, and a further complication develops when her gay friend, Carol Stevens, also becomes interested in Martin. Another main character is a gay friend of Mr. Roberts named Drew, and the confusion over names and sexes increases as a drag ball approaches and gay nicknames begin to be used.

To the drag ball, an obligatory scene in most of the gay novels of the thirties, come the following: Miss Roberts or Roberta, who says of Rio: "Her hard-boiled act doesn't fool me a bit"; Miss Stevens or Carrie, wearing a tiara and a leopard cape, who, when told she looks gorgeous, responds by saying, "I'm so glad you like me. I didn't want to look tacky"; plus, among others, Beulah (a retired manufacturer), Kate (just back from doing the Indians again in Chile), Miss Murphy (in her dime-store black lace), and Daisy, who as her contribution to the entertainment sings:

> I'm a little Prairie Flower
> Growing wilder every hour![3]

Though McIntosh re-creates the drag scene with more perceptiveness than Mrs. Niles in *Strange Brother,* the chitchat is still wooden and never approaches the fast-paced spontaneity of the snippets of party conversation overheard in *The Young and Evil.* What casts the greatest doubt on the believability of the party, though, is the appearance, in a pale canary evening gown and yellow satin slippers, of Miriam, who is none other than Martin Devaud! Soon after Miriam's arrival, pandemonium erupts: Rio crashes the party, knocks Miriam down; Drewena whips Rio; Martin leaves with Rio; and Drewena, upset at Martin's escaping from his clutches, vows to leave for Paris as soon as possible. At the end of the novel, Rio ships out again with Martin, who tells his buddy that someday they will find a "cloud and hold it."

Throughout the novel, McIntosh is either ambivalent or confused in establishing Martin's sexuality. When Carol tries to seduce him, Martin says that it gives him "the creeps" to think of having sex with another man, but he later tells Rio that both of them are probably gay and that homosexuality serves as a "resilient salient between the rigidity of the sexes." From a gay standpoint, a basic weakness of the novel is that while the author drops every hint that he is sympathetic toward homosexuals, he limits Martin's gestures of approval to those which are rather unlikely or unconvincing. In short, McIntosh was playing the game of writing a gay novel which, if need be, could be interpreted as otherwise.

The Novels of Carson McCullers

While Carson McCullers was apparently gay herself, it should be made immediately clear that she does not qualify as a writer of "gay novels" from the point of view of the male-gets-male or female-gets-female plot summary.[4] In each of her novels there is a male who has at least some sort of crush on another male, but however relevant Singer, Captain Penderton and Cousin Lymon may be to this study, perhaps it is the plight of the unbearably lonely, androgynous Biff Brannon at the end of *The Heart Is a Lonely Hunter* that symbolizes McCullers' vision most fully—he is ready to love "anybody decent who came in out of the street to sit for an hour" and just talk with him in his New York Café. What strikes a particularly responsive chord for many gay readers of McCullers' novels, then, is not so much who gets whom or even who loves whom as it is her underlying philosophy of love.

Simply to say that McCullers wrote about the irrationality of love falls short of capturing the essence of her brooding reflections about what happens when the beloved enters the life of the lover. The idea of Cupid shooting his arrows blindly has always been a staple of heterosexual fiction, and it is true that many straight literary romances have withered because of unrequited love. In the lives and works of the "average" heterosexual, however, the concept of irrational love is usually counterbalanced by the concept of the possibility of felicitous love. After all, heterosexuals are falling in love with the traditionally *proper* sex, and if at first they don't succeed, their chances are good that out of all of the hundreds of millions of heterosexuals around them they will eventually find someone who will be in a position to love them in return. In McCullers' novels, however, the irrationality of love has no such hopeful counterbalance—Singer and Penderton and Lyman are forced to cope with their feelings as best they can because, as is spelled out in *The Ballad of the Sad Café,* they can never translate their love into terms that will be understandable or acceptable to the beloved:

There are the lover and the beloved, but these two come from different countries. Often the beloved is only a stimulus for all the stored-up love which has lain quiet within the lover for a long time hitherto. And somehow every lover knows this. He feels in his soul that his love is a solitary thing. He comes to know a new, strange loneliness and it is this knowledge that makes him suffer. So there is only one thing for the lover to do. He must house his love within himself as best he can; he must create for himself a whole new inward world—a world intense and strange, complete in himself.[5]

This often-quoted passage goes on to say that the "beloved can be of any description" and that the "most outlandish people can be the stimulus for love"—but for the lover the impossible outlandishness "does not affect the evolution of his love one whit." The examples of irrational love that McCullers cites (preacher and fallen woman, great-grandfather and girl) are both heterosexual, but perhaps the ultimate in hopeless love is experienced by those who desire straight members of their own sex. This passage was especially relevant for gay readers of a generation ago because, for any number of reasons (e.g., the immediate unavailability of other gay men, the self-loathing which made only straight men worth loving), the initial and even subsequent love objects of most gay men used to be straights who could not love them in return and who often didn't even know they were being "loved" at all. Since these gay "lovers" could express their feelings neither verbally nor physically, they were forced to try to house their loves within themselves as best they could.

Even the McCullers characters who are not specifically gay—Mick Kelly and Frankie "Jasmine" Addams, for instance—have little success at falling in love "wisely." Mick fancies she is in love with a gay deaf-mute, and Frankie falls in love with, of all things, a wedding, and thus McCullers' thirteen-year-olds share a predicament with her gay characters. Both are confounded by their twilight state—the one being neither total child nor total adult and the other being neither total man nor total woman, with the possible distinction being that while the adolescent is expected to emerge eventually into clear-cut "normality," the gay character may continue falling in love over and over again with the type that cannot love him in return.[6]

McCullers did her best writing during the forties, and her important novels that came out during the decade were *The Heart Is a Lonely Hunter* (1940), *Reflections in a Golden Eye* (1941), and *Member of the Wedding* (1946), with *The Ballad of the Sad Café* coming out in 1951 and her final novel, *Clock Without Hands,* being published in the early sixties. The love that Singer has for Antonopoulos and the crush that Harry Minowitz has on Jake Blount did not prevent reviewers from praising *The Heart Is a Lonely Hunter* as an impressive first novel from a young lady who was then only twenty-three years old, but with the publication of *Reflections in a Golden Eye* the critics began to charge that McCullers was obsessed with abnormality, and the tone of Hubert Creekmore's review in *Accent* was fairly typical:

> The whole thing has the atmosphere of snickering in a privy. Most people know about the juicy items she displays, but one feels that Mrs. McCullers has just been told. . . . She ought to learn how to write, how to build characters that are more than a pathology diagnosis, how to

move them for her story, and how to be interesting without being abnormal.[7]

Thus, McCullers' novels have often been subject to the same homophobic attack that writers of more explicitly gay novels have had to endure from critics in this country. Since in the minds of some reviewers love was sane, predictable, rewarding, and above all *sensible,* most felt free to tag the attachments in McCullers' fiction as perversions of True Love—freakish, grotesque, and even morbid. But for gay readers there was naturally nothing surprising in the love of one man for another, and the special comfort they find in McCullers is the almost palpable sense that while she is brooding over Singer and for Captain Penderton, she is, in her soft, tremulous Southern way, brooding over them as well.

THE FOLDED LEAF:
ABNORMALITY NIPPED IN THE BUD?

While much of William Maxwell's *The Folded Leaf* (1945) reads like a genuinely gay novel, there are moments of strange Harlan McIntosh clumsiness in the final scenes, as Maxwell grinds gears and shifts into a "straight" ending. This ending is found eminently satisfactory by W. Tasker Witham, who, in *The Adolescent in the American Novel,* blithely assures us in a phrase that is more pretty than perceptive that by the end of this novel "the relationship between the two boys becomes a normal friendship, while the folded leaf of their undeveloped manhood unfolds into maturity."[8] Maxwell was born in Lincoln, Illinois, in 1908, grew up there and in Chicago, alludes to Tennyson in his title, and has written other fiction that has been characterized by, as Witham might say, the naturally unfolded maturity of adult heterosexuality.

The Folded Leaf focuses on the relationship of two young men as they grow up in Chicago in the twenties, and Maxwell's tone of bemused sentimentality places him closer to the tradition of Tarkington than to that of Farrell. However, a convincingly gay attitude is established in the first chapter, "The Swimming Pool," and is

repeated throughout the novel: the skinny Lymie Peters gets great
joy in looking at the athletic physique of Spud Latham. From
Lymie's first view of Spud when they are lined up to play water polo
in high school, on through to their college days, when Lymie tags
along to the gym dressing room to act as towel boy for his friend,
Spud's naked body exerts an irresistible fascination:

> He [Spud] had been a life guard all summer long at one of the street-
> end beaches in Chicago and the hair and eyebrows were still bleached
> from the sun. His skin was so tanned from the constant exposure that it
> looked permanent. He could have been a Polynesian. Though Lymie
> had seen him dress and undress hundreds of times, there is a kind of
> amazement that does not wear off. Very often, looking at Spud, he felt
> the desire which he sometimes had looking at statues—to put out his
> hand and touch some part of Spud, the intricate interlaced muscles of his
> side, or his shoulder blades, or his back, or his flat stomach, or the
> veins at his wrists, or his small pointed ears.[9]

This strange, gingerly, and deliberately anticlimactic detailing of
Spud's anatomy makes even Walt Whitman's cataloguing of the
male body sound gutsy, but Maxwell's strategy throughout is to
provide a multiple-choice explanation for Lymie's interest in Spud,
with one of the choices always genteel enough to satisfy the city
librarian of Lincoln, Illinois. For instance, in the above paragraph,
one may choose to interpret Lymie's interest as aesthetic rather
than sensual and assume that when his eyes wandered down to
Spud's crotch, he immediately averted his glance and busied himself
picking up those towels. When Lymie and Spud are snuggling up
close to each other in the double bed they share at their college
roominghouse, Maxwell again provides an innocuous motive. Their
landlord turns off the heat every night at 10 P.M., the Illinois win-
ters are cold, and they purely and simply want to keep warm.

From Spud's point of view, keeping warm was indeed the main
reason he wanted to snuggle, for Maxwell makes it clear that he is
quite straight. During their freshman year in college, Spud falls in
love with one of Lymie's classmates, Sally Forbes, and for a while
they are a gleesome threesome eating chocolate sundaes together at
the Ship's Lantern. In the spring, Spud forsakes Lymie by moving

into a fraternity where he belongs, and the bereft Lymie tries to commit suicide and fails. Spud never understands, of course, that he has been loved by Lymie all these years, even though this fact is quite clear to the gay reader and, I should think, to most straight readers.

Up to this point, the relationship between Lymie and Spud is a perfect illustration of McCullers' concept of the lover and the beloved, especially as Lymie illustrates her closing thought that the lover "craves" any possible relationship with the beloved, even if it brings nothing else than pain. After the attempted suicide, however, the consistency of Lymie's character ends in an uncertain turnabout. Rejecting the two possible "gay" endings (Lymie dying or Spud discovering that he himself is gay), Maxwell suggests that the convalescent Lymie is really straight after all, because he is considering an invitation to a spring house dance from a girl symbolically named Hope. But at the same time Maxwell never resolves the triangle that still unites Lymie with Spud, Spud with Sally, and Sally (in a sisterly way) with Lymie. The last lines of the novel reveal that the relationships are essentially unchanged and, furthermore, that the invitation from Hope has receded into insignificance.

[Sally] took his hand in hers and Lymie's hand in her other hand, and with her eyes shining with mischief she said, "Well, here we all are!"

"You guys," Spud said disparagingly, and made Lymie raise his knees, so that he and Sally could go on a camping trip up and down the cover.

It was some time before the nurse came in and put an end to this childish game.

From the standpoint of today, at least, it could well be that the real "game" in this novel has been played by William Maxwell. While it might be argued that he had a perfect right to end the novel as he pleased and that he himself might well be living proof that an adolescent can graduate from hero worship to heterosexuality, at the same time it must be said that within the context of the novel there are no convincing hints that Lymie is anything but genuinely gay. Regardless of Witham's comforting theory, when Lymie's leaves unfold, the blossoming will very likely be homosexual: he is exactly the sort of person to spend the rest of his life searching for a substitute for Spud.

TWO FLUSTERED MARRIED MEN

During the years 1946 and 1947, two novels were published that brought several "inevitable" comparisons from the reviewers— Charles Jackson's *The Fall of Valor* and Stuart Engstrand's *The Sling and the Arrow*. What they had in common was that the main character in each was a flustered married man, but while Jackson's John Grandin has recognizably gay impulses, Engstrand's Herbert Dawes most assuredly does not.

THE FALL OF VALOR: Another Amazing Physique

The Fall of Valor was published two years after *The Lost Weekend* (1944), Jackson's first and best-known novel about the disintegration of an alcoholic. Jackson's first published story, "Palm Sunday" (*Partisan Review*, 1939), focused on a lecherous small-town church organist as remembered by two grown-up brothers, but Jackson was never tagged publicly as a gay writer. Born in New Jersey in 1903, he married in 1938, was the father of two children (thus qualifying as normal), did some lecturing on the novel at universities, and died in 1968.

Jackson's title is taken from a passage in *Moby Dick,* where the fall from "immaculate manliness" is regarded as "sorrowful—nay, shocking," and his novel details the "fall" of John Grandin, a forty-four-year-old English instructor who leaves Manhattan to spend a few days of early summer vacation with his wife, Ethel, on Cape Cod. The year is 1943, and everywhere around him Grandin notices big, beautiful servicemen—they're all over the magazines and newspapers, and they are sitting next to him on the train to Massachusetts. On the train ride, he recalls having been distracted all spring by the young men wearing nothing more than shorts on the tennis courts outside his classroom, and the book he is carrying contains the poems of A. E. Housman.

This deft psychological scene-setting is completed with the information that the Grandins are troubled about their marriage—they hope to salvage it during their time together on the beach without the children—and thus Jackson has prepared the reader for Grandin's reaction to a handsome, well-built, disarming young Marine captain named Cliff Hauman. The first meeting between the Grandins and the honeymooning Haumans is unpromising enough—Billie Hauman turns out to have been one of Grandin's less talented creative writing students—and the age and personality gaps between the two couples are so great that there seems to be little basis for a deep friendship during their stay at the beach. The novel turns on Grandin's gradual discovery that his interest in Hauman is greater than, by the standards of prevailing American morality, it has any right to be. The first time the two men are undressing for the beach,

. . . out of a kind of furtive curiosity, Grandin could not keep from stealing a glance or two at the exposed and splendid physique. It was heroic: Hercules, Hector, a younger Odysseus, seen as they were never seen in the storybooks, and made modern by the startling whiteness of the hips above and below the tan. While he did not display himself exhibitionistically, Hauman nevertheless stalked about in the nude as if he were alone, apparently completely unconscious that his was a figure to be looked at. . . .[10]

To begin with, Grandin tries to filter the raw male beauty through the refinement of William Maxwell's vision: as long as he can convince himself that he is appreciating Cliff's body in literary and legendary rather than sexual terms, everything remains innocuous. Later Grandin comes up with another perfectly respectable basis for his increasing interest in Cliff: envy or "nostalgia for youth." In a passage that parallels McCullers' explanation of Captain Penderton's fascination with the easygoing, roughhousing camaraderie of the enlisted men in *Reflections in a Golden Eye,* Jackson says:

The war photographs which had been drawing his attention for so many months—what were they but a nostalgia for youth? He envied the solidarity, fraternity and fellowship of servicemen . . . and felt keenly his forty-four years. The thousand pictures of GIs at chow, the young flyers strapping on their parachutes as they ran for the bombers tuning up in the gray dawn, the helmeted half-naked leathernecks grinning for the camera at the wheel of bulldozers. . . .

In other words—in McCullers' words, to be exact—Grandin is trying to convince himself that his interest in the Marine is based on nothing more than a desire to belong to the *we* that Hauman symbolizes, a hearty band of heroic young warriors with whom, after all, the whole country seems to be in love. Midway through the novel, however, Grandin admits to himself that his private obsession with servicemen has become particularized, and it is with a sense of bewildered shock that he finally accepts the fact that he is "in love" with Cliff Hauman.

The crucial line in the novel which sets into motion the final scene is a seemingly offhand comment made by Cliff one day while he and Grandin are sunning on the beach by themselves. Cliff has been telling "Johnnie" about a helpful English prof who once made a pass at him, and after he says that he naturally rebuffed the advances, Grandin gets up to go into the water. Cliff's line is: "Of course, I was a lot younger then . . ." With nothing more to encourage him than this comment, Grandin eventually invites Cliff to drop by and see him after he gets back to his Manhattan apartment, where he will be alone for a while. Cliff does so with his usual buddy-buddy naïveté, and the final scene is thus fraught with great tension for Grandin, who wants everything to happen and yet is almost deathly afraid that it might. Cliff arrives on a hot, sticky morning, asks to take a shower, and does. "You son-of-a-bitch," Grandin thinks while Cliff splashes. "I will not be played with in this fashion. I will not be made a monkey of." Later, though, Grandin hears himself saying the words, "Cliff, I've grown very fond of you; I can't help it," and he starts to embrace the Marine, who, "as if by reflex," hits him over the head with fireplace tongs, knocks him out and leaves. Grandin is bloody and bowed when he regains consciousness, and he wishes that Cliff had "finished the job."

As in *Reflections in a Golden Eye,* there is no villainous character in *The Fall of Valor.* Jackson portrays his main character as essentially the victim, and if there is any villainy at all, it is not to be found in Cliff Hauman himself but in the "as if by reflex" rejection which American men feel obliged to display when confronted with tenderness from another male. In other words—to invert Melville's phrase—while Cliff finds Grandin's fall shocking, Jackson conceives of it as essentially sorrowful. *The Fall of Valor* is far more honest and courageous than *The Folded Leaf,* as Jackson's unresolved ending is infinitely more satisfactory and convincing than Maxwell's pretty resolution. The critical reaction to Jackson's novel was mixed. Quaintly enough, the *Library Journal* cautioned: "Subject, and especially bluntness of presentation, limit library use," and warned librarians to be sure to "read before purchase." *The New York Times* reviewer felt that Jackson had chosen an "embarrassing subject" and implied that married men could not presume to handle this theme with expertise. Edmund Wilson commented that Jackson had removed homosexuality from the "privileged level" of Proust and Gide and made it middle class, and Clifton Fadiman offered the dull thought that Grandin might symbolize a "larger and more pervasive disease of our own time, a universal failure of nerve."[11]

THE SLING AND THE ARROW:
Engstrand Misses the Mark

Stuart Engstrand's *The Sling and the Arrow* is the sort of novel that gives homosexuality a bad name. The inclusion of this title in gay literature bibliographies is misleading, because rather than being gay, Herbert Dawes is what we would today call a latent transsexual with voyeuristic tendencies.

In this work the author, who was probably more comfortable writing straight novels-of-the-Midwestern-soil, has written a clinical case study in fictional form, set on the California coast. Because of unresolved childhood conflicts, fashion designer Herbert Dawes has married a woman he regards as his "husband." His wife Lonna has an affair with a sailor who, if Herbert were gay, would also be a tempting bed partner for him; however, in his voyeuristic fantasies, Herbert is content to imagine himself as Lonna in bed with the sailor. At the end of this weird novel, when Lonna tells her husband that she is expecting the sailor's baby, Herbert kills her, goes to his dress shop, puts on matron's drag, speeds out of town, and is apprehended and jailed.

In *The New York Times,* Helen Eustis wrote: "This honest, clinical novel will be compared with Charles Jackson's *The Fall of Valor* . . . if for no better reason than the fact that we have so few novels of homosexuality in English. . . . If Mr. Jackson's novel was on the one hand more tightly composed and graceful, on the other hand we must give Mr. Engstrand the credit that is due his book for being more extensive and more courageous."[12] These comments are imperceptive even for the forties, and are all the more disappointing coming from *The New York Times,* whose critics are expected to enlighten rather than add to the general confusion.

JOHN HORNE BURNS: The Star Rises . . . and Falls. . . .

"Everyone's still wearing their veil," an American second lieutenant calls out early in the evening in the gay bar which provides the setting for Burns' "Momma," and then he adds, knowing full well what is going to happen, ". . . but wait . . ."[13] In this portrait of Momma and her bar, set in the middle of *The Gallery* (1947), Burns gradually lifts up the veil to reveal with piercing clarity a glimpse of gay American GIs spending an evening together with their British, French, and Italian counterparts in occupied Naples *circa* 1944. At the end of "Momma," the veil comes down over the rest of the portraits and promenades in *The Gallery,* and it remained more or less coyly arranged when Burns wrote *Lucifer with a Book* (1949) and almost totally in place for *A Cry of Children* (1952), published a year before his death. But as Gore Vidal points out, Burns "had his moment" and that moment was "Momma," which remains one of the most brilliant pieces of gay writing in English of this century.[14]

Burns was born into an Irish Catholic family in Andover, Massachusetts, in 1916, went to Harvard, and taught English at the Loomis School from 1937 to 1942. After a stint in the infantry, he spent the war years as an officer reading POW mail in Italy, where he was able to soak up all of the sun and warmth and love and sex so often denied the inhabitants of our bleaker shores. "In the classic tradition of northern visitors to the South," Vidal comments, "Burns is overwhelmed by the spontaneity of the Italians," and in a gay context *The Gallery* shows Burns to be most overwhelmed by the Italians' freewheeling bisexuality, which dazzles and melts the more straightlaced gay GIs.

As was perfectly acceptable if not downright obligatory in war novels of the time, there was a good deal of sexuality in *The Gallery*. In writing his sexual scenes, though, Burns had to be ambiguous and clever enough to appeal to his gay readers without giving himself away to his straight readers, and he did so with oblique references to street-corner cruising and caresses meant to console for "every hurt the world had ever inflicted." In fact, from a homosexual standpoint, most of the portraits in *The Gallery* have a direct correlation with the explicitly gay "Momma," which forms the cornerstone of the work. With scattered allusions to the Astor bar and the swishy set and midnight pickups in Algiers, Burns drops "bobby pin" clues that the dominant awakening in this novel is gay and that he is only bringing in occasional female characters in order to play the game and pass.

Even in "Momma," however, Burns had to be careful to filter the evening at a gay bar through the eyes of a heterosexual woman, who is in the first part of the portrait dutifully described as she treads water before she is allowed to open her Galleria Umberto bar at 1630 hours. But Momma is quite different from McAlmon's straight persona who viewed European gay life in the twenties—she is maternally *simpatica* as she stands at her cash register, taking an interest in each of her regulars. One by one, or two by two, they enter her bar and begin drinking and cruising and talking: the wary Desert Rat, who once loved perfectly; the campy Negro second lieutenant who admires her hat with its cherry-eating bird; the lesbian WAC who comes to read and growl; the newlyweds, a lance corporal and a Grenadier Guard; the Italian civilians who flutter over some American parachutists and sailors who are deciding to be "trade" for the evening; the Italian count, dying of love, who greets Momma with a "tender wretchedness"; French officers who wish each other *bon appetit;* Ella, the Australian who wears flowers and feathers in his fedora; and Esther and Magda, two British sergeants who wear shorts "draped like an old maid's flannels."

It is to Esther and Magda that Burns gives the longest and most sustained conversation, because, spinsters that they are, they have come not to cruise but to analyze, dissect—and get drunk. Early in the evening they try to claim retroactively the sexual swirl now excluding them by calling up glories of their younger days:

"For some hours I've known, though they'll never come again, I'd cheerfully pass all eternity in hell."

"And I too, Magda. That's the hell of it. We have all known moments, days, weeks that were perfect."

"All part of the baggage of deceit, Esther. God lets us have those moments the way you'd give poisoned candy to a child. And we look on all those wonderful nights with far fiercer resentment than an old lady counting the medals of her dead son."

"But we've had them, Magda; we've had them. No one can take them away from us."

"Momma" ends with Esther and Magda passing out in each other's arms after they agree that "some compromise must and will be reached" in the future; a drunken American roaring "Ya will, willya!" when he decides he doesn't want to be trade after all; a fight breaking out; the Desert Rat, "roused from his torpor," leaping in to "defend the fallen"; the MPs coming in with their nightsticks; and Momma "fainting."

The critical reaction to *The Gallery* was generally favorable, with the *Boston Herald* announcing that a "new literary star has risen," the *New York Herald Tribune* calling it a novel of "extraordinary skill and power," and *The Saturday Review* terming it one of the "best" of the novels to come out of the war.[15] Few American critics could fault Burns' thesis, which might be thought of in terms of a bouquet to the people of Italy in gratitude for those moments of perfect "lovin":

I remember that I came to love the courtesy and the laughter and the simplicity of Italian life. The compliment I pay to most Italians who haven't too much of this world's goods is that they love life and love. I don't know what else there is, after all.

In 1947 Burns told Gore Vidal that he was certain it was necessary to be gay to be a good writer and quickly named six other celebrated authors who, with himself, formed a "pleiad of pederasts" on the American literary horizon.[16] As he later put it, Burns decided to "come out of the cloister" with his second novel, *Lucifer with a Book,* which focused on the love affairs of the teachers and students at a coed prep school in New England.

Unlike war novels, American school novels of the forties were not supposed to be suffused with sex, especially the sort that pervades *Lucifer with a Book.* While it is true that Guy Hudson, the veteran turned history teacher, ends up courting the ex-WAC Betty Blanchard, the inclusion of the alternating chapters about Betty and the girls' school appears to be as perfunctory as Burns' mention of hot-blooded Italian women in *The Gallery.* Hudson is the dominant character, and all the males around him—students or staff— are appreciated or deprecated in sexual terms. Among the students are Ralph DuBouchet, who has a crush on Hudson; the dumb muscular Buddy Brown, who, in open pajamas, tries to seduce Hudson; plus the campy Abbott, Abbess, and Bishop, who invite willing types such as The Body to their gay Little Evenings at Home at "The Abbey" for pleasures not hard to divine. Among the faculty are "Auntie" Sour, who teaches Romance languages and meets his students in Provincetown during vacation, and spindly Philbrick Grimes, a closet case who delights in playing the role of campus busybody as if he were the reincarnation of Alexander Pope. The novel is steamy with post-practice shower-room scenes in which teacher and student share the same stall, and during vacations Hudson has a lot of sex in New York with unspecified "bed companions for the night."

In order to have a respectable rationale for this would-be gay novel, Burns uses the supplementary theme of criticizing secondary education in postwar America, especially as it takes place in snobbish private schools, and thus the portraits of Grimes and Sour could be regarded as part of this indictment. It was this theme, "the parlous state of American private school education," that the reviewers felt more comfortable in analyzing, and many of them believed the novel was weakened by Burns' "righteous indignation," "gall," and "fury." Maxwell Geismar in *The Saturday Review* took a fairly unruffled view of the sexual side of the novel:

> The central love affair of the novel, through which Guy Hudson finally realizes the difference between sex and love, is not altogether convincing. What is apparent, however, just as in the English sophisticates, is the dominant sexuality of the novel and a sexuality that finds expression in harsh and even violent terms. There is an inverted Puritanism . . . a remarkably sophisticated sense of evil and malice. . . .

On the other hand, the reviewer for the *Catholic World* was, as might be guessed, scandalized by the sexual overtones:

> His sole attempts at realism are confined to the introducing of vulgar words and indecent scenes. Moreover, the book is filled with cynical obscenities, and Krafft-Ebing, who is named only once, seems to have inspired the author frequently.[17]

In an early piece of gay literary criticism, "The Ambiguous Heroes of John Horne Burns," in *One* for October 1958, Daniel Edgerton points out that *Lucifer with a Book* was weakened by Burns' trying to squeeze the essentially gay Hudson into a nominally straight mold. In spite of Burns' pride in being one of the postwar smart set of gay writers, there is justification to Edgerton's criticism that Burns ultimately does surrender to the demands of the straight reader who is expecting a straight romance. Given the intense homoerotic interest that both Guy and Ralph have in each other and in other males throughout the novel, their last-minute conversions to heterosexuality are not believable for Edgerton, who says that while "the problem of homosexuality was strongly, if not primarily, on the author's mind . . . he was unwilling to deal with it openly."[18] As a result, Burns was generally forced to expand on "themes in which he was not especially interested in order to cover up the forbidden theme." Burns has less difficulty in *The Gallery,* Edgerton says, because there he could expound wholeheartedly on the need for everyone to have love and understanding. In *Lucifer with a Book,* however, with the gay motif not closely related to the condemnation of private schools, the result is that "neither theme is treated successfully."

The other "ambiguous hero" Edgerton discusses is David Murray, the young would-be straight concert pianist in Burns' strange novel, *A Cry of Children.* While David has an affair with Isobel Joy, Burns hints that it was really her handsome brother whom David had loved when both were in the Navy. Edgerton cites all of the allusions indicating that Burns has once more dressed up a gay man in straight clothing, and he concludes that reality has been distorted in both of the later novels. (For a variety of reasons, straight reviewers were also greatly disappointed with *A Cry of Children,* one of them finding just a "few vague echoes of his original talent," and another wondering "what has happened to John Horne Burns.")

What was happening to Burns in the early fifties, according to Gore Vidal, was that he "was drinking himself to death in Florence. Every day he would go to the Grand Hotel and stand in the bar and drink Italian brandy, which is just about the worst thing in the world. . . . He was living with a doctor, an Italian veterinarian. They had a rather stormy relationship, but nothing sinister about it. One day he was drunk at a bar, wandered out in the hot midday sun and had a stroke. Cerebral hemorrhage . . . I think he wanted to die."[19] At the end of his appreciative biography of Burns, John Mitzel writes that "Americans have always had a particular love for the beautiful young author of just a few books who dies early in life: Poe, Hart Crane, Fitzgerald, West, Burns, Sylvia Plath . . ."[20] It seems to be the case, though, that the straight readers who liked him for *The Gallery* have almost entirely forgotten him, and the vast bulk of gay readers, who should love him for *The Gallery,* have never even heard of him.

END AS A MAN: What Happened to Southern Chivalry?

Another postwar school novel containing a gay motif was *End As a Man* (1947) by Calder Willingham. The author was born in Georgia in 1922, went to the Citadel, and set his satiric novel in a military academy in the South.

The gay aspects in *End As a Man* are totally different from those in *Lucifer with a Book,* as Willingham is far more forthright in his unflinching and unflattering portraits of Perrin McKee and Carroll Colton, the two gay cadets at the academy. In Willingham's novel, the only coy winking is done not by the author but by Perrin and Carroll, who cope as best they can in a sultry atmosphere where heterosexual braggadocio is the order of the day. In their literary preciousness, Perrin and Carroll are much like the Abbess and the Abbott, but rather than being indulged or even tolerated, as Burns' gay students are, these two cadets are clearly out of step in a Southern military academy preparing officers for World War II. Perrin falls in love with dashing Jocko de Paris and then makes the mistake of reading from his private notebooks to freshman Robert Marquales, whom he has gauged to be sympathetic:

> I have been wondering about this business of love at first sight. Of course it sounds foolish. But isn't it true that the shape of a face or the look of an eye can do more to determine love than the deepest spiritual compatibility? Isn't it true that the man who loves is not rational?[21]

Willingham is not McCullers, however—Marquales is not at all gay, and Perrin and Carroll are treated with derision by the other cadets, who, while they may be Southern, at least pride themselves on not being *decadent. End As a Man* was regarded as obscene by the New York Society for the Suppression of Vice—but generally for heterosexual rather than homosexual excesses, and Willingham's caricature of the silly and simpering fags must have been cruel enough to satisfy the most insistently homophobic readers. It might be added that Willingham had little respect for the institution he was satirizing and that nearly all his characters seem monstrous, but this is cold comfort indeed for the gay reader who waits in vain for the author to allow that in at least a few ways his gay cadets, the only ones *not* caught up in the macho madness, are really the best of the lot.

THE CLEVER STRATEGY OF TRUMAN CAPOTE

Truman Capote is one of the few post–World War II novelists who has been shrewd enough to have been able to prevail during the past thirty years as both a writer and a nationally known personality. Because of media exposure, Capote's idiosyncrasies are now equated with his being gay, not only by homosexuals but also by heterosexuals who feel free to snicker when television comedians go into their Capote act. Nonetheless, this doughty Southerner has skillfully avoided being pigeonholed as a gay writer through the (perhaps carefully calculated) versatility that has produced such double-barreled works as *In Cold Blood.* Although there are gay overtones in this and most of his other writings, the focus in this chapter will be on his best-known novel of the forties, *Other Voices, Other Rooms.*

In 1948 the American reading public was not nearly so knowing about homosexuality as it is today; however, the famous picture on the back of *Other Voices, Other Rooms* served notice to all that this was a novel written by a very special person. Although in tone and atmosphere this book may be regarded as gay, in actual fact Capote avoids having his main character come to grips with the problem by keeping his thirteen-year-old safely prepubescent. In this sense Capote has played it safe by retreating far enough back into his Southern childhood so that Joel Harrison Knox, however gay he might be expected to turn out eventually, is allowed to remain sexless within the terms of the novel. *Other Voices, Other Rooms* is thus similar to some of McCullers' novels in which the homosexual sensibility is conveyed although none of the main characters is required to make a definitively gay commitment.

Cousin Randolph does indeed provide a gay motif, but this is just one of the threads woven into the fabric of the novel. Viewed as a gay male, Randolph has much to say that is apt: recalling the "rainy lilac April" when he was in love with the beautiful prize-fighter, Randolph says:

It was different, this love of mine for Pepe, more intense than any-thing I felt for Dolores, and lonelier. But we are alone, darling child, terribly, isolated each from the other; so fierce is the world's ridicule we cannot speak or show our tenderness; for us, death is stronger than life, it pulls like a wind through the dark, all our cries burlesqued in joyless laughter; and with the garbage of loneliness stuffed down us until our guts burst bleeding green, we go screaming round the world, dying in our rented rooms, nightmare hotels, eternal homes of the transient heart.[22]

But Randolph can also be viewed symbolically, and should be, ac-cording to William Nance (*The Worlds of Truman Capote*), who says that he "is meant to function not primarily as a sexual deviate but as a generalized symbol of all humanity in its need for love— an ideal object for the complete, undiscriminating commitment of which Joel is now almost, but not quite, capable."[23] Joel, in accept-ing Randolph, is prepared to accept everyone else. So the reader is free to interpret Randolph's plea for those who have fallen in love with someone from "another country" as the universalized hope that all human beings will somewhere find affection:

The brain may take advice, but not the heart, and love, having no geography, knows no boundaries: weight and sink it deep, no matter, it will rise and find the surface: and why not? Any love is natural and beautiful that lies in a person's nature. . . .

Surely Randolph speaks for all humanity—men as well as women, heterosexuals as well as homosexuals—when he tells Joel that "What we most want is only to be held . . . and told . . . that every-thing . . . everything is going to be all right."

W. Tasker Witham, that self-appointed one-man Watch and Ward Society, interprets Randolph as a sinister deviate "whose schemes to get and keep Joel for his own perverted pleasure" motivate much of the plot.[24] "Normal" is one of Witham's favorite words, and he goes on to say that "it is Joel's struggle to 'wake up,' to escape from the death world of Skully's Landing and move on toward a world of normal maturity that forms the main conflict" of *Other Voices, Other Rooms.* Witham's view of Randolph is witless—people who go screaming around the world and die in rented rooms are victims, not villains.

Capote's more recent writing is also discussed by William Nance, whose comment about the "chosen dreamers" in *The Grass Harp* suggests that these dreamers could very well be symbolizing gay people:

> *The Grass Harp* contains Capote's fullest expression of antagonism between his chosen dreamers and the rest of society. The Capote characters we have met don't fit in and, since Joel Knox, they don't seem to want to. They are innocent pilgrims wandering in search of some better place. Society for its part considers them "crazy" and tries to put them into its prisons and its starchy straitjackets. . . .[25]

These are the characters, of course, whom gay people can identify with, and the special qualities of sensitive understanding and feisty individualism are more important than any isolated homoerotic scenes for the homosexual reader of Capote. For instance, while the gay reader can recognize the importance of Collin going swimming with and being hugged by Riley in *The Grass Harp,* the greater charm of the story lies in the delightful sense of coziness that Collin shares with Riley, Dolly Talbo, and Catherine Creek up in that treehouse. In short, Capote's appeal for many gay readers is probably based not so much on what he says as on the peculiarly delightful way in which he says it.

HUBERT CREEKMORE'S *THE WELCOME:* THE IRRECOVERABLE PAST DOWN SOUTH

If Capote skirted the issue of homosexuality in *Other Voices, Other Rooms* by keeping his main character too young, Creekmore skirts the issue in this little-noticed 1948 novel by making his main characters too old. In *The Welcome* Don Mason and Jim Furlow are not too old for sex, of course, but they are too old to be able to recapture that seemingly perfect adolescent affection they had for each other as high school buddies in Ashton, Mississippi.

It may be remembered that Creekmore is the critic who in 1941 faulted McCullers for the snickering over the juicy items in *Reflections in a Golden Eye*. Something must have happened to this Mississippi-born poet-novelist-reviewer in the intervening years, because the relationship between Don and Jim is certainly juicier than that between Captain Penderton and Private Williams. Moreover, Creekmore's thesis in *The Welcome*—"If only people could forgive each other for loving"—is nothing short of a corollary to McCullers' philosophy of love.

Set in the thirties, *The Welcome* begins with Don Taylor coming back home to Ashton from New York to live with his mother, and Creekmore emphasizes the difficulty that single people have in trying to belong in a small town where nearly everyone else is married. The closeness that Don and Jim Furlow enjoyed in high school has faded, but midway through the novel Jim, now married to a frigid wife, begins to wonder if it cannot be recaptured. The two go out into the woods on a hunting trip, and as they go to bed, Jim says, "Gosh, this is wonderful . . . just us out here . . . and no one to bother. . . ."[26]

Toward the end of the novel, two threads of the plot are crisscrossing. On the one hand, Don gets a job on the *Ashton Herald* and, in order to feel that he somehow still belongs, begins to spend time with Miss Isabel, the town bohemian who falls in love with him. On the other hand, Jim grows more and more dissatisfied with his marriage and begins to wonder why he ever rejected his friend:

> Jim couldn't understand to what compulsion he had yielded that made him forsake the close perfection of those days [with Don] for marriage with Doris. As he grew older, he feared the town or himself; he doubted the endurance of this adolescent happiness which dragged on into young manhood. He forced himself to scoff at it. . . .

However, by the time Jim makes up his mind to go over to Don's house and propose that they go away together, it is too late. "During all those years behind us," Don tells him, "I loved you. But you always threw it away, because you could always be sure it was there." Don tells him he has decided to marry Miss Isabel in order to qualify as an accepted member of the community. The novel

closes with the wedding, and after the ceremony Jim rushes up-
stairs to Don's old bedroom to try to find something to hang on to.
There are tears in his eyes as he pulls out a book:

> The title danced before his eyes and at last waved away while the
> words of a poem, "pity this busy monster manunkind Not . . ." wriggled
> across his brain as if written in water. And beside the water he lay with
> Don, wet from swimming, hot in the sun on the yellow sand, and Don
> reading to him, and the quiet of the woods all around. . . .

GORE VIDAL AND HIS ALL-MALE EDEN

Only with the publication of Vidal's *The City and the Pillar* in
1948 did there emerge a main character whose gayness was not
camouflaged by his being too young, too old, sexually ambivalent,
frightened, silly, or pathological. Though hesitant to admit it to
himself, Jim Willard turns out to be definitely gay, and thus *The
City and the Pillar* is the most forthright novel of the decade. Moreover, it appears to be the first major American novel written by a
respectable man of letters to break a one-hundred-year-old national
taboo: in the nineteenth century males could kiss each other but
not disrobe; in the twentieth century they could undress together
but not kiss; in *The City and the Pillar* they do both.[27]

When Vidal said he was tired of playing it safe, the earlier work
he was referring to included *A Novel* (1943), *Williwaw* (1946),
and *In a Yellow Wood* (1947). *A Novel,* a 175-page typescript
now owned by the Wisconsin State Historical Society, was begun
while Vidal was at Phillips Exeter Academy.[28] The hero of this
"abandoned" and unpublished story was a dead gay American
writer, a befriender of tennis players, who is remembered in flashbacks by three men at his funeral. In his first published novel,
Williwaw, there was almost no sexual overtone of any kind—it was
a short and perhaps deceptively simple tale of the crew of an army
freight/passenger ship facing a storm in the Aleutians. *In a
Yellow Wood,* however, does have gay aspects. The title and theme
are from the Frost poem, "The Road Not Taken," and the novel
focuses on the inability of veteran Robert Holton to break out of a

conventional, snug niche in postwar America. During the course of one day in Manhattan, where he works in a brokerage house, Holton rejects an offer of escape made by an old war buddy, rebuffs a gay man at a cocktail party, and rejects the milieu of a gay bar which he visits with a former lover (female). The novel ends with Holton deciding not to take the bohemian road but rather to stay on Wall Street.

In his afterword to the revised version of *The City and the Pillar* of 1965, Vidal mentions that the manuscript was actually written in 1946, and it is likely that a practical reason for postponing publication was the author's desire to establish his credentials as a novelist of undeniable worth. With the publication of his first two novels, Vidal did indeed make what he has called the "OK List of writers in 1947 and 1948," along with Burns and Willingham. "Capote and Mailer were added in 1948. Willingham was soon dropped; then Burns (my own favorite) sank, and by 1949 in the aftermath of *The City and the Pillar* I too departed the OK List."[29]

It is understandable that in writing *The City and the Pillar,* Vidal felt he was trying to do something that no American had done before, particularly with his emphasis on the naturalness of homosexuality. (It should be remembered that Vidal was only about seven when the spate of gay novels was published in the early thirties, and although as a boy he had access to thousands of books up in his grandfather's attic library, it is unlikely that Senator Gore had purchased *Better Angel* or *Strange Brother.*) In his afterword to the revision of *The City and the Pillar,* Vidal went on to explain his aims:

> I decided to examine the homosexual underworld (which I knew rather less well than I pretended) and in the process show the "naturalness" of homosexual relations. . . . In 1946 . . . it was a part of the American folklore that homosexuality was a form of mental disease, confined for the most part to interior decorators and ballet dancers. Knowing this to be untrue, I set out to shatter the stereotype by taking as my protagonist a completely ordinary boy of the middle class and through his eyes observing the various strata of the underworld.[30]

Naturalness is the keynote of the flashback chapter into adolescence near the start of Vidal's account of this ordinary boy, Jim

Willard. The early events of Chapter 2 are quite as normal and rugged as Ernest Hemingway: Jim and his buddy with the dark red hair, Bob Ford, play some tennis and then decide to spend the weekend at a deserted cabin by a river. It is June, and Bob, who has just graduated from high school, has decided to leave the small Virginia town and go up to New York and perhaps out to sea. At the cabin, Jim and Bob gather firewood, go swimming, lie in the sun, cook, eat, complain about the present and wonder about the future. "The air was gold. The leaves on the trees were green-gold . . ." and Jim "was feeling at peace, as if he were part of the day." All is so natural and idyllic that what happens after they start wrestling by their fire Saturday seems to follow as perfectly inevitable:

> Their bodies, warm in the warm night, met with a primal violence; to be one, to be one not two, to be whole not halves, that was the rage that held them together . . . so they met. Eyes tight shut against the irrelevant world. In the sky, summer stars fell. . . .

There is something of a Boy Scout benediction upon this campfire sex because it is so spontaneous and reverent and kind. Because of the magnetic magic and because it all seemed as natural and sublime as the trees and the stars, this experience with Bob, as Ray Lewis White points out, "becomes the point in Willard's life that remains his ideal, his secret touchstone for measuring all later adventures."[31]

Of course, Jim never recaptures the perfection of this moment in all of these later adventures which take place with a certain degree of calculated cunning in places like Hollywood and New York. No one that Jim has sex with—from the movie star Ronald Shaw to the vaguely masochistic writer Paul Sullivan—can ever measure up to Bob Ford, and there is in the whole novel the same sense of inevitability that marked Chapter 2: Jim "maintained his secret and it grew inside him and became important to him, a part of himself that no one might ever know or share: a memory of a cabin and a brown river. Someday he would relive that again and the circle of his life would be completed."

At the end of the novel, when Jim goes back home to Virginia for Christmas, he is not at all upset to learn that Bob has married a high school sweetheart, because according to the psychology of the forties a special premium was attached to seducing someone who was "straight," "trade," or at least "jam."[32]

Jim would have been surprised if Bob had become homosexual; he would have liked him less, for his love of Bob came from the fact that Bob had been drawn to him as a person, in spite of the object, and the original force would not have diminished over the years, could not have diminished. He was glad that Bob liked women. It would make their affair more unusual for both of them, more binding.

Throughout the novel Jim has not only clung to these illusions about Bob, he has also maintained a few about himself (e.g., he is not just another chichi cocktail party faggot: his bed partners have to be "young men like himself who were still natural and not overly corrupted"). Thus Jim fancies himself an exceptionally worthy object for Bob's desire, which is supposed to be rekindled in a dingy New York hotel room where the lighting is now provided by a naked light bulb and where the warmth comes from whiskey. Although Jim tries verbally to re-create the idyllic campfire setting as the two men lie on the hotel bed, nothing works, and when he takes Bob in his arms, the response is: "You're a queer; you're nothing but a damned queer. Go on and get your ass out of here!" Jim does leave, but not before he strangles (in the 1948 book)/rapes (in the revised edition) his uncooperative friend.

Although Vidal remembers that most reviewers were "hostile" in 1948, there was indeed some praise for *The City and the Pillar.* In *The Saturday Review,* John Aldridge's first reaction was that the author's achievement was "impressive" because he was making a "tragic affirmation in the midst of futility." The *Atlantic Monthly* called it a "brilliant exposé of subterranean life," and Christopher Isherwood thought it was "one of the best novels of its kind yet published in English. It isn't sentimental, and it is frank without trying to be sensational and shocking."[33] Vidal recalls that "the book was a best seller, not only in the United States but in Europe, where it was taken seriously by critics, not all engaged. André Gide presented me with a copy of *Corydon,* as one prophet to another.

E. M. Forster invited me to Cambridge . . ." Vidal says that later that year, "Dr. Kinsey revealed what American men were actually up to, and I was somewhat exonerated for my candor. I even received a nice letter from the good Doctor, complimenting me on 'your work in the field.' "[34]

At the time, Vidal was more affected by the negative reviews. "When the book was published in 1948," he recalls, "it was received with shock and disbelief. How could that young war novelist (last observed in the pages of *Life* magazine posed like Jack London against a ship) turn into this? *The New York Times* refused to take advertising. . . ."[35] According to *The New Yorker,* the novel was "unadorned tabloid writing . . . the kind of dreary information that accumulates on a metropolitan police blotter." *The New York Times* reviewer said, "Presented as the case history of a standard homosexual, this novel adds little that is new to a groaning shelf. Mr. Vidal's approach is coldly clinical . . . he has produced a work as sterile as its protagonist." Two adjectives from this review, Vidal says, have "popped up to haunt that book":

"Clinical" is used whenever one writes of relationships which are not familiar. I dare say that if the story had dealt with a boy and a girl instead of two boys the book would have been characterized as "lyrical." "Sterile" is an even deadlier curse upon the house, and comes from a dark syllogism in the American *Zeitgeist:* the homosexual act does not produce children therefore it is sterile; Mr. X's book is concerned with the homosexual act therefore the book is sterile.

While Vidal was quite right in charging his detractors with homophobia, it must also be said that to illustrate his theme, he had to look askance at the unseemly lives of most of his gay characters (who composed "one of the most astonishing collections of strange men ever to people a novel," according to one reviewer). However fallacious it was of Jim to place Bob Ford up on that pedestal, the fact remains that he did so, and by contrast Jim's experiences with Shaw and Sullivan and others who are comparatively unnatural and overly corrupted are necessarily depicted as less fulfilling. Vidal succeeds in showing the utter naturalness of homosexual relations only in the campfire scene.[36] Jim never finds any later relationship to be as innocent and charming and worthwhile as the one he had with Bob; indeed an adequate substitute must *not* be found, or he would have no compelling need to search out his old friend at the end of the novel. Viewed from the post–gay lib seventies, there is actually a certain homophobic strain in Vidal's theme, however it might be explained away as a faithful representation of gay psychology of the forties. The concept that the really worthy and desirable bed partners are straight and the corollary that having sex with just another fag is not much to boast about unwittingly played into the hands of straight reviewers, who therefore sensed that the Bob Fords of everyday life and they themselves were a slightly superior breed in contrast to the Shaws and the Sullivans. While it is true that in recent years Vidal has turned the tables with a malicious vengeance in *Myra Breckinridge* and *Myron,* it nonetheless seems that in 1948 some of the reviewers' points about the unsatisfactoriness of gay life were not only understandable but inevitable. If in *The City and the Pillar* Vidal here and there perpetuated rather than shattered the stereotype of the homosexual, he had only himself to blame.

In the few scholarly analyses of American gay fiction that have appeared over the last twenty years, *The City and the Pillar* has almost invariably been cited and occasionally discussed with considerable astuteness. In *The Apostate Angel: A Critical Study of Gore Vidal,* Bernard Dick views the novel as embodying a "homoerotic paradise myth—an all-male Eden" complete with its brown river running through the pastoral bower of bliss. Quite rightly, Dick stresses the importance of bodies of water in the novel, noting that the story begins and ends with the image of a river:

> In a New York bar, Jim Willard recalls a period from 1937 to 1943 as his fingers idly trace islands and rivers in the water that spilled from his drink. At first the crude cartography seems like drunken doodling, but out of the geography of reminiscence a watery Eden appears on the charred tabletop—a savage parody of the idyllic retreat where he first made love to Bob Ford.[37]

But out of apparent ignorance of other similar homosexual scenes, Dick regards this myth as springing out of the classic tradition of merely latent homoeroticism as defined by Fiedler: ". . . the boy-hood idyll, the intrusive women, the miraculous sea, Cooper's red-skin brother-surrogate for the white male in the guise of the red-haired Bob Ford, the lost frontier friendship."[38] A much more truly gay interpretation of the bower of bliss has been offered by Rictor Norton, who, viewing literature from Theocritus' *Idylls* down through the present literature of many countries, has sug-gested that the pastoral tradition is indeed *the* homosexual genre. In discussing the transformation of the "Hylas Ritual" so that two waterside wrestlers are now able to love rather than kill each other, Norton fits the male bathing scenes in Whitman's "Calamus" poems, Sanford Friedman's *Totempole* and Richard Amory's *Song of the Loon* into a ritual that is characteristically homosexual.[39] For what-ever reason, there are indeed many variations of the idyllic poolside scene in our homosexual fiction (e.g., *South-Sea Idyls, Bertram Cope's Year, The Fall of Valor, The Welcome, The Divided Path, The Bitterweed Path, The Captain, Quatrefoil*), and it is likely that archetypal theories can offer only a partial explanation for all of this undressing and swimming.[40]

The City and the Pillar has also been discussed by Stanton Hoff-man in his 1964 *Chicago Review* essay called "The Cities of Night," which compares Vidal's novel with *Giovanni's Room* and *City of Night*. Although many of his points are sound, Hoffman's analysis suffers from a glib usage of such phrases as "fall from grace" and "sense of lost innocence" with the implication that these terms are transferable from heterosexual to homosexual fiction.[41] Hoffman believes that in the Jim-Bob fireside scene Vidal was trying to show the American obsession with a "fall from grace," and elsewhere Hoffman notes that gay characters define themselves in the "de-structive context" of a "love-mad culture" which "manifests itself in their consciousness through a sense of lost innocence, a fear of experience, of love and the dangers of love. . . ." Hoffman's use of these terms is somewhat understandable since he is discussing com-paratively dark and brooding novels, but the general principle of applying heterosexual literary terms to homosexual fiction is, by and large, presumptuous and unthinking. Without any qualifying quo-tation marks, for instance, Hoffman looks for a return to innocence as it was conventionally defined in Chester Eisinger's *Fiction of the Forties:*

> With the end of innocence comes the yearning for innocence. The dream of Eden drives the writer's imagination back to the years before knowledge came to corrupt the soul and complicate the world. At the same time the end of innocence—or the ending of it, the act itself—takes on the fascination of dreadful and inevitable novelty in the American experience, and many writers, thus compelled, return to the theme repeatedly.[42]

While for most heterosexual males the end of innocence is tinged with the wistful realization that carefree days are fading and that the syndrome of marrying, getting a job, buying a house, and supporting a family has begun to claim them, the term has no such connotation for homosexual males. At least within the sexual context, the end of innocence for gay men is an exhilarating and dramatic moment of definition, and the initiatory sex act is something that has been dreamed of and desired rather than dreaded. This act serves to liberate the spirit, mark an end to years of waiting and alienation, and provide reassurance that one is not, after all, alone in the world. Rather than corrupting the soul and complicating the world, the gay male's new knowledge that there are other men who will love him in return cheers the soul and helps to make more sense of a world that had previously been baffling and upside down. If finally finding someone to have sex with is a "fall from grace," from a gay point of view it is surely a tumble well taken, and thus if "the end of innocence" has any meaning at all in the gay experience and in gay literature, it has little to do with the longing to return to some state of cherubic prepubescence.[43]

THE DIVIDED PATH:
ANOTHER CABIN, ANOTHER POOL

The year following the publication of *The City and the Pillar,* Greenberg brought out Nial Kent's *The Divided Path,* which utilizes a pastoral motif and ends with a supposed fall *into* grace. Kent's contriving to close the novel on a note of hopefulness recalls the equally upbeat ending of Richard Meeker's *Better Angel,* and it might be said that *The Divided Path* is somewhat of an updated, more vibrant version of Meeker's 1933 pastel novel. In 1949 this book may well have been pleasant reading for gay men, but today's reader is likely to smile at Kent's sentimentalization of small-town life and his crafty ending that promises more than it can deliver.

The Divided Path does include a few realistic glimpses of what the hero, Michael, is forced to endure while growing up in a small town. As a boy, Michael is bored by the dullness of the Methodist church, with its sepia portrait of Frances E. Willard and its ladies who use imitation palm-leaf fans provided by the local undertaker. (Quite characteristically Michael is later dazzled by the rich theatricality of the local Catholic church.)[44] As a freshman in high school, Michael goes through a painful crush on Hal Manning, a handsome basketball star who is a senior, and the first time he sees his idol naked in the locker room, he is transfixed:

> Michael's eyes devoured him . . . he wanted to remember forever every detail of that exposed body which moved with such admirable grace. The swelling pectorals, the rhythmic ripple of his thighs, the swinging of his genitals as he walked—there was a pain in Michael's chest that had never been there before.[45]

Altogether, though, Kent focuses more generally on the snug, secure, comforting aspects of small-town life. In a scene right out of Sarah Orne Jewett, Michael goes to visit Aunt P'liney, who gives him freshly baked grape pie and milk kept cold in her well, and then, when they sit down to watch the sunset, she says such homey, wholesome Aunt Jennyish things as, "Of all the day this is the hour I love the most. When it's quiet and the birds are goin' to bed and the flowers smell so strong and the sky is so beautiful . . . it's peaceful then, and I don't feel tired anymore." And of course it is in the small town where Michael, during a summer vacation home from the conservatory, falls blissfully in love with Paul, a "sexy-looking" young man with a wedge-shaped torso, black hair, square jaw, deep voice and "brooding, moody eyes."

Like Vidal's Bob Ford, Paul is predictably "straight," and, as in Vidal's novel, there is a cabin by a pool where he and Michael spend lazy weekends together. The difference is that Paul and

Michael never wrestle themselves into sex, but Michael is fairly content just to be alone with his friend:

At the cabin they could be completely alone in their own private
world. And Michael could have Paul all to himself. He was happier then
than he had ever been, or would ever be again. . . . Michael was filled
with love to overflowing. They seldom wore more than shorts, in which
they also slept, and Paul often went without even those during the day.
When they walked to and from the pool, Michael loved to watch the
way the sun came through the leafy roof here and there and fell upon
Paul's bare skin, bright flecks sliding caressingly across the burnished
bronze body as it moved with Arcadian naturalness . . . both were at
peace.

Although the author puts Michael and Paul to bed on many occasions—they often sleep over at each other's house—there is never
any overt display of affection on Michael's part, and only once
does Paul become demonstrative. One night toward the end of the
summer, after having pie and milk, they get into bed pajamaless—
because of the heat—and Michael takes a last look at Paul before
turning out the light:

Paul was propped up on one elbow, and his eyes were very dark. He
said, "Michael, I want you to know how very much I appreciate you,
and all you've done for me. . . ."
And without warning he leaned suddenly forward and kissed Michael
full on the mouth. Then he dropped back on his pillow, and Michael
quickly turned out the light . . . weak and shaken. . . .

In the last half of the novel Paul joins the service and Michael
goes to New York City, where he comes out. They see each other
once during the war, and, out of motives that appear to be those of
pure and simple friendship, Paul gives Michael a carnelian ring. At
the end of the novel both are back home—Michael on vacation
and Paul out of the service—and they decide to spend a weekend
together up at Paul's cabin. But on the last pages Kent throws in a
thunderstorm, Michael smashes up his car, and Paul discovers the
wreck near the cabin the next morning:

The hand that he clasped was cold and wet. A lock of hair stirred
faintly, showing golden lights, but there was no sound, no other movement.

"Michael!" he cried in a voice that wept, and in the silence the crow answered him, cawing dismally in the distance.

The cold hand that he held between his warm ones wore a heavy carnelian ring. Limply it lay in his grasp, but slowly, imperceptibly at first, then unmistakably, it tightened on his fingers.

Kent's ending sentence is clever from the standpoint of craftsmanship, but the implications of the ending are rather unconvincing from the standpoint of reality. Like Vidal in *The City and the Pillar,* Kent contrives to substitute an act of violence for an act of sex at the end, but in *The Divided Path* we are led to presume that the car smashup will merely postpone sexual consummation and that, as soon as Michael can grasp more than Paul's fingers, the two men will hit the hay or sandbank or whatever. Realistically speaking, however, Michael's having sex with Paul is based on little more than wish-fulfillment, as there is no guarantee that his buddy is going to be much more sexually acquiescent than was Bob Ford at the end of *The City and the Pillar.* So even though the last sentence of the novel is designed to start visions of tender-sex-by-the-pond floating through the heads of gay readers, the only conclusion really warranted by this sentence is that, for the moment, Michael is still alive.

As was often the case during this time, the reviews revealed as much about the reviewers as they did about the work. J. P. Quehl complained in *The New York Times* that *The Divided Path* missed "by a mile" as "a serious study of aberration," while the comment in *Kirkus* was even more quaint. This novel was for "the sensation-seeker," the *Kirkus* reviewer decided, because its treatment of the gay theme was "overt" rather than "fastidious."[46]

THE BITTERWEED PATH: THE WILD TENDERNESS

Since his novel was being published by Greenberg, Nial Kent was free to write a novel that would primarily appeal to and be read by gay people. In 1949 Thomas Hal Phillips was making arrangements with Rinehart to publish *The Bitterweed Path,* and the editors there were not nearly so indulgent as the people at Greenberg since they knew their line was expected to appeal to the general reading public. Moreover, the twenty-five-year-old Mississippi State College graduate had written the novel for his master's thesis in the rather conservative creative writing department at the University of Alabama. For these reasons there are heterosexual goings-on in Phillips' novel, but because of its plot structure *The Bitterweed Path* is at least climactically gay.

A distinguishing feature of this book is that it is a thoroughly Southern novel: it not only starts in the South, it continues and ends in the South. Thus there is no flight to New York for either Darrell or Roger, the novel's two main characters. The touchstone at the beginning and at the end is the idyllic, close-to-the-soil rural South, and from a gay perspective the only flight anyone takes is the flight of both men into the haven of heterosexual marriage.

The novel opens in horse-and-buggy days with Roger Pitt and Darrell Barclay as adolescents undressing in a boathouse in preparation for the Vicksburg Spring Races. Darrell is handsome but poor, and soon the Barclays come to live with and work for the wealthy Pitt family, and Darrell and Roger become playmates. Their relationship is occasionally sensual, but it is of a sort of childlike sensuality that remains innocent. When they go swimming at the creek, they look at each other's bodies, wrestle and get aroused, but only once do they kiss each other after a spat:

"Will you forgive me?"
"Yes."
"All the way?"
"Yes."
"Bend over." Darrell leaned over close and his hand, half on the pillow, touched Roger's hair. Roger touched his other hand.
Then Darrell kissed Roger's lips. They were soft and warm and the very touch seemed to pain him with tenderness. Darrell stood up. Roger let his hand go. "We won't ever fuss again, ever."
"No," Darrell said.[47]

While it is love rather than lust that characterizes the relationship between the two boys, the relationship between Darrell and

Malcom Pitt, Roger's well-built, masterful father, seems to develop gradually into something more overtly sexual. Darrell's mean father disappears early in the novel, Roger soon goes off to school, and thus in each other Darrell and Malcom find father/son substitutes. On a riverboat trip, Malcom suggests that Darrell sleep with him; Darrell shivers when he feels "the great maleness" of the older man, and Malcom, with his lips against Darrell's cheek, says, "You go to sleep . . . honey-boy." Of course, terms of endearment in a Southern novel do not always mean as much as non-Southern readers might think, but Phillips does make it clear that the relationship is an unusual one for a Southern gentleman farmer and a hired hand.

During the middle of the novel, much happens to separate Darrell and Roger. While Darrell stays home and has Malcom to rely on for friendship, Roger gradually becomes estranged from both, always off at school preparing to become a doctor. Eventually there is news that Roger is marrying, and Darrell decides he should marry as well, and he does, with his wife giving him a set of twin boys. At the end of the novel, Roger and Darrell are brought together by two deaths: Malcom dies and Darrell's wife later dies in childbirth. Moreover, Roger quarrels with his wife, who leaves him to go back to New Orleans, and in the last chapters, for a while at least, Roger and Darrell have only each other.

The climactic scene takes place on a foggy night in Vicksburg, where the two men have gone on a business trip. After deciding that "whatever we're looking for" won't be found at the Showboat, they walk along the riverfront for a while, reminisce about Malcom, and finally go back to their room at the Yellow House. They undress and climb into a double bed and manfully confess their love for each other:

Then Roger put his arm around Darrell and they were very still. Somewhere along the waterfront a bell rang sharply, like the clamor of new-sharpened shovel plows dropped suddenly to earth. A coldness came to Darrell and crept along his skin like blackberry winter. He ached with the longing that Roger would speak and hold back the coldness, even for an instant. For a full minute Roger neither moved nor spoke and his arm lay like years across Darrell's body. Suddenly Roger whispered, "Do you think it's right?"
"I don't know . . . we're grown now . . ."

"What did Father ever say?"

"Nothing . . . he never said anything . . ." Darrell held his breath, for they seemed to be on the river: the room swerved and he listened to the barely audible seeping of the wind outside and the lashing of water. . . . It is only a dream, he thought; but he knew the wild tenderness was now upon them.

The next chapter begins:

In the bright light of day their eyes burned with a tenderness against each other, as if to say: now it is done; we have reached the just-beyond; there is no going back to something less. . . .

The novel ends with Roger sending a note to Darrell that he is taking the night train out of town; they meet in the village churchyard and embrace silently in the darkness, and Darrell goes home and weeps. In the last few pages Phillips makes his gay statement, which seems all the more impressive because of the heterosexual experiences the two men have had. Of course, the word "gay" is never mentioned, but when the "wild tenderness" comes upon them, the two men are caught up in a lyrically beautiful moment that is not surpassed in poignancy in any of the other more self-consciously gay writing of the forties.

Critical comments on *The Bitterweed Path* ranged from the squeamish to those which were more positive: "Not a book for the general public," *Kirkus* warned. "Unfortunately there is no better word than homosexuality to describe the basic theme of this unusual novel," the *Library Journal* complained. The *New York Herald Tribune* reviewer said he wished Phillips had "chosen a more rewarding theme." However, *The New York Times* reviewer conceded, "He knows the country he describes, its colors and moods and seasons, its odors and winds and dirts, its flowers and trees and grasses."[48]

STRANGER IN THE LAND:
MURDER IN THE POND

In a number of ways *Stranger in the Land* (1949) by Ward Thomas departs from the more traditional motifs of other relevant fiction published during this time. This novel inverts the associations of the archetypal "Hylas Myth," with its blissful pool around which gay characters are supposed to lose themselves in love—Thomas uses the pond outside Chatsworth, Massachusetts, as the setting for a murder of the "beloved." The town itself, with its bigoted and cruel residents, serves almost as the villain in Thomas' novel, and there never seems to be any chance of escape for the hero, a twenty-eight-year-old English teacher named Raymond Manton. Rather like a gay Ethan Frome, Raymond is trapped at home out of a sense of duty to his invalid mother, and the only occasional outlet for his affection is twenty-year-old Terry Devine, who is what used to be called a juvenile delinquent.

From the standpoint of credibility, Thomas' novel is uneven. On the one hand, the author believably evokes the dreariness faced by high school English teachers who are expected to bring literature to life for dull, uninterested students. In contrast to the academy in *Lucifer with a Book,* where moments of wit and displays of erudition are appreciated, Woodrow Wilson high school in Chatsworth seems dedicated to the lowest common denominator of mentality. Another believable aspect of the novel is the author's handling of the teacher's attraction to the hood. Terry is everything that Manton is not—beautiful, devilish, ungrammatical—one from "another country" who attracts the teacher *because* they hardly speak the same language. But what remains unbelievable throughout the novel is that in such a small town a cautious, paranoid closet case should risk being seen so often with Terry in the local taverns. Chatsworth is basically an updated Grovers Corners—when Manton walks down Main Street at night after having supper with his mother, he bumps into Judge Hartshorne and Officer Garvey, and everyone seems to know everyone else's business, just as in *Our Town.* Although Manton says things like, "We really mustn't meet like this so often," he keeps meeting Terry at the Krazy Kat Kafe and at the Golden Goose, where it must be clear to everyone that it is hardly the boy's mind he is interested in. Thomas' allowing Manton to flirt with Terry in public is almost as astounding as if Wilder had allowed Simon Stimson to fondle George Gibbs under the soda-fountain counter of Morgan's Drug Store, and even when Orville

Finch is arrested on a morals charge and gay men are rounded up and jailed and the town becomes even more suspicious of bachelors, Manton continues to meet Terry at the Golden Goose.

Since Terry isn't gay but only poor "shanty Irish" trade, he decides to take advantage of the town's aroused homophobia by blackmailing Manton, who by the end of the novel has become exasperated with his devious friend. The resolution comes on a warm June night out at Benson's Pond, where Manton drowns Terry. English teachers do not drown other human beings without some brooding afterthoughts, of course, and these are Manton's on the last page of the novel:

He had killed his own soul when he killed the body of Terry Devine: death was seeping into his spirit from the stagnant marsh, death was all he would get from his act of deliverance . . . and the humid night, bizarre with the flickering of the fireflies, closed in around him.[49]

While *The New Yorker* praised Thomas for his "perceptive" analysis of a small town and his hero's dilemma, the *San Francisco Chronicle* quite rightly pointed out that Manton was "so weak as to be almost completely uninteresting."[50] Through most of the novel, Manton plays the role of helpless puppet, and so his decision to drown Terry comes as a surprise not only because the circumstances don't seem to warrant such drastic action but also because the teacher doesn't seem to be the type who would even consider a murder to solve his problems, let alone perform one. The murder at the end of *Stranger in the Land* is about as contrived as the one at the end of *The City and the Pillar*. It appears that Thomas, like Vidal, was willing to sacrifice character consistency for a blockbuster ending. At the same time, though, such frenzied finales were most satisfactory in the minds of straight publishers and readers, and it is likely that the Houghton Mifflin editors would have had serious reservations about publishing *Stranger in the Land* if Thomas had ended with Manton and Terry moving to Greenwich Village and setting up a happy gay household. In its own way, this upbeat ending would have been equally sensational—but in the minds of many heterosexuals not nearly so "true-to-life" and comforting as the downbeat ending that Thomas provided.

THE GAY YEAR:
THE BROADWAY SHOW-BIZ SET

So many homosexual novels have a Manhattan setting that, unless they are distinguished by style or characterization, their plots tend to run together in the reader's mind as interchangeable and forgettable. Typical of the undistinguished New York novel is *The Gay Year* by Michael de Forrest, published by the Woodford Press in 1949.

De Forrest details in soap-opera fashion the frenetic lives of a show-biz set, and in retrospect the weakness of the novel is its predictability. Perhaps in 1949 the gay reader did not find *The Gay Year* to be as cliché-ridden as it seems today, but even then many of the characters and situations must have seemed slightly stock. For instance, what is Joe Harris going to be reminded of when spring comes to Central Park? "At home now, there would be scarlet tulips with waxy petals and tiny powdered yellow pistils." By summer Joe is disenchanted with the empty whirl of Manhattan gay life, so what does he think of as he goes swimming in the ocean? "Why not lose himself in something he could be part of? You could be part of death. You could be part of the ocean."[51]

About the only surprise in this otherwise gay novel is the emergence of the idea that happiness/salvation is a heterosexual woman, a theme that was to become common in many of the paperback originals published in later years. A straight woman saves Joe from drowning, and on the last page he is hoping to be worthy of someday finding a girl who will be able to love him.

Other Fiction of the Forties

During this decade a number of other writers included gay characters in their novels, and several of these writers who have since identified themselves as gay were able quite successfully to preserve the illusion that homosexuality was no more central to their work than it should have been.

Among the war novels, Norman Mailer felt obliged to make his latently gay officer play the role of fascist villain in *The Naked and the Dead* (1948), while in Richard Brooks' *The Brick Foxhole* (1945), the gay man is an interior decorator who picks up soldiers and is murdered. Kenneth Millar's *The Dark Tunnel* (1944) was set in this country during the war and concerned a "liberal" college professor who uncovers some murdering pro-Nazi German spies who are either gay or transvestites or both.

In novels which featured amoral young punks, Willard Motley's *Knock on Any Door* (1947) gives a sympathetic portrait of an older, lonely gay man charmed by Nick Romano, but Charles Gorham was less kind in his novel of a slum kid on the make, *The Future Mr. Dolan* (1948). There was no American counterpart of Jean Genêt in prison novels, and *Four Steps to the Wall* (1948) by Jon Edgar Webb was typically ingenuous in that his hero left gay sex to the silly queens and depraved jockers. George Sylvester Viereck's semi-prison novel, *All Things Human* (1949), was only slightly more revelatory. Hiding behind the pseudonym of "Stuart Benton," Viereck tells the story of a middle-aged inmate who takes a fatherly interest in a younger man whom he will only kiss, lest their intimacy turn "into something less holy and wholesome."

The decade was not without its tough guys and lady authors. Writing in the spirit of James Cain's *Serenade,* Marc Brandel set *The Barriers Between* (1949) in Mexico, where the main character tries to kill a gay acquaintance who dares to bring up the subject of repressed homosexuality. Isabel Bolton's fairly intelligent *The Christmas Tree* (1949) was weakened by a melodramatic denouement, Helen Eustis' *The Horizontal Man* (1946) was spooky and unconvincing, but Janet Shane's *The Dazzling Crystal* (1946) was the worst of the lot. Shane's theme of "straight-lady-to-the-rescue" anticipated that of *The Gay Year,* and the gay male villain in her triangle is as diabolical as the one in *A Marriage Below Zero.*

Merle Miller played it safe in *The Sure Thing* (1949), and Christopher Isherwood played it almost as safe in *The Berlin Stories* (1946). The romantic interest in Tennessee Williams' plays was ostensibly heterosexual, but he did have some gay short stories published in a limited edition of *One Arm* in 1948. In addition to the title story, which concerns a beautiful male hustler who gave many great pleasure and warm memories, relevant overtones characterize "Desire and the Black Masseur," "The Angel in the Alcove," and "The Night of the Iguana" (which had to be heterosexualized for the stage adaptation).

How did "non-status" come about? In analyzing the extremely complicated and shifting relationships between straight critics and gay authors which have produced the many double-edged varieties of playing the game, one first has to examine the question of cause and effect. Does the homosexual novel in America not officially exist because it has not been written by gay authors or because it has not been recognized by major critics? Although there is no clear-cut answer to this question, it seems that the greater burden of the blame must rest on the shoulders of the critics, who, after all, have made up the rules. As with any minority, gay writers have been forced to respond to these rules as best they could in order to be published; gay camouflage and subterfuge in the novels of a generation ago, however tiresome they might be for today's liberated reader, must be regarded as the penalties one had to pay in order to play the game at all. It is particularly lamentable that, in more recent years, critics have had neither the insight nor the grace to admit their complicity in this game, as the following observations of literary historians reveal.

In covering the homosexual novels of the forties, these historians have generally opted either to ignore the formerly "groaning shelf" completely or to treat these books condescendingly as curious sports or gothic freaks. In his 1963 *Fiction of the Forties,* Chester Eisinger categorizes Vidal as a "war novelist" for *Williwaw,* omits any mention whatsoever of *The City and the Pillar,* terms Capote a gothic novelist of "the twisted self," and equates homosexuality with sterility. Although in one paragraph of *Love and Death in the American Novel* Fiedler says that it is now "impossible for the right-minded to reject either fairy or Jew," in the next he proceeds to poke fun at the former in fiction while praising Robert Phelps' homophobic *Heroes and Orators.*[52] In Frederick J. Hoffman's appendix on "Marginal Societies" in his *The Modern Novel in Amer-ica* (1963), the only post-1940 marginal groups worth discussing are "the Southern, the Negro, the Northern and urban Jewish, and the 'Beat.' " In *Radical Innocence* (1961), Ihab Hassan regards the gay male as someone who "perverts the sexual will," and homo-sexual fiction is given backhanded mention in contrast to the Jewish, black Southern, and war novels in his *Contemporary Amer-ican Literature* (1973). The most even-handed of these critics has been Walter Allen, who, perhaps because his being British obviated the need to defend the virility of American letters, was able to be Fiedlerian without being anti-fairy. In *The Modern Novel* (1964), Allen said:

The relationship between man and man, often idealized and never overtly sexual, but involving a virtual exclusion of woman, is a common theme in classic American fiction, so common, indeed, as to argue the existence of a strong homosexual strain, however repressed, in American experience. But the point is, it *was* repressed, and one has the feeling that the tabu on male homosexuality was much more binding, at any rate until very recently, in American society than in English. From Burns's *The Gallery* onwards, however, the open homosexual becomes increasingly frequent in the American novel, figuring, indeed, rather as the Negro and the Jew traditionally appear, as the representative of an unaccepted minority in American society and therefore of what might be called the self-outlawed, the nay-sayers to the notion of conformity that for good historical reasons has always been so compelling in the United States.[53]

Unfortunately, Allen's giving the homosexual equal billing with the Negro and the Jew generally has been regarded as an assessment coming from someone who just didn't know any better, because the conventional wisdom and "definitive" criticism on post-war gay fiction was handed down by John Aldridge's *After the Lost Generation* (1951). Viewing the "strong preoccupation with homo-sexuality" in *The City and the Pillar, Stranger in the Land, The Gallery, Lucifer with a Book,* and *Other Voices, Other Rooms* as a vogue that was "most curious" and "interesting indeed," Aldridge goes on to dismiss the homosexual talent as a "narrow one, subject to all the ills of chronic excitation" and to view a writer's gayness as probably no more important than a taste for "dry martinis."[54] In the game that was played during the fifties, the views of Aldridge held sway, and although they were as crackpot as anything Dr. LaForest Potter had written in the thirties, they were nevertheless generally accepted as gospel during the Eisenhower years by Those Who Knew Best.

NOTES

1. Gore Vidal, *The City and the Pillar* (Revised) (New York: Dutton, 1965), p. 245.

2. White, *Gore Vidal* (New York: Twayne, 1968), pp. 49-50. National hypocrisy about sex was a major obstacle to any reassessment, and Philip Wylie devoted a chapter to this subject in his *Generation of Vipers*. Writing in 1942, Wylie observed that homosexuality was common in the Navy and Army, that "husbands and sons, good Americans all" were, as he wrote, busy "practicing pederasty," and yet everywhere people were "engaged in a violent vocal repudiation of that which they are simultaneously engaged in doing." One of the other frank analyses of homosexuality to appear in this country during the war was Robert Duncan's "The Homosexual in Society" (*Politics,* August 1944), which gave an insider's view of the unhappy effects of closet mentality on gay art and artists.

3. Harlan McIntosh, *This Finer Shadow* (New York: Lorac, 1941), p. 188. Other quotes are from pp. 172, 178, 232, and 264.

4. Although McCullers was married (to someone who was about equally gay), she spent most of her adult life falling in love with other women, according to Virginia Carr's recent biography, *The Lonely Hunter.*

5. Carson McCullers, *The Ballad of the Sad Café* (Boston: Houghton Mifflin, 1951), p. 24.

6. The idea of the twilight state of adolescence was first pointed out by Oliver Evans in a *College English* article and later included in his critical biography, *The Ballad of Carson McCullers.*

7. *Accent,* Autumn 1941, p. 61.

8. W. Tasker Witham, *The Adolescent in the American Novel* (New York: Frederick Ungar, 1964), p. 127.

9. William Maxwell, *The Folded Leaf* (New York: Vintage Books, 1959), pp. 108-9. The final quote is from p. 274.

10. Charles Jackson, *The Fall of Valor* (New York: Signet, 1949), p. 82. Other quotes are from pp. 108, 165, and 186-91.

11. *Library Journal* (September 15, 1946). R. G. Davis reviewed it in

The New York Times (October 6, 1946); Wilson reviewed it in *The New Yorker* (October 5, 1946); and Fadiman's review appeared in the *New York Herald Tribune* book section (October 6, 1946). It might be added that the careful reader can today perceive that Jackson's hero in *The Lost Weekend,* Don Birnam, is as much of a closet case as was Charles Grandin.

12. *The New York Times* book section (May 11, 1947). Surprisingly enough, the *Kirkus* reviewer was far more perceptive in this case, calling Engstrand's novel an unnecessary and "sensational exploitation of scientific case history material."

13. John Horne Burns, *The Gallery* (New York: Bantam, 1950), p. 147. This paperback version is longer and more candid than the original edition published by Harper in 1947. Other quotes are from pp. 152, 163-64, and 285.

14. Vidal's essay on "The Revelation of John Horne Burns" was reprinted in *Sex, Death and Money,* pp. 153-57.

15. According to the back cover of the Bantam reprint, the *Boston Herald* reviewer said, "There are passages in it which can only be described as 'terrific' . . . a new literary star has risen." The novel was praised in the *Herald Tribune* book section (June 8, 1947) and in *The Saturday Review* (July 19, 1947).

16. Vidal, "The Revelation of John Horne Burns." (p. 153.)

17. The novel was reviewed in *The Saturday Review* (April 2, 1949) and in the *Catholic World* (June 1949). *Lucifer with a Book* invites comparison with a boys' school novel published several years later, Nathaniel Burt's beautifully written and almost equally homoerotic *Scotland's Burning* (Boston: Little, Brown, 1953).

18. All of Edgerton's quotes come from the October 1958 issue of *One,* which was published in Los Angeles by One, Incorporated, a pioneering homophile society founded in 1952.

19. Vidal discussed Burns in an interview that appeared in the Boston gay quarterly, *Fag Rag* (Winter–Spring 1974).

20. John Mitzel, *John Horne Burns: An Appreciative Biography* (Dorchester: Manifest Destiny Books, 1974), p. 132.

21. Calder Willingham, *End As a Man* (New York: Vanguard, 1947), p. 230.

22. Truman Capote, *Other Voices, Other Rooms* (New York: Signet, 1949), p. 92. The later quote is from pp. 92-93.

23. William Nance, *The Worlds of Truman Capote* (New York: Stein & Day, 1970), p. 59.

24. Witham, *The Adolescent in the American Novel,* pp. 240-41.

25. Nance, *The Worlds of Truman Capote,* pp. 63-64.

26. Hubert Creekmore, *The Welcome* (New York: Appleton-Century-Crofts, 1948), p. 231. Other quotes are from pp. 247, 256, and 305.

27. At least we can assume that, among the other things they do, they kiss, even though Vidal never specifically says so. In spite of the relative forth-

rightness of the fireside scene, it should be noted that Vidal included an "out" for those who needed one: immediately afterward, Bob Ford dismisses it as "kid stuff."

28. Information on *A Novel* is given by Bernard Dick in his *The Apostate Angel: A Critical Study of Gore Vidal* (New York: Random House, 1974), pp. 27-30.

29. Vidal discusses the "OK Lists" of what he now thinks of as the Golden Age of American Literature in his 1960 essay on Norman Mailer, "The Angels Are White," reprinted in *Sex, Death and Money*. It should be added that Vidal's last novel of the decade, *The Season of Comfort* (1949), with its teenage romance between Bill and Jimmy, helped to confirm the critics' opinion that he was no longer OK.

30. Vidal, *The City and the Pillar* (1965), p. 245. The quotes here from the novel itself are taken from the 1950 Signet edition, pp. 24, 28, 127, 178, 150, and 187.

31. White, *Gore Vidal*, p. 51.

32. Vidal first prized the mystique of the heterosexual in *A Novel*, where his gay hero tells a straight college roommate, "I like you the way you are. I don't think I would have had you different." For an autobiographical explanation of the appeal of "normal" men a generation ago, see Chapter 12 of J. R. Ackerley's *My Father and Myself* (New York: Coward-McCann, 1969).

33. These critical comments appeared on the back dust jacket of *The City and the Pillar*, pp. 247-48, with Aldridge's originally appearing in *The Saturday Review*.

34. Vidal mentions Gide, Forster, and Kinsey in the afterword to *The City and the Pillar* (Revised). "Engaged," of course, was a mid-sixties euphemism for homosexual.

35. Vidal compares himself with Jack London in his 1965 afterword, and Ray Lewis White cites the quotes from *The New Yorker* and *The New York Times* in his study of Vidal. White also includes Vidal's comments on the reviewers who felt his novel was "sterile," on p. 127.

36. In his 1965 afterword, Vidal claims that "all human beings are bisexual," but *The City and the Pillar* hardly proves this. In *The Apostate Angel*, Bernard Dick points out that "Jim Willard clearly was not," and neither, quite obviously, was the adult Bob Ford.

37. Bernard Dick, *The Apostate Angel*, pp. 31-32.

38. *Ibid.*, p. 39. However, in his essay, "The Origins of Homosexual Fiction" (*Colorado Quarterly*, Spring 1974), Dick fits *The City and the Pillar* into the quaintly archaic tradition of the homosexual pastoral.

39. This information is taken from Norton's doctoral dissertation, "Studies of the Union of Love and Death" (Florida State University, 1972), much of which served as the basis for his *The Homosexual Literary Tradition: An Interpretation* (New York: Revisionist Press, 1974). Norton also mentions the "recognition scene while skinny dipping" in his "The Homosexual Literary Tradition" in *College English* (March 1974).

40. Since the one sensuous nude/near nude experience American society permits young males to have with each other is related to some variation of "the old swimming hole," it is not surprising that many of the more autobiographical novels contain swimming scenes. The traumatic shock of recognition that one is "different" often goes back to some early and indelible fascination with the naked body of a slightly older male (e.g., Michael's seeing Hal Manning in *The Divided Path*), and furthermore it is not uncommon for the physical characteristics of this person to serve as the ideal against which all later love objects are measured (e.g., Jim's search for a replica of Bob Ford in *The City and the Pillar*—and Vidal's search for a red-haired replica of Ford in several of his later novels). Sharing some golden moments with an adored near-naked buddy is the closest many gay males come to perfection during their peculiarly troubled adolescence, and thus it seems that the appearance of these poignant pool scenes can also be understood in terms of the novelist recapturing the golden moments of his youth.

41. Stanton Hoffman, "The Cities of Night: John Rechy's *City of Night* and the American Literature of Homosexuality," *Chicago Review* (17:2-3, 1964), p. 196 ff.

42. Chester Eisinger, *Fiction of the Forties* (Chicago: University of Chicago Press, 1963), p. 17.

43. A gay concept of the end of innocence as it meshes with the pastoral tradition is discussed in the next chapter in connection with *The Night Air*.

44. An irresistible pull toward the opulent trappings and vestments of the Roman Catholic Church or high Episcopalianism has become something of an inside gay joke if not a recurrent theme in American gay fiction. Perhaps the most dramatic account of a gay writer fantasizing on this subject is the British writer Frederick "Baron Corvo" Rolfe's *Hadrian the Seventh* (1904), in which the author-hero ascends to the papacy.

45. Nial Kent, *The Divided Path* (New York: Greenberg, 1949), p. 29. The spell is broken when Hal walks by Michael, their eyes meet, and Hal asks, "What's the matter, sister . . . ?" Other quotes are from pp. 179, 242-43, and 447.

46. The reviews of the "Kent" (pseud. of William Leroy Thomas) novel were generally negative, with the San Francisco *Chronicle* terming it too Pollyannaish and *The Saturday Review* complaining that "Surely there is more to say of the world of the homosexual than this." *The New York Times* review appeared November 6, 1949, and the *Kirkus* review September 15, 1949.

47. Thomas Hal Phillips, *The Bitterweed Path* (New York: Avon, 1950), p. 82. Other quotes are from pp. 73 and 252-53.

48. *Kirkus* (April 1, 1950); *Herald Tribune* (July 2, 1950); *Library Journal* (June 15, 1950); and *The New York Times* (September 10, 1950).

49. Ward Thomas, *Stranger in the Land* (Boston: Houghton Mifflin, 1949), p. 373.

50. The reviews come from the *San Francisco Chronicle* (August 7, 1949) and *The New Yorker* (June 18, 1949).

51. Michael de Forrest, *The Gay Year* (New York: Woodford Press, 1949), pp. 127, 162.

52. Fiedler deplores our "gothic" gay fiction (calling Brando's shirtlessness the ultimate in inverted strip teasing) in *Love and Death in the American Novel*, p. 452.

53. Walter Allen, *The Modern Novel in Britain and the United States* (New York: Dutton, 1964), p. 299.

54. John Aldridge, *After the Lost Generation* (New York: McGraw-Hill, 1951), p. 100 ff.

THE FIFTIES

FOR A MOMENT in the late forties, when John Horne Burns was crowing about the "pleiad of pederasts" who were the seven rising young stars of the postwar literary scene, the outlook for gay writing must have seemed bright. In fact, Gore Vidal now calls the 1948 era "the golden age," because at that time "none of us knew where history had placed us," an oblique way of saying that the seven homosexuals and their literature had not yet been tagged as such.[1] When the critics began calling a "fairy" a fairy, however, the golden age was over. By the early fifties Burns was no longer roaring with delight, and the general spirit of self-congratulation had given way to feelings of disenchantment, bitterness and defensiveness: the pleiad must have realized that if they were to continue to shine, they would have to do so on a strictly unpederastic basis.

The gray-flanneled deadliness of the fifties made it hard to be a happy homosexual unless one escaped American society altogether by becoming an expatriate or a member of the new beat generation. At the beginning of the decade many gay citizens felt particularly outraged by Senator Joseph McCarthy's State Department purges, and they were not much happier to think that their family and friends were reading such *Coronet* articles as "New Moral Menace to Our Youth" and "Third Sex: Guilt or Sickness?" The Eisenhower years were not propitious for the sympathetic treatment of gay themes in nonfiction or fiction, and by the end of the decade a number of magazine writers and literary critics were viewing homosexual novels with dismay or even alarm.

One of the earlier scaremongers was Alfred Towne, who deplored "The New Taste in Literature" for the *American Mercury* in 1951. Towne's thesis was that struggling young novelists dare not struggle with unnamed "lisping critics, and certain Brooks Brothers–suited book reviewers" if they wanted to succeed, and the *Mercury* promised its readers other fearless articles that would examine "the sinister influences, the peculiar values of the effeminate supersensitive 'new taste' that is seeping through the arts in America."[2] In his 1954 study, *The Literary Situation,* Malcolm Cowley was hardly much kinder when he discussed gay men who were creating "fairy-Freudian" novels or trying to write about "normal love." With apparent satisfaction Cowley noted that the "fairy-Freudian" novel (about a "sensitive and so artistic young man" who comes to New York to find "release in the company of other sensitive young men") didn't often reach the bookstores, because it provided "a high proportion of the manuscripts that publishers reject." Cowley felt that many gay writers were "handicapped" by their "inability to present any characters in whom and for whom the reader feels an ordinary human warmth," and he went on to explain how this handicap prevented them from successfully depicting the "normal passions":

> . . . the reader may feel that the sexes have been transposed and that the women in a novel are really boys; or he may feel that the heroine is being hounded to death or insanity for the crime—as it appears to the homosexual author—of having normal passions; or again he may feel that the author, in depicting love between the sexes, has made it seem brutal or even bestial.[3]

In 1958 Stanley Edgar Hyman told *College English* readers that he found the emergence of gay motifs in modern American literature to be a most "unattractive trend," and a year later in *Harper's* Alfred Kazin vented exasperation at being asked to sympathize with characters so obviously "bent the wrong way":

It is astonishing how many novels concerned with homosexuality, on the order of Truman Capote's *Other Voices, Other Rooms,* are apologies for abnormality, designed to make us sympathize with the twig as it is bent the wrong way. . . . As in James Baldwin's *Giovanni's Room,* sympathetic justice is always accorded homosexuals. No Vautrin as in Balzac, no Charlus as in Proust, no honest homosexual villains![4]

According to Gore Vidal, it was John Aldridge's excoriation in *After the Lost Generation* (1951) that did the most to place gay writers on the defensive, and Aldridge's critical turnabout helped to rationalize the homophobic backlash that developed during the decade. In 1947 Aldridge had praised *Williwaw* and *In a Yellow Wood* and had initially regarded *The City and the Pillar* as a "distinct gain" for Vidal. In a recent interview, Vidal remembers that at first nearly all the critics liked him and John Horne Burns because they were war writers: "To be a War Writer was pretty gutsy. You cannot knock a War Writer. Then *The City and the Pillar.* Then *Lucifer with a Book.* They [the critics] said: 'Oh my god, what is this we have been admiring?' " Giving his opinion of Aldridge's aboutface in this interview, Vidal says:

The ineffable John W. Aldridge began his career with a piece in *Harper's* Magazine, out of which came his book *After the Lost Generation.* He reversed all of his judgments later. He began his career as our great admirer. He discovered we were dealing with the horrors of homosexuality. He then exactly reversed himself and began to applaud the Jewish giants who are still with us today. Aldridge is nothing if not a rider of bandwagons.[5]

In *After the Lost Generation,* Aldridge had dismissed the homosexual talent as "necessarily . . . narrow" because he felt that all homosexuals led comparatively narrow lives and thus could never come "to grips with whole areas of normal emotion" which provided the foundation for great heterosexual writing:

. . . the homosexual experience is of one special kind, it can develop in only one direction, and it can never take the place of the whole range of human experience which the writer must know intimately if he is to be great. Sooner or later it forces him away from the center to the outer edges of the common life of his society where he is almost sure to become a mere grotesque, a parasite, or a clown.[6]

During an era that rewarded high school and college students for being "well adjusted" to a society that was supposedly worth adjusting to, Aldridge's absolutism sounded right: normal was normal, abnormal was abnormal, and that was all there was to it. And where at this time were all those powerful gay "lisping critics" who were said to dominate the literary scene in Manhattan? If they murmured anything at all in rebuttal to Aldridge, they were either not heard or perhaps just not understood.

Unrelenting homophobic criticism caused most of the gay stars of the forties to stop—or at least postpone—writing on explicitly homosexual themes. John Horne Burns produced his strange, ostensibly straight novel, *A Cry of Children,* and then died. Rather than writing a novel in which his hero came to sexual grips with himself or someone else, Truman Capote transcended to airier themes in such works as "House of Flowers," "The Duke in His Domain," and *Breakfast at Tiffany's.* Gore Vidal began to shift gears from fiction to nonfiction, with his saucy political streak dominating the essays, criticism, television scripts, and plays that he wrote to pay for his country house on the Hudson. He continued to jab at homophobes, however, and in 1959 he observed that "the poor old homosexualists" were totally excluded from "the short List of the OK Writers" in America, which had room only for "two Jews, two Negroes and a safe floating *goy* of the old American Establishment (often Wright Morris) . . ."[7]

With the atmosphere in this country causing even "name" gay writers to sidestep rather than advance, it is not surprising that many younger gay novelists who wanted to be published were obliged to follow suit. What resulted was that much of the more explicit homosexual fiction was being turned out by mediocre writers, and this situation was analyzed by a gay critic writing for *One* in 1955. In his article, "Literature and Homosexuality," David L. Freeman first deplores the quality of most gay fiction:

While society pronounces homosexuals degenerate and psychiatrists usually consider them emotionally unbalanced, many homosexuals believe themselves to be uncommonly gifted, intelligent or sensitive. Contemporary literature by and about homosexuals, however, seems to verify the general opprobrium, for almost without exception it is morbid, bohemian, introverted, unrealistically romantic and perverted. Without more than one or two exceptions, it is also badly written.[8]

But then Freeman goes on to draw the logical connection between all the bad writing and the people who were producing it: "Since few top-notch writers will risk their reputations with a homosexual subject, the field is left to the mediocre." Believing that the "negative aspects have been emphasized long enough" in gay fiction, Freeman ends his article by calling for a "healthy, new homosexual literature" that stresses ordinary, everyday realism:

We homosexual writers must portray our lives as they are really lived—not jumping off cliffs on the French Riviera or . . . nurturing delicate neuroses at elegant cocktail parties on Park Avenue. We must show homosexuals as human beings, as very like their neighbors—working at dull jobs with inadequate wages, struggling to meet the payments on furniture from Sears for the sixty-or-seventy-a-month apartment on unromantically named streets like Sixth or Central or Main. Most of us, after all, . . . come from places like Rockford, Illinois, or Minot, North Dakota. . . .

Another gay critic, Arthur Krell, made many of the same points in his exhortatory "We Need a Great Literature," published in *One* the year before. Krell began by commenting on the cultural deprivations of gay people in contrast to other minority groups:

The Negro or Jewish individual does not stand alone; he is guided by group tradition and linked in warm human relationship.
The homosexual finds no bond between his love feeling and the familiar values about him. The emotion that can seem to him the very gleam from his soul, he finds despised. Either he must reject himself or be rejected by his esteemed peers.[9]

Krell added that a solution to this dreary state of affairs would be the writing of positive gay fiction, and he ended with a call for the same sort of honorable literary tradition to which other minority groups could lay claim at the time:

We can only hope that gifted writers with important things to say will come forward to fill the vacuum. We can only hope that some will describe heroes other men might emulate—instead of poor bastards whose story is a . . . funeral march. . . . When the homosexual appears widely in literature, not as a doomed weakling, but as a man whose supposed handicap becomes the very foundation of his achievement, the same literature that sets useful patterns for the homosexual will be read more widely, affecting society as well, creating human friendliness toward the whole man where none existed before.

It is clear that no one was especially pleased with most gay writing during the 1950s: the few gay critics objected because it was too downbeat, suicidal or unreal, and the straight critics usually objected simply because it was too gay. Obviously the more influential critics were the establishment heterosexuals, whose squeamishness affected editors and publishers and thus ultimately dictated what was going to be read by the average American on this subject. What is surprising is not that some mediocre novels were written but rather that in spite of the likes of Alfred Towne, Malcolm Cowley, Stanley Edgar Hyman, Alfred Kazin, and John W. Aldridge, a few novelists had the courage to write and the luck to get some first-rate fiction with a gay theme published.

"TRADITIONAL" GAY FICTION OF THE FIFTIES

Many variations of the characteristic "apprenticeship problem" novel appeared during the fifties: some writers emphasized growing up; others emphasized homosexuality as a problem; and a few of the more daring, original authors stressed neither angle. Amid this great variety, any attempt at neat categorization will appear to be arbitrary; nonetheless, a distinction should be made between the "traditional" gay novel and the more "untraditional" gay writing that began to surface in the fifties. Especially as homosexual fiction is viewed from the perspective of today, it can be posited that the more traditional writer worked within the confines of realism as he and his characters explored the implications of being gay for the American male. In the two untraditional approaches—softcore pornography and beat/counterculture writing—the writers were less interested in coping with the everyday problems of being gay than in escaping this reality through sexual fantasy or dizzy sur-realism. To oversimplify greatly, the more traditional writers such as James Baldwin were playing the game, while such people as Jay Little and William Burroughs were not.

Even among the writers of traditional gay novels of the fifties, however, there was a great range in sexual explicitness, because some had to play the game more carefully than others. Men who had already established themselves as promising non-gay novelists could not afford to be totally outspoken, while beginning novelists writing under pseudonyms and being published abroad could enjoy the luxury of flouting many of the rules. Two novels that illustrate the range of freedom and candor in the fifties were James Baldwin's *Giovanni's Room,* published by Dial in 1955, and *The Gaudy Image,* a more carefree work written by "William Talsman" and published by Olympia Press in Paris three years later.

GIOVANNI'S ROOM:
A SLIGHTLY ABASHED NOVEL

Although in many ways Baldwin was playing the game in *Giovanni's Room,* it still seems rather remarkable that in the middle of the Eisenhower years he was willing and able to write—and to get published—such a gayish work. How did this happen? First of all, *Giovanni's Room* was published only after the 1953 publication of *Go Tell It on the Mountain* had secured Baldwin's reputation as one of the most promising black writers in the country. Although there was in Baldwin's first novel the same sort of lyric, adolescent homoeroticism that characterized his 1951 short story, "The Out-ing," *Go Tell It on the Mountain* was basically an evocation of a religious family in Harlem, and it was quickly assigned a place right alongside the works of Wright and Ellison. Secondly, by the mid-fifties, black writers were becoming especially fashionable, and Baldwin's blackness established him as someone whose "difference" had to be respected, as someone who was saying incisive and worth-while things to the American reading public. Finally—and most significantly—*Giovanni's Room* could be published and distributed here simply because it allowed for multiple interpretations, not all of them definitively gay or pro-gay. On the dust jacket, Baldwin wrote that David's problem—"the dilemma of many men of his generation"—was not so much "sexual ambivalence as a crucial lack of sexual authority," and, furthermore, Baldwin removed himself from immediately identifiable commitment by transforming his hero into a naïve white ex-football player adrift in the Old World decadence of Paris. Had David been a black, slightly older version of Johnnie (from *Go Tell It on the Mountain*) who went to gay bars in Harlem, straight critics and readers would have been forced to conclude that *Giovanni's Room* was another gay novel by a writer who was clearly *engagé*. Baldwin, however, played the game and was quite successful at it. By keeping his persona both white and just bisexually confused and by setting him in the midst of foreign rather than domestic depravity, Baldwin was able to confound the Alfred Kazins in this country for quite a while.

After the publication of *Giovanni's Room,* the underground was abuzz with the news that James Baldwin had written what in those days passed for "a really gay novel"—gay readers were, after all, old hands at recognizing pertinent fiction disguised by multiple-choice interpretations. These readers could completely identify with the central struggle of the novel, as it was basically a description of coming out, which was much the same for young American men in Peoria as for those in Paris. No outsider could have so successfully captured the electric atmosphere during the crucial evening in Guillaume's bar, with all the darting eyes, wistful wisecracks, tiny defeats and breathless victories. Also ringing true of the gay experience was the trenchant wisdom of Jacques' advice when he makes to David the annunciation that Giovanni is his to take: "Love him . . . love him and let him love you. Do you think anything else under heaven really matters?"[10] In addition, some gay readers of *Giovanni's Room* could also hear echoes of other recent writing that had managed to convey moods that were singularly evocative or meaningful: Jacques' comment that "not many people have ever died of love, but multitudes have perished, and are perishing every hour—and in the oddest places!—for the lack of it," recalls Capote's Cousin Randolph, and Baldwin's final scene of the breeze blowing tiny blue fragments of Giovanni's letter back to David captures the delicate closing moments of Williams' *The Glass Menagerie*. At the beginning of the novel Baldwin quotes Whitman—"I am the man, I suffered, I was there"—and surely the gay readers of the fifties who had also been "there" realized intuitively, even without the aid of grapevine gossip, that this was a novel that had been written especially for them.

Most of the reviewers of *Giovanni's Room* were slightly uncomfortable with the book—they were accustomed to Baldwin writing as a black about blacks. Most seemed to have no very clear idea of the sort of game he was playing, and many opted to praise his eloquence while expressing surprise and even displeasure at the new choice of subject matter. In the *Atlantic Monthly*, C. J. Rolo took Baldwin to task about his dust-jacket notes suggesting that the novel was concerned not so much with homosexuality as with national confusion over role models. "This sounds to me pretentious nonsense," Rolo said. "We know that David's problem is not uncommon, and it merits compassion. But there is surely no 'lack of authority' as to whether boys should like girls or other boys." Rolo goes on to say that the subject "is one of which I have had my fill," but he concludes by asserting that *Giovanni's Room* "belongs in the top rank of fiction concerned with homosexuality." In *The New York Times* Granville Hicks said about the same thing (". . . even as one is dismayed by Mr. Baldwin's materials, one rejoices in the skill with which he renders them"), while in *The New Republic* William Esty wrote that generally he liked the book, noting that its "message" was uttered by the Belgian-American auntie, Jacques, and made the valid criticism that Baldwin's persona, the "blond-athlete-type hero . . . never wholly emerges from dimness."[11] While Esty felt that the Europe-versus-America theme was central to the novel, Anthony West in *The New Yorker* expressed disappointment that Baldwin had strayed so far afield from the genuinely important

American concerns that he had previously dealt with so well. West concluded his review by saying:

> It is to be hoped that Mr. Baldwin, a gifted writer, will soon return to the American subjects he dealt with so promisingly and with so much real understanding in his novel *Go Tell It on the Mountain* and his brilliant collection of essays, *Notes of a Native Son.*[12]

This comment reveals not only our xenophobic tradition of wishing to label homosexuality a non-American concern, but also—with the backhanded implications of the phrase "so much real understanding"—the sort of penalty often imposed on gay writers. Everyone recognized that in *Go Tell It on the Mountain* and *Notes of a Native Son* Baldwin was writing with "real understanding," because he was viewing black subjects from an unabashedly black point of view. What appears to have been at least somewhat sacrificed with Baldwin's strategy (the dim blond-athlete-type hero) in *Giovanni's Room* is that sense of immediacy and authorial commitment which had characterized his earlier works, and what the reviewers never seemed to perceive was that during this time most gay writers—unlike members of other minorities—were obliged to make some sort of smokescreen sacrifice if they wanted to have their novels published and sympathetically reviewed in this country.

THE GAUDY IMAGE:
AN UNABASHED NOVEL

While playing the game imposed certain penalties on the gay novelist who wanted to be published in America, the decision not to play the game carried with it penalties that could ultimately prove to be far more severe. Although it might be said that Baldwin's obliquity dimmed aspects of an otherwise brilliant novel, *Giovanni's Room* was nonetheless widely read, has been generally praised, and is today one of the most famous pieces of gay fiction in American literature. For William Talsman, sadly enough, the situation has been reversed. Although the Olympia Press was willing to publish his unapologetic novel about everyday gay life in an American city, Talsman's explicitness so scandalized customs officials that they seized the novel, which has remained almost completely unread and, of course, unpraised.

With its refreshing honesty and frankness, its playful humor and startling bursts of wit and poetry, *The Gaudy Image* has more in common with that other published-in-Paris novel, *The Young and Evil,* than with most of the traditional gay works published during the forties and fifties. Like Tyler and Ford—and unlike Baldwin in *Giovanni's Room*—Talsman sets his novel in the United States, creates characters that are delightedly and delightfully one-hundred-percent gay, and includes a generous number of those perfect moments that make homosexuality neither perplexing nor regrettable but "worthwhile." Though both Talsman and Baldwin have a gift for lyrical evocation, the dominant moods of their novels are quite different: in *Giovanni's Room* it is a wistfulness over a love that has been lost; in *The Gaudy Image* it is a dreamy anticipation of loves that can be found night after night in the French Quarter of New Orleans. There is never any brooding about sexual authority or sexual ambivalence in *The Gaudy Image*—Talsman's characters are as pleased to be gay as were Karel and Julian in *The Young and Evil,* and they only seem perplexed when they wonder who is going to do what to whom once they get each other in bed.

The other American writer who invites comparison with Talsman is Tennessee Williams, and *The Gaudy Image* can indeed be viewed as the gay counterpart to *A Streetcar Named Desire.* Not only are the settings the same, but Talsman's hero, "Tit" (*né* Thomas Schwartz, but now Titania, Queen of the Fairies), displays a gossamer airiness and a gift for disarming speech that recalls Blanche DuBois. They are, you might say, each other in drag. Furthermore, there are in Talsman's seedy underworld a number of Stanley Kowalski tough guys who, for various interesting reasons, enjoy getting those "colored lights" going with another male. In his own somewhat more believable way, Tit is as dependent on the kindness of strangers as was Blanche, and the sort of male he searches for throughout the novel is someone very like the torn-T-shirted Marlon Brando who personifies "the gaudy image":

The gaudy image was a group of characteristics which varied by the instant as if by the owner, but they varied only slightly as the essence remained constant. To wit: black hair, the curl was optional. An imposing build, firm roundness, full compactness, O, you know, he was decidedly suave with muscle and possessed the humility which accompanies such a body, a humility fostered by flattery and admiration. . . . His smile was slight, less than a ripple. As a snake weaves to hypnotize his prey, the image smiled to immobilize his victim. Nakedness became him, like so few. He was incapable of the vulgar, the awkward, of the unappetizing position. . . . His face resembled a sky which was illuminated with black stars, his eyes. . . .[13]

Unlike the gay underworld of Paris that Baldwin felt obliged to sketch through the remove of a McAlmonish outsider, the gay underworld of New Orleans comes immediately and vividly to life through the eyes of Talsman's extremely knowledgeable insider. Other than a brief flashback showing the adolescent Thomas Schwartz first inciting "wonder in a male," Talsman's focus is on Tit's daily game of searching for dazzling males who measure up to the "image." First there is Nickie, then Destiny (who "seemed kind, gentle, good-looking, and Italian. Not much of a godhead, perhaps, but many religions have flourished on less"), and then Bengal the Greaser, the first "husband." After they have been married for three weeks, Tit asks Bengal for an anniversary present:

"You're a little early, ain't ya? You know I don't do the department stores 'til Thursday."
"O, I don't want something you just go out and clip. That's too easy. I want something special, something you make with your own hands, no matter how simple, how formless."
"I don't do that. You think I'm common?"
"Go on, make something with your own hands."
Firstie [Bengal] scratched his head before he obliged. He gave her a bruise.

Tit's great love during the last half of the novel is Pelvis, who is too beautiful for her to watch ("You hurt my eyes. I can't stand the glare of perfection"). After sex, which Talsman always sketches with oblique cleverness rather than hardcore grossness, Pelvis is critical:

"You act like you don't like it," he told Titania. "All you do is 'enh.' "
He gave a short, high-pitched grunt.
"What do you do?"
"Kick up a storm," he said. "Didn't you notice?"
He had imitated Titania with derision. His "enh" was curt, his first point, which was well made; and his second point was to inject the tone of a soprano, which was also well made.

Tit's tumultuous relationship with Pelvis is typical of those he has with tough guys throughout the novel—the two constantly engage in verbal sparring matches, with Pelvis compensating for a lack of sharp-wittedness with his own brand of manly but playful bluntness. Indeed, throughout *The Gaudy Image* it is the contrast between the compact, muscular sentence fragments and body movements of the "guys" and the airy, graceful responses of Tit and her "sisters" which provides the basis for Talsman's tension, excitement and humor. But the author is utterly unpredictable and full of stylistic surprises—in some scenes Talsman toys with creating a tone of studied masculinity, while in others he allows lacy Ronald Firbank chitchat to go on for pages, unchecked by so much as one masculine grunt or growl.

The most notable example of a tough-guy episode occurs near the start of the novel while Titania is temporarily off-stage. The scene begins as if Talsman is parodying James M. Cain ("Gunner and Nickie divvied up the haul after the holdup") and takes place in a sleazy Tennessee Williams-like roominghouse where the two young hoods share the bathroom with a boxer and a wrestler. Eventually they share even more, because there's not too much else to do while "laying low" and the only female in the house is the fat, ugly, snooping landlady. Gunner tells Nickie that the wrestler "loves it. Lets you in from the front," and adds that the wrestler gets into the boxer when the latter "ain't payin' his rent." But occasionally Talsman intersperses flashes of humor to add a bit of sparkle to his leaden prose style. At the start of the sex scene between Nickie and the boxer, for instance, the two men obviously have conflicting preconceived notions of who will be doing what to whom:

> . . . Nickie landed face down on the bed. With some fleet movement the boxer fell on top of Nickie and pinned him to the bed. The boxer was a silent, dead weight for some time. That time ended when he started his hips in an easy, forward motion.
>
> Nickie was numb. He felt as if he had stacked a deck of cards only to discover, after he had looked at his hand, that the gods had intervened and had reshuffled the deck on the sly.
>
> "Do ya like it?" the boxer asked.

"Strangely enough," Nickie does, and after a few paragraphs there is an interruption—the broom-swinging landlady bursts in and starts yelling—and at this point it is not clear to the reader what is happening on the bed other than that a "symphony" has been underway.

> "Get out a here 'fore I punch ya silly . . ." the boxer yelled.
> "You're the one's getting out. If you and that bathrobe ain't out of here by nightfall, I'm callin' the cops."
> "Don't worry!"
> "That goes for Lady Godiva there, too."
> The landlady slammed the door. . . .

Only with the next sentence can the reader deduce that this blasé boxer didn't feel that his tiff with the landlady was important enough to warrant disengaging himself from Nickie: ". . . The boxer resumed, and in no time at all he reached the climax of the symphony by spouting a galaxy of stars."

Illustrating Talsman's other stylistic extreme is the campy banter over beers in Sparafucile's bar, where Tit goes to gossip with her two friends, Rose, who is faded, and Denis, who is fat. Although they usually talk about sex, they do so in terms that suggest they might have spent the afternoon reading the metaphysical poets.

> "You look like you swallowed a couple too many boulders, Hector."
> "O, this? This is my armor," Denis admitted, jiggling his jelly.
> "But did you have to swallow it?"
> "Well, yes," Denis said, curling his hands in the air as if they were

smoke caught in an updraft. "I wanted the world to bloom in wild cherries, thin skinned but, O, so red, so gorged with blood." He opened his palms. They blossomed, all pink and white, on the ends of his arms which were stalks. Then he tightened his fists and constricted the blossoms. "I needed pits to sow," he said.

"I know just what you mean," Rose said. "You were thinking double."

"No," Denis said coyly.

"Backwards?"

"No."

"Upside down?"

"At least! . . ."

"Do tell us about it," Rose urged.

"Well," Denis began, "it was this long."

Rose gasped.

"Strenuous but nice, that sort of thing."

"You're impossibly vulgar," Tit told them.

If they are not sharing their sexual adventures, Tit and Denis and Rose chat about their health, always vaguely related to some aspect of having sex or not having sex. None of them is ever well—they "die" from time to time, each of them predicting and mourning their various "deaths," and then they are magically reborn after ghastly love affairs or one-night stands. Further on in this conversation at the bar, Titania suggests that it has been only her poor health that has kept her from her usual number of sexual conquests:

". . . You're overupholstered, Denis. You should travel in your own class."

"You mean heavyweight?"

"No, overweight!"

Titania's gaze trembled, then fled to the bar for shelter, but Pelvis still lurked as the only possibility.

"You girls know that I haven't been feeling well lately. It must be the weather and so forth and so on and so be it. You admitted yourselves that I haven't been able to keep up with the social events of the season. Why, you've hardly seen me at all. Well, I didn't want to tell you this, but"—Rose and Denis leaned forward to absorb his confidence—"my system has not been all that it should be."

"None of us is perfect," Rose conceded.

About the only evaluation of *The Gaudy Image* in print seems to be the afterword by Olympia publisher Maurice Girodias at the end of the Nickie-Gunner segment in his 1965 anthology, *The Olympia Reader*. Quoting the letter he wrote in 1959 after customs difficulties arose, Girodias correctly asserts that the novel is not pornographic but just "frankly homosexual. . . . I would even say it is the first book with this theme which is completely uninhibited and straightforward in style and treatment."[14] By this time, frankly heterosexual novels were allowable reading in this country, and of course the unstraightforward homosexual novel was no longer regarded as *ipso facto* obscene. But Talsman's accounts of bedroom acrobatics, however lightly sketched, were apparently regarded by the customs officials of 1959 as just too shocking, and it must be said that his penalty for writing an unabashed novel has been disgracefully severe. Today only a few fly-specked, pirated editions are to be seen in the hardcore sections of secondhand bookstores, and hardly anyone has read this breezy star-spangled poem in praise of hunting, finding, and loving a grinning muscular male with black hair.

WAR/MILITARY THEMES

During the fifties a number of novels focused, with varying degrees of sympathy and explicitness, on gay servicemen. The official Department of Defense and unofficial middlebrow taboos against homosexuals in uniform were so strong that major publishers usually shied away from touching this theme unless the gay character was a neurotic villain or (as in the case of *The Gallery*) the homosexuals were sketched as outlandish members of the international set. These various taboos have been so formidable that candid depiction of gay love and sex in the military has in general been relegated to those "adult" paperbacks about simpleminded sailors who can hardly be held back from each other. During the fifties, of course, novels of this sort were comparatively restrained—even those published by Greenberg, which brought out both *Quatrefoil* and *The Invisible Glass* in 1950.

QUATREFOIL: Love Returned in the Navy

James Barr's *Quatrefoil* is one of the most intelligently written of American gay novels, with the author's lofty intellectualism appearing somewhat of a mixed blessing as the novel is reread today. The two main characters are Phillip Froelich and Tim Danelaw, naval officers who meet in Seattle in 1946, fall in love, and finally become lovers. Both are wealthy, erudite, civilized: they can speak in French or German, discuss art and philosophy with epigrammatical grace, and they value themselves as vastly superior to the average homosexual, who is always sliding "further toward degeneracy."

While the military setting is not especially crucial to *Quatrefoil,* Phillip's experiences in the Navy establish the tension that dominates the first third of the novel. After Tim helps to quash the court-martial proceedings that are being brought against Phillip for insubordination, the two men fly to San Francisco, where Phillip finds that going to bed with another man is not as "indecent and ugly and diseased and perverted" as he had assumed. Much of the second half of the novel focuses on Phillip in his hometown, Devereaux, Oklahoma, where he goes to sort out his life. Tim comes to Devereaux and goes swimming with Phillip on the extensive family estate, and the two sit around the idyllic pond, with Tim inspiring and Phillip listening in the ancient Greek tradition. At the end of the novel Tim is killed in an air crash, and Phillip's first impulse is suicide. However, he decides that having been loved has made him "strong enough to face the ordeal of living" when he remembers Tim's last words: "And now, my life is a part of yours, and your life is a part of mine. Never again shall we stand entirely alone."[15] We are helped to understand the ringing affirmation of this novel by the author's explanation that a psychiatrist had suggested that writing it could be "a key to solving my problems at the time . . ."

The positive aspect of Barr's approach in *Quatrefoil* is one that can be appreciated today more in sociological than in literary terms. Not only did the book serve as therapy for the writer, but its two thoughtful, masculine heroes also provided a corrective to the many mindless, pathetic or flighty gay characters of the forties. *Quatrefoil* is one of the earliest novels that could have produced a glow of gay pride, and in this regard it can be viewed as *The Front Runner* of the fifties. From today's point of view, however, this insistent positivism weakens the novel. Barr's desire to update the Greek "listener-inspirer" theme was admirable, but the effectiveness of this motif was minimized by the two men talking in stilted sentences. Not only, for example, does Phillip ask, "And what is truth?" but, worse, Tim answers without a moment's hesitation ("That lies within the mind of each man").

THE INVISIBLE GLASS: **Love Denied in the Army**

The first barrier between two men loving each other in the military is the sexual taboo, but it helps if the men are of about equal rank. If one man is a white officer and the other is an enlisted man who is black—and straight—not too much can be expected of the affair. Loren Wahl chose an interracial relationship to depict in *The Invisible Glass,* or perhaps this rather unusual situation chose him, since he dedicates the novel to Eddie, who is "Chick," and to George, who was "Steve."

Chick is a black former UCLA student who isn't happy in the all-Negro company commanded by a racist Southerner, Captain Randall, and Steve is Lieutenant La Cava from San Francisco, who joins Randall's unit in northern Italy in the spring of 1945: although he isn't sure he is completely gay, Steve is just getting over a love affair with a sergeant who was killed by a German shell while they shared a foxhole at Rapido crossing. Chick's romantic interest is Anna Castiglione, whom he wants to marry and take back to the States. Both Chick and Steve are trying to break through their versions of an "invisible glass" (the quote is from Du Bois' *Dusk of Dawn*): Chick wants the color barrier to be smashed so Steve and other whites can like him as a worthy human being, and eventually Steve wants the sex barrier to come down so Chick can love him as a worthy human being.

Neither color nor rank means very much to Steve, who quickly becomes a good friend of Chick's, and they are often dinner guests together at Anna's house. One night the dinner honors Anna's brother, Angelo, who has just returned from the front, and after the meal Steve and Angelo go for a walk by an olive grove. Angelo, who had also fought the Germans at Rapido, startles Steve by saying:

> "I saw you and the sergeant lying together with your arms about each other and I wished it were I that was with you. . . . It is still the same, now that I have seen you again."[16]

However, Steve does not fall in love with Angelo as he has already fallen for Chick, who toward the end of the novel drives him up to Pavia to visit relatives. Steve is not completely aware of his feelings for Chick until they arrive at his uncle's house and climb into a huge bed together to go to sleep. Heady with red wine, Steve confesses his love, and Chick allows him to have his way, but in the middle of the night Chick awakes, sober and shivering, and goes to sleep on the floor. After this act of rejection, the novel races toward a slam-bang finish. Steve and Chick leave the next morning and ride silently into Milan, where they separate. Steve inadvertently wanders into a gay bar, where an American sergeant tries to pick him up:

> "You must be carrying the torch for someone. Believe me, sir, it isn't worth it. He isn't worth it, whoever he is. None of them are. Play the field. One-night stands. It's the only thing to do, or you'll go through life with one heartache after another. None of us ever really finds, and keeps his ideal. That's the tough thing about gay life. I know. I've had to learn the hard way." He rested his hand on the officer's crotch. "How about it? Want to go? I've got a grand room a few blocks off."
>
> Lieutenant La Cava flushed. He wasn't angry, but he felt tricked and cheated. Tricked into admitting he was gay. And cheated somehow, cheated of so much. He didn't dare think what. He drank his cognac and turned to the sergeant. "Thanks, kid. But I've got to be taking off."

Drunk and crying, Steve bumps into Chick on the street and pleads to be driven back to camp that night. When they arrive, Chick jumps out of the jeep, while Steve, thinking "Dear God, why?" shoots himself. The novel ends with Captain Randall assuming that Chick murdered Steve and stole his watch, which the lieutenant had actually insisted Chick accept as a gift when they were in bed together the night before.

In spite of its "pathetic" ending, *The Invisible Glass* reads better today than *Quatrefoil,* because Wahl was generally content to recreate reality rather than write a story to uplift both writer and reader. Though not as dazzling as *The Gallery,* Wahl's novel succeeds in evoking the war-ravaged atmosphere of Italy, and to his credit Wahl was consistently more candid than Burns in depicting homosexuality. For years it has been fashionable to deprecate the grim endings of older gay novels, but, realistically speaking, the Steve-Chick relationship was indeed doomed to fail one way or another.

TWO DELIGHTFUL EXTRAORDINARY SAILORS

In *The Literary Situation,* Malcolm Cowley tells us something we already know about the cast of characters in the typical American war novel written after 1945:

> There will be a Jew and an Italian (one of them from Brooklyn), a Texan, a farm boy (always from Iowa), a hillbilly, a Mexican, and an Anglo-Saxon from an Ivy League college—these are the required characters—and sometimes there will also be a Boston Irishman, an Indian from Arizona, a Pole from the Midwestern steel mills, and a Swedish lumberjack from Puget Sound. The Texan or the Irishman creates dissension by his racial prejudice, but the Jew and the Mexican turn out to be heroes, the Texan is killed or converted, and the squad becomes a family of blood brothers.[17]

Cowley's list is especially interesting for what he omits—he does not mention that some war novels also include a gay character who is usually depicted as stereotypically as the others. Even if a gay type had been listed, of course, Cowley would have been forced to exclude a "fairy" from deserving hero status in war fiction, although in fact gay servicemen were more than likely just as heroic as Jews and Mexicans—and perhaps more so, having so much more to prove. However, Cowley's disdain for fairies reflects the conventional attitudes of the fifties, and for this reason it is all the more remarkable that two marvelously butch gay men did appear in war novels—maybe not as heroes, but certainly as charmers.

"The Theban Warriors"

Published by Little, Brown in 1955, Lonnie Coleman's *Ship's Company* is less a conventional novel than a collection of vignettes about the crew of the U.S.S. *Nellie Crocker.* Merely the mention of the name of the ship in the first sentence alerts the gay reader that some mischief may be afoot, and when William Montgomery clatters down the ladder with his sea bag, that reader is not disappointed. Like *The Gallery,* much of *Ship's Company* can be read by heterosexuals without eyebrow-raising, but sandwiched in the center of Coleman's book is a vignette called "The Theban Warriors" which is just as gay and clever as "Momma."

Montgomery is delightful. He is dark, good-looking, with "big muscular thighs, and a good back and good arms," and, more important, he is a boxer, and, most important, he beats the best boxer aboard the first Sunday at sea en route to Algiers. On the other hand, about the first thing he says when he clatters down the ladder is, "Now would you be a dear and help me with my bag?"[18]

The sailor he addresses is the narrator, Barney Casper, who is also big and muscular—but tied to a girlfriend named Doris back home in Baltimore. After the fight, Barney comes into the shower area to congratulate Montgomery, who tells him he is going to get him sooner or later—and he doesn't mean in the ring.

"Barney, the world of straight men is a fraud. They can all be had if anyone wants them enough to work things the right way. And wait his chance. Like I'm waiting my chance with you."
I shook his hand away. "Don't wait too long, Monty."
He laughed. "You see, you like me. You're calling me Monty already."
"I'm calling you Monty because in spite of pretending to be queer as a three-dollar bill, you're a nice guy basically."
"You don't know how nice I can be."
"Oh, hell, you're impossible."
"I'm the most possible thing you ever met up with."

"Look, Montgomery, don't make me mad. It's all right to kid the others but—"

". . . there's no hurry. I can wait. When I get you, it's going to be for good, and nobody's going to pretend afterwards that nothing happened. When it happens, we'll both want it to happen. Understand?"

This, then, is an unfolding plot in a respectable novel that came out in the middle of the Eisenhower years. At the beginning of the story, Montgomery isn't serious about anything at all. ("What shall it be today, girls?" he asks a dumbstruck work detail. "Let's get out the carriage and horses, put on our red dresses and high-heeled shoes, carry our sauciest parasols, and drive right by the Methodist Church like we're good as anybody!") But by the middle of the story Montgomery begins to dedicate himself to the goal of getting Barney. Barney insists he has other plans when they get to Algiers: he's going to have sex with Rina, "a well-stacked piece" at the Sphinx Club. Montgomery decides to tag along with Barney "to keep posted on what the competition has to offer" and to be available when Barney changes his mind.

At the Sphinx Club, Montgomery says, "Isn't it all too thrilling?" as they head for the tacky rooms containing Rina and Marjane. Barney is preoccupied by listening to what is going on next door (first Montgomery is laughing and then Marjane is "grunting like a hog"), and his experience with Rina is thus not all it might have been. At the end of the story, he and Montgomery are sitting on a park bench. They eye each other's bodies, and Barney seems jealous that Montgomery took so long "with that French whore" ("I was being kind," Montgomery says, "she knows she's ugly . . ."). Montgomery becomes quiet and subdued as he tells Barney that what he has to offer is something better than "a whore shreiking ooh-la-la":

". . . I'm offering you myself, and I'm promising you that I'll take you and hold you and keep you as long as—such promises last. I love you, Barney."

It was that that made me cry. My mouth was open, and I was biting my knuckles, and I couldn't see for the tears.

"Barney, this is what we're going to do. I found out about a place a few blocks from here. It's a sort of hotel where we can rent a room for

a few hours, and they don't ask any questions about why two sailors want to rent it. We can take a bath, get clean again, and then we can be together until it's time to go back to the ship. Wouldn't you like that?"
    It was a long time before I could answer. "I guess I'd like a bath."
    He stood up.
    "Are you sure this place is safe?" I said.
    "Come on."

That an American sailor is able to seduce a buddy in a novel issued by a major publishing house must be hailed as a singular bit of gay outflanking, but it hardly need be added that had successfully predatory gay sailors dominated *Ship's Company,* Coleman would have been turned down by Little, Brown. As it stood, Montgomery's homosexuality was a sufficiently minor motif that Coleman's reputation was not immediately tarnished and tagged as gay. By the mid-fifties, the Georgia-born author had established himself as a versatile literary man—he had written novels about Central America and the South, was an editor at *Collier's*—and his gay novel, *Sam,* was not to appear until 1959.

THE CAPTAIN

Russell Thacher's *The Captain* is a fairly conventional novel about the crew of an LST in the South Pacific, told from the point of view of a typically no-nonsense captain. The relevant twist is provided by Esposito, a tough guy who sometimes talks and acts as if he had wandered in from *The Gaudy Image.* He has a brawny body which he doesn't mind exposing, a broken nose, a sly sense of street-gang humor, and a quality of "insouciant sensuality" that the Captain finds "annoying."
    The first inkling that Esposito is polymorphously perverse comes during an early scene set on the beach at night. The crew is in a festive mood, and Esposito, wearing only a gold cross around his neck and two flashy rings, splashes out of the surf to challenge the Captain to a swimming race out to the rock. The Captain undresses and obliges, Esposito gets a "cramp," and when they get to the

rock, the Captain massages his leg, only to discover that Esposito has become sexually excited. "I'm sort of a touchy kind of guy," Esposito explains in a "dreamy" voice.

"That isn't the word I'd use," the Captain replies.

Esposito laughed, and it was abrupt and shattering. He crouched behind the Captain and put his arm over his shoulders. . . . He peered up into his face, his expression solemn except for the eyes. "Anything I can ever do for you—anything, sir—say the word."

The Captain swung at him, and Esposito rolled easily out of range, his laughter splitting out over the dark water and echoing back at them. When he finally stopped laughing, he looked over and said—mocking, but there was more to it than that—"Trouble with you, sir, everything's too serious the way you live—too serious. And where does it get ya, huh, where the hell does it get ya? Think anything anybody does matters to anybody but them? Not on your life."[19]

During the novel the Captain does not make use of any of Esposito's proffered services, but the bosun's mate does find a friend in another officer, "Gil" Gilchrist, who has received a Dear John letter and who reads *Leaves of Grass* in the wardroom. By the end of the novel it is clear that Esposito and Gilchrist have had a hot shipboard romance—Gilchrist is discovered "excitedly awake" in the middle of the night, fully dressed, returning from or going to Esposito, whose ring he begins to wear. In the last chapter, Gilchrist is killed by the Japanese during a landing, and Esposito comes to see the Captain. "I wanta tell you somethin'," he says, and he goes on to blame the Captain for getting "moral" with Gilchrist:

"I'm the only guy on this rotten ship that ain't sorry or ashamed. I got nothin' to feel bad about. I wasn't doin' him no harm, maybe I even done him some good. A guy I once knew—a bum guy too, but plenty smart—he said to me once that love ain't a one-dimension business. I still ain't sure what he meant, but I've got a good idea; and you ought to know with all your college and gold braid, you ought to have no trouble knowin' what he meant."

. . . He came close to him, insistent and menacing and pleading. "But I want you to know about him and me, see? I don't give a frig what you do to me or what you think a me. I ain't ashamed a nothin', and I want you to know it; and I hope you'll tell the rest a them bastards that have been shootin' off their fat mouths. See? 'Cause all we did was talk—talk

—talk; that was the important thing—all that counted. . . . And I liked to hear him talk, and I liked for someone to like me enough to want to talk to me. Is that bad? . . . We talked, talked, talked—God damn your lousy soul! And—and—" He gasped. "The other—that other—it had nothin' to do with nothin', 'cause . . ."

His voice faded; all belligerency left him, and his whole body was surprised by a pain he could not subdue. He looked at the Captain mutely . . . turned and began to run; and the pain was on him still.

On the last page, as he is leaving his ship and his command to go ashore where Gilchrist is buried, the Captain says to Esposito: "So long, lover, keep yourself out of trouble." The bosun's mate gives him the gold cross to stick on Gilchrist's marker.

The Captain swallowed. "Rate you're going, you won't have any jewelry left."

"That worry you?" Esposito glanced over his shoulder. . . . "Keep your feet dry, Capt'n. Ain't no one gonna be around to take care of ya."

Interwoven into the fabric of the whole novel, Esposito's hot-blooded sensuality makes the gay statement in *The Captain* somewhat stronger than it is in *Ship's Company,* but it was still minor enough so that a straight reviewer could call Thacher's novel merely "salty, bawdy, and vital for ex-servicemen." For the gay reader, Montgomery and Esposito are refreshing reminders that once in a while homosexuals have indeed gotten a fair shake in ostensibly straight fiction, especially as these two sassy, indomitable sailors are contrasted with their dismal counterparts in other war novels.

THE STEREOTYPICAL FAG IN WAR NOVELS

A more conventional approach to depicting gay characters in a military setting—in keeping with the equation implied in Melville's *Billy Budd* and Lawrence's "The Prussian Officer"—was to show the homosexual as depraved, neurotic and/or villainous. In 1955 Norman Mailer confessed that when he was writing *The Naked and the Dead,* he felt there was an intrinsic relationship between homosexuality and "evil," that it was symbolically just to make General Cummings villainous because he was gay. (In a piece written especially for *One*, Mailer goes on to confess that after he read Cory's *The Homosexual in America*, he found himself thinking, "My God, homosexuals are people, too.")[20]

One of the best-known war/military novels of the decade featuring a villainous homosexual was Dennis Murphy's *The Sergeant* (1958). Murphy perpetuates the black and white extremes of moral judgment quite as if no advances into gradations of psychological gray had been made since the publication of "The Prussian Officer." Sergeant Callan is assigned the Claggart role—darkly troubled, unhealthy—while Pfc. Tom Swanson is the 1950s embodiment of Billy Budd—healthy, normal, natural, noble—in short, heterosexual. At the end of the novel, when Callan presumes to touch Swanson's crotch, the private roars with "lightning strength" that comes "clean as a vision" and crashes the sergeant into a wall. When Callan shoots himself, Murphy seems to be signaling the victory of the all-American boy over the clammy forces of evil. "There is a great deal of truth and beauty in this book," John Steinbeck said on the jacket blurb, but because Murphy trumpets truth and beauty in triumphantly heterosexual terms, there is for the gay reader very little truth and even less beauty.

Neurotic gay villains also appear in Martin Dibner's *The Deep Six* and Ralph Leveridge's *Walk on the Water*, while Marc Rivette's homosexual character in *The Incident* is simply neurotic. Dibner's Ensign Mike Edge is willing to rape and murder to "get his piece," and the "pogue" he chooses in *The Deep Six* is a mentally disturbed crewman named Gray. However, Edge gets killed before he gets Gray. Leveridge's sadistic character, Tuthill, is depicted as being supermacho to compensate for his fear that he may have homosexual tendencies of his own. Tuthill shares a foxhole with Adams, a piano-playing sissy trying desperately to be a man; when Tuthill unbuttons his fly and says, "Chow down, you bastard," Adams is so unnerved he wanders into Japanese territory, where his fingers are cut off.[21] Leveridge is sympathetic to the plight of Adams ("I've got a hunch I won't come back. Then it will be all over. At last there will be peace. And then nobody can hurt me any more"), but at the same time he sketched this gay character as very much a stereotype. About equally predictable is the latently gay crew member in *The Incident,* the guilt-ridden Loosely, who commits suicide after being rebuffed in a lifeboat.

In his famous *From Here to Eternity,* James Jones allows his heroes to be entertained by members of the Honolulu gay set without compromising their own sense of masculine self-esteem. Though Kinsey would have tagged Prew and Angelo as bisexual, the two soldiers clearly regard themselves as perfectly normal when they have this discussion on the way to pick up their dates at a gay bar:

"You know, they're funny things, queers. This Hal is really a pretty good joe, if he dint hate everything so much. He hates everybody. Everybody but me. I guess he's bitter about being a queen. I spent a lot of time, tryin to figure out what makes them tick. Lots of guys tell you if you even talk to them you're queer yourself, that you ought to beat them up all the time. I don't figure like that. I figure those guys just hate them."

"I don't like them," Prew said thoughtfully. "But I don't hate them. I just don't like to be around them." He paused. "It's just that they, well for some reason they make me feel ashamed of something." He paused again. "I don't know what of."

"I know," Angelo said. "Me too. I spent a lot of time trying to figure it. They all say they was born like that. They say they been that way ever since they can remember."

"I wouldn't know," Prew said.[22]

Altogether, the war fiction that emerged after 1945 tended to preserve the illusion that gay males had either been weeded out at the induction centers or were quite justifiably being hounded out of the platoon or crew by sharp-eyed heterosexuals. Thus, Montgomery and Esposito go against the grain, as do these thoughts in *Walk on the Water:*

In war (leastways this war was honest enough to admit it) it happened all the time. And nobody gave a good goddam, unless it was some of the stupid people who had stayed home. . . . So what if the whole outfit was some renaissance of Sparta and the battalion of lovers? Who cared?[23]

Well, obviously the major publishers didn't care too much as long as their writers subordinated hints of irregular love to the more acceptable themes of war fiction, such as killing and torture. If World

War II was indeed "honest enough" in one way or another to admit that American servicemen were having sex with each other, most of the people back home preferred to think that their favorite military characters weren't touching each other even in fun and that their blood-brothership was based on something other than affection.

OTHER TRADITIONAL NOVELS OF THE FIFTIES: *A MIXED BAG*

THE NIGHT AIR: You Can't Go Home Again

Although Harrison Dowd's *The Night Air* (Dial, 1950) was not regarded as great gay fiction, it did get some fairly good reviews— *The Saturday Review* called it "excellent" and the *New York Herald Tribune* called it "forceful." Since it came out so early in the decade, it not surprisingly echoes some familiar themes of the forties, particularly that of the hero going full circle in trying to recapture the freshness and beauty of his idyllic boyhood.

In the midst of a hectic, troubled show-biz life in Manhattan, Andy Moore remembers his grandmother's kitchen in Vermont: "pans of milk standing on the cold pantry shelves, gathering tough yellow skins of cream which he liked to puncture with his forefinger . . . gingerbread cookies, featherbeds . . . the smell of cedar and dripping Christmas candles . . . it was his world, undamaged and complete, with no threat, no danger . . ." Into this world comes his slightly older cousin Harold, who teaches him about sex and, perhaps, love. "Harold was big, with a handsome mouth and dark red hair; he could high dive and swim four times across the river and back; his chest and legs were hard as a colt's."[24]

In New York Andy searches for a suitable facsimile of this sense of security that had been provided by his grandmother, her house, and Harold. Neither his marriage to a woman nor an affair with a fellow actor works out, but toward the end of the novel Andy thinks he has found what he has been looking for: Mike Colsak, a big, balding, masculine gay man. By the time he meets Mike, Andy has become an alcoholic, and his acting career seems about over, so when he goes to bed with Mike he is thinking not only of sex but security:

> He didn't feel cold any longer. He looked at Mike's heavy pale face and strong mouth and felt like . . . all the withering lonely women in the world, frail, immeasurably pathetic. He was home at last; this was where he belonged. He sighed, contentedly.
> "Mike."
> Mike grunted, turned away, then half waking, looked back over his shoulder. "Huh?"
> "Do me a favor, will you?"
> "What's that?"
> "Marry me."

Mike doesn't marry him, however. He calls Andy a lush and tells him that he'll end up in the booby hatch if he doesn't stop drinking. At the end of the novel, Andy gets on the bus and goes "home at last" to South Pond, Vermont, where Harold's son shows him around the old farm, which is now for sale. It is a spring day, and the last sentences of the novel sound a hopeful note:

> Andy bent down and tugged at one of the plants; it stuck tenaciously to the black dung, bringing some of it along on its tough, elastic little roots. He lifted the clump to his nostrils and inhaled, and the smell was one of spring rain and sun, of melted snow, of death and rot and fertility, and of green, inextinguishable life.

However, the "tough, elastic little roots" should not be interpreted as a symbol that Andy has finally decided to settle down. "No, the answer wasn't here," he had realized earlier as he looked around the farm. "He hadn't come home."

Andy's dilemma at the end of this novel is peculiar to gay characters in fiction and to gay people in general. The back-to-nature impulse often found in post–World War II American thought and literature makes sense mainly for heterosexuals, who have the greater capacity to be content and successful if they move back to the old home town. However disenchanted gay men may be with life in the big city—and this disenchantment is a stock feature of homosexual fiction—there are two reasons that compel most of them to stay in an urban area. First, the city provides anonymity, sexual opportunities, perhaps acceptance, and the chance to be caught up in the metropolitan whirl. Equally important is the awareness that by returning "home" (as in Creekmore's *The Welcome*), one courts the reputation of once more being the misfit— and it is the unpleasantness of provincial homophobia that drives gay people away from Minot and Rockford in the first place.

Along with such other novels as *City of Night, The Night Air* underscores the fact that the whole subject of "idyllic innocence" is one which teases, frustrates, and confounds many gay people. As was pointed out in the last chapter, they hardly regret their sexual knowledgeability, but at the same time most gay people can recall their pre-adolescent years with a singular sort of wistfulness. After puberty homosexuals are gradually forced to give up their hold on that familiar, snug, and comfortable world of dimly Eden-like "normalcy" in which they lived for a time, but it is usually not the end of their own innocence that is shattering. Rather, it is the end of the innocence of *others* that is hard to bear: one is dropped by high school chums, given strange looks by parents, and the old home town becomes, in Housman's words, "the land of lost content" where you "cannot come again."

Understanding this situation is essential for appreciating the final conflict in *The Night Air*. While Andy senses an overwhelming tug at the sight of the wholesomeness and rightness of South Pond, he and Harrison Dowd realize that the answer isn't there. He cannot stay. The "answer" may not be found in Manhattan, either, but eventually Andy will have to get back on the bus and return to New York, where he and his kind more properly "belong."

SAM

Lonnie Coleman's *Sam,* published at the end of the decade (David McKay, 1959), presents a less sordid view of the gay milieu in New York City. The title character, a book publisher named Sam Kendrick, has this to say about gay novels: "The only ones I see are trashy or sentimental. A dream world of television drama, with the sexes changed a little. They all end with a suicide or a murder."[25] Taking pains to avoid trashiness and sentimentality in *Sam,* Coleman at least succeeds in avoiding trashiness, ending on a note as upbeat as the final scene of "The Theban Warriors." The blurb on the back of the Pyramid paperback edition calls *Sam* the "story of a successful man who is also an *unashamed homosexual"* (these words in flaming red ink), with the implication that the two conditions generally exclude each other—or at least should. However, in both "The Theban Warriors" and *Sam* Coleman seems to be insisting that gayness is not only no cause for shame but can actually be the foundation for quite a delightful, rewarding life. Thus, the theme of *Sam* is merely a restatement in broader, civilian terms of that of "The Theban Warriors," but the novel is not quite as impressive as the short story. "The Theban Warriors" remains a tour de force because of the breathtaking twist of the plot, while the ending of *Sam* comes dangerously close to being as idealized as that of *Quatrefoil.*

Although the world of Coleman's novel is familiar to gay readers, everyone in Sam's set of friends, gay or straight, is more of a thirty-year-old success than a pathetic twenty- or forty-year-old knockabout. The foursome at the beginning includes Sam; his lover Walter, an ambitious actor; the pregnant Addie; and Addie's homophobic husband, Toby. By the end of the novel the foursome is Sam; his new and better lover, Richard, a debonair doctor; the childless Addie; and her new and better husband, Dan. What saves the denouement from being slushy is Coleman's restrained style and his dry, playful dialogue. In the hands of a more effusive writer, Richard would turn out too good to be true—he's not only sincere and loving and generous, he has a charming country house on a fifteen-acre wooded lot with a stream running through it. Just as in "The Theban Warriors," though, Coleman knows how to underwrite, and he is quite successful in depicting the Sam-Richard relationship as one that has not only love but logic to recommend it. A main difference between *Sam* and *The Night Air*—or *Giovanni's Room,* for that matter—is that in Coleman's novel the main character is able not only to endure but actually to prevail in day-to-day living.

Sam Kendrick may not have been what David Freeman had in mind in the *One* article calling for Sears customers living on Sixth Street, but Freeman would surely have agreed that the over-all concept of *Sam* was a step in the right direction.

OLDER VOICES, YOUNGER MEN

The main focus of several novels of the fifties was the relationship between an adolescent and an older male, and in three of the novels—*Finistere, Never the Same Again,* and *Parents' Day*—the setting seems to be especially important in shaping the plot.

FINISTERE

Fritz Peters' *Finistere* (Farrar, Straus, 1951, with the Lancer paperback title being the more "telling" *The World at Twilight*) is set in France, where Matthew's divorced mother takes him to live and to go to school. Matthew is rescued from being drowned in the Seine by Michel, a handsome young teacher, with whom he falls in love. Michel turns out to be gay, the love turns out to be mutual, and if there were no other Americans in the novel, the ending might have turned out to be cheerful. The French characters are tolerant of Matthew's incipient gayness ("Not everybody is the same . . . be happy while you can"), but the American characters are scandalized once they finally catch on. Scott, whom Matthew loved as a father substitute, writes a note suggesting they not see each other again, and at the end of the novel Matthew's mother becomes hysterical and says she wishes he were dead. Apparently Matthew does too, because he drowns himself in the Atlantic Ocean that very night. The particular significance of the foreign setting is that the sixteen-year-old youth has only his mother and Scott to rely on for approval, and there is simply no one else to turn to after they reject him.

Peters was generally praised by the reviewers for being "serious," "sincere," and "knowledgeable," and what seems today to be the slightly benighted vision of *The New York Times* critic ("The best novel this reviewer has ever read on the theme of homosexuality . . . and its tragic consequences") was a common one for the early fifties. In *The Saturday Review of Literature,* Gore Vidal used the magic phrases, praising Peters for resolutely focusing on "his great theme: the corruption and the murder of innocence."[26]

NEVER THE SAME AGAIN

"Corruption" and "innocence" might be said to be components of Gerald Tesch's *Never the Same Again* (Putnam's, 1956), but as usual these terms demand especially careful definition if they are to make sense in gay literature. Although thirteen-year-old Johnny Parish is innocent at the start of the novel, his contact with thirty-year-old Roy Davies cannot be termed corruption from any valid point of view. At the end of the novel Davies leaves town, Johnny remains a saddened but otherwise "normal" growing boy, and the only cries of "corruption" are shouted by the dreadful townspeople of Wilkinson City, Illinois. It is on the end of *their* innocence that the novel turns, and the only one who will never be the same again is Roy Davies.

Perhaps it needs to be made clear to heterosexuals that most gay people would view the age differential between thirty and thirteen as an insuperable barrier to serious romance. While love between two thirteen-year-old males or two thirty-year-old males can be accepted as normal in the gay experience, the idea of a thirty-year-old man courting a thirteen-year-old boy is viewed by many gay people as something rather close to child molestation. Though the nature of child molesters is a source of continuing confusion in the minds of many heterosexuals, there is almost complete agreement on this subject among gay men in this country: the desired sex object is a physically mature male, not a budding child. In all fairness, however, it must be conceded that among the gay population of America there is a small fraction of pedophiles. They have their own magazines full of pictures of naked boys, and they have their own champion, J. Z. Eglinton. A theme of Eglinton's lengthy *Greek Love* (Oliver Layton Press, 1964) is that sexual attraction between two mature males is merely "androphilia," an unfortunate perversion of the more venerable tradition of "Greek love" between a man and a boy.

Identifying with the hero of *Never the Same Again* is easy for anyone—androphile, pedophile, or heterophile—because the main character is simply an average mid-American kid whose curiosity matches his ignorance about sex. Relying chiefly on documentary realism interlarded with occasional patches of overwritten sentimentality, Tesch depicts Johnny as the paper boy next door who loves to look at his Aunt Margaret's "billowing bowl of mashed potatoes" with its golden-yellow melting butter "running down the snowy sides." The role that Roy Davies plays throughout most of the novel is merely that of a swell father substitute for Johnny, who helps out at his service station, goes on fishing trips with him up to the lake, and tells him, "You're the nicest guy inna whole wide world, Roy."

By the last part of the novel, however, Roy is asking Johnny not to tell anyone what they do in the car, and apparently what they do—this is never specified—is have some mild sort of sex. How the novel itself climaxes is clearer: a closet-case villain materializes in the form of Mr. Bentley, a slimy church boys' club adviser who wants Johnny all to himself. Bentley insists that Johnny "tell on" Roy to the town judge, Roy inexplicably tells him to go ahead, Johnny finally does, Roy moves away, Johnny is crushed, and the novel ends.

Both the *Library Journal* and *Kirkus* reviewers were old-maidish about this novel—the former objected to certain "lurid passages" and the latter warned "Caution—here." The more worldly *Time* critic objected because Tesch wrote badly: ". . . but Tesch, an off-and-on Handy colonist since 1952, has apparently been trained to write this way."[27] In fact, the book reveals too little rather than too much training (the blurb notes that Tesch's formal education extended only through the sixth grade), but it is conceded that the simplicity of the author's style was in keeping with his story.

PARENTS' DAY

One of the most unusual American novels with a gay motif was written by Paul Goodman in the late forties and published as *Parents' Day* by the 5 x 8 Press of Saugatuck, Connecticut, in 1951. By the time this novel was published, Goodman had acquired the reputation of doing the sort of "writing that seems acute even when you're not quite sure what it means,"[28] and with a streak of spirited University of Chicago iconoclasm, he was busy analyzing everything from city planning to anarchistic politics.

Parents' Day succeeds more as an evocative memoir than as a gripping novel because of the remarkably tolerant atmosphere of the setting. Goodman's Summerhillish school has little in common with the prep schools in *Lucifer with a Book* and *End As a Man,* as its purpose is to do away with all of the taboos that restrict the blossoming of the individual. Goodman's main character is a teacher who tells everyone he is gay, but no one minds as long as he doesn't seduce his students. There are moments in the novel when Goodman comes close to the malicious satire of Mary McCarthy's *The Groves of Academe,* but, unlike McCarthy, he remains essentially sympathetic with the spirit of his fictional school. The antagonist turns out to be the headmaster, who at the end of the novel asks the teacher if he has ever had sex with any of his students. The teacher considers:

I had toyed with the idea of baiting him a little, for sport and instruction. I could have asked a question or two: "What are sexual relations? Are we, now, Mark Anders, having a sexual relation? And what are overt sexual relations? Where do *you* draw the line? Is it overt if the persons rub together? or must the parts rub together? or suppose they touch and, say, both know what they are doing but avert their eyes and talk on as if they did not know? Must the parts be exposed? For instance, sometimes at night, sitting on Davy's bed and entertaining him with the habits of the world, I masturbated him through the blankets and then, sick with longing, fell on him and came in my pants. Was this an overt sexual relation?" . . . But I had no heart for small victories, and I said, "Yes, I did."[29]

The teacher is asked to leave the school, and he does. *Parents' Day* is a loose story about a loose year in a loose school, and as a result there is little conflict until the end of the novel. Goodman seems to have been mainly interested in approaching the question of "normality" from an intellectual perspective, and by asking—if not always answering—provocative questions, he implies there are shades of gray in male-male relationships which defy the neat Dennis Murphy categorizations of "good" and "evil."

THE EMERGENCE OF THE "UNTRADITIONAL" TRENDS

Assigning separate status to softcore pornography and beat literature is something that can only be done from the vantage point of the seventies: during the fifties the Jay Little books were regarded as merely bold gay novels, and beat writing was not recognized as fundamentally gay at all. One is now able to see, however, that as softcore has become hardcore and as the seeds sown by the beats have blossomed into counterculture-gay liberation literature, these two trends have posed important competition for what is now regarded as the old-fashioned gay novel.

Softcore Pornography and the Novels of Jay Little

The mysterious history of homosexual erotica in this country goes back to and perhaps well beyond J. P. Starr's "Boys, Men, and Love," that quaint typescript which included a number of "boys-in-the-barn" stories written during World War I. By the 1950s many gay men in America had acquired copies of typewritten "fuck stories," which were much more hardcore than anything in the Starr collection.[30] These stories were circulated and exchanged with great secrecy—they were often confiscated by the police during raids—and they were always safely out of sight along with the crypto-gay muscle magazines when Mother came to call.

Whatever doubts one may have about the quality of Jay Little's novels, it must be said this man did make a contribution of sorts by opening the bedroom door. Using a pseudonym and the services of a vanity press, Little was able to get away with more than his contemporaries who had to observe the traditional taboos. But it is not explicitness alone that identifies *Maybe-Tomorrow* as softcore pornography; *The Gaudy Image* was also explicit, but it was not fundamentally pornographic. The characteristic that defines sexual scenes as pornographic is their relative unbelievability. In *The Gaudy Image*, Tit's sexual adventures are so naturally interwoven into the plot and conveyed with such twinkling humor that the reader accepts them as a delightful but hardly surprising part of the underground life of the French Quarter.

Little's sexual scenes, however, are not only less real, they are also self-consciously written, revealing that the author is quite obviously compensating for past frustrations through the ploy of wish-fulfillment fantasy. So it could be said that it is the aspect of believability which separates traditional writing from softcore pornography and, in turn, softcore from hardcore pornography. The more traditional novel is at least theoretically convincing, because the author is relying more on memory than on desire to sketch the daily life of his gay characters. Traditional novels become softcore when the author contrives to have some gorgeous, untouchable straight type tumble into bed in a way that defies all the rules of probability. Softcore turns into hardcore when *everything* becomes incredible, but since the purpose of the hardcore novel is to create some sort of masturbatory intensity, nobody really cares— the last thing on the reader's mind when a whole locker room full of professional football players start taking off each others' jockstraps is verisimilitude.

MAYBE-TOMORROW: Dreams Come True in Cotton, Texas

The compensatory aspect was especially evident in Little's first novel, *Maybe-Tomorrow* (Pageant Press, 1952), in which the town sissy has unheard-of success with the local football star. From the standpoint of both gay life and gay literature, Little was departing from a truth that had been almost universally acknowledged. In those pre–Dave Kopay days, you were expected to suffer through your high school crushes as best you could until you were able to go away somewhere and find people who would be able to respond. In gay novels, this pattern was seen in everything from *Beyond the Street* to *The Folded Leaf* to *The Divided Path,* and even the enchanted moment in *The City and the Pillar* was finally conceded to be a fluke. Jay Little might have thought that football players were pushovers in small Texas towns, and indeed no less an authority than Gore Vidal has claimed that in "Texas—that relentless Bible belt—there's nobody who is not available."[31] However, that Cotton is different from its counterparts in other states and that Vidal says what he does is surely more traceable to a desire for rather than a memory of complete wish-fulfillment. The Bob Blakes in real life were never *that* available to the little Gaylord LeClaires who adored them.

Maybe-Tomorrow opens with Gaylord (or Gay) brooding with "melancholia" because he doesn't know how to cope with his crush on Bob, the bronzed, muscular Cotton High athlete who goes out with girls. To his credit, Little does try to establish Bob's extraordinary sense of gallantry just before the shower-room scene. Two little girls are inexplicably playing jacks in front of the gym door, and Bob is humane enough to ask Marion what happened to her "two pretty teeth." Then a sound, and Bob becomes Superman:

What was that? Sounded like a scream from the gym. . . . Blake perked his head and listened. . . . Yes, there it was again, faint but real. Someone was in trouble. He'd better hurry.[32]

It is Gaylord, in fact, who is in trouble—he is about to be raped by three mischievous boys, and Bob arrives just in time, warning the toughs that if he ever catches them doing this again, he'll forget that he is a "gentleman." The boys are sent away, Bob undresses ("Gaylord watched Blake's thick fingers strip off his trunks, pull them down over his hips. Then they fell of their own accord to his feet, a circle of white, whiter than the sudden exposed buttocks"), and he and Gay share a shower. Gay begins to sob, Bob comforts him by taking him in his arms, and the chapter ends with his kissing Gay's "upturned lips" as "the spraying water formed a glass curtain of protection around them. . . ."

Almost overnight, Bob's gentlemanly concern is magically increased to include sexual desire. On their first date, after an evening of hamburgers, Cokes, and a movie over in Egan, Bob parks his car in Lovers' Lane and begins to undress Gaylord, who

. . . swayed unsteadily as the silence rose up around him, when his clothes left his body. He lay back feeling Blake's body, hard and rigid as timbers against him, and hot with an animal's vitality. He threw his arms around the naked back above him, felt Blake's firm mouth on his own. Felt Blake's tongue forcing itself into him. Ways of kissing that had never occurred to him were sought for and discovered. . . . His hands worked gently up against the oily hair. He caressed it until the darkness went out of him, and the slow joy too. He could feel the pounding of Blake's blood, rolling out to meet his, leaving a weakness in him, a tropical languor . . . a melting . . . a dying . . . a flame.
It was accomplished there in the darkness between them.

And there is more! Bob Blake loses nearly all his interest in girls and becomes sex-crazed over Gaylord. They sit out in front of Gaylord's house in Bob's car, making love "as if they were obeying unspoken orders."

"You don't have to go in, do you, Gay?"
"No," Gaylord whispered. "I don't . . . I want to be with you . . . just you . . ."
"You do?"
"You know I do."
"Want to take a little ride?"

In fact, the conflict toward the end of the book comes not with Gaylord's jealousy over Bob's interest in a girl but with Bob's jealousy over Gaylord's friendship with another boy. On the closing pages this conflict is happily resolved when, one night after a spat, Bob confesses he was a fool to be jealous, and in "the warm night air," while the trees stand "silent and friendly," they decide to flee Cotton and move to New Orleans.

Little's turning the tables with his characterization of Bob Blake must have been a source of immense satisfaction for the more frustrated gay readers of the 1950s, who could find all wrongs made right and all hurts smoothed over with comforting kisses. Once a reader detached himself from vicarious emotional involvement, however, he would have to admit that reality had been suspended to permit the acting-out of adolescent fantasies. The suspension of belief must take place during the locker-room scene, as very few gay men have ever been kissed by their high school heroes in the shower. Once this allowance is made, of course, nothing comes as much of a surprise.

SOMEWHERE BETWEEN THE TWO:
More Wishes, More Fulfillment

In 1956 Pageant Press published another Jay Little novel, *Somewhere Between the Two.* Little's dedication was "With my respects and admiration to every professional female impersonator," and the novel sentimentalizes the hectic show-biz career of Terry Wallace, indomitable drag queen.

Softcore sex, though subordinated to a less important role than it played in *Maybe-Tomorrow,* is not altogether absent. Midway through the story Terry is driving home into New Orleans after finishing his act out at Sunset Cottage, and he has a flat tire. Of course, he doesn't know a thing about changing one, and to the rescue comes butch Nick Lazzo.

His skin was so golden brown that Terry wondered if this was its natural color or just a good tan. Although his clothes were cheap, he wore them well. The white pull-over sweat-shirt molded his well-built physique, as did the faded blue jeans.[33]

Nick, who can fix flat tires blindfolded, is thus a highly suitable candidate for the softcore sex scene that unfolds after Terry asks him up to his apartment for a drink. Almost before Terry can finish saying, "I love the gulf, too . . . it gives one a sort of free feeling," the sweat-shirt and the faded blue jeans come off and the well-built physique is in bed.

They were in each other's naked arms again, and Nick's hot breath was on his flesh. All his embarrassment and shyness was in a heap on the floor with his clothes. He was holding Terry hard against him. He was kissing him hard, driving on, forcefully, in his maleness. . . .

A warmness put itself across his flesh like melted wax. A burning flame was ebbing out by receding waters, a surge of exquisite pain, a deep sigh, then limpness. . . .
Love had lifted them up as on wings of flames.

For some reason, Little begins lapsing into Song of Solomonese during his lyrical love passages, and at the very end of the novel Terry's meeting a young admirer at the club sets off such thoughts as "Oh, desirable one, delectable youth, you are stately as a palm tree and your lips are like its clusters. I say I will climb the palm tree and lay hold of its branches. Oh, am I dreaming in vain when I say unto you . . ." The desirable one turns out to be, neatly enough, Gaylord LeClaire!

Critical reaction to Little's novels was limited mainly to gay reviewers, since they were too brazen for establishment critics—Gaylord was too irredeemably perverse, for instance, to fit comfortably into W. Tasker Witham's *The Adolescent in the American Novel.* The *One* critic found Little's second novel not so "startling" as his first but granted that *Somewhere Between the Two* did have "pinpricks of excitement." This critic described Little as a "very earnest young man" whose writing was weak because of inexplicable character motivation. The *Mattachine Review* praised *Somewhere Between the Two* in contrast to other contemporary novels that were so "etherealized that the reader may wonder whether homosexuals ever have sex," but at the same time found Little's sex scenes "predictable" and conveyed in the "oddest combination . . . of fancy language."[34]

Little's novels probably produced their greatest impact on naïve, virginal readers in the hinterlands, who, after receiving their copies in plain brown wrappers at the post office, could take them home, lock the door, and listen to their hearts thud as they read of Bob Blake dropping his shorts and exposing his white buttocks. For the more experienced and sophisticated gay readers of the fifties, however, Little's softcore approach must have been less satisfactory. The literate reader demanding convincing character motivation would have been more amused than excited by the thought of a halfback becoming enamored of the school sissy or an Italian laborer desiring a plucked-eyebrowed drag queen. Moreover, the hardcore fuck-story fan wanting the writer to describe the parts in thundering detail would have found such phrases as "driving on, forcefully, in his maleness" hopelessly ineffectual.

Jay Little apparently wrote no more novels, and his softcore approach had few imitators here during the fifties. However, softcore did continue to be written and published during the sixties, growing more and more explicit as it inched its way toward hardcore. Gay softcore might be defined as writing that would like to be hardcore if only it dared, and by the freewheeling standards of today, yesterday's softcore novels seem little more than quaint reminders of an era when caution was still necessarily the watchword.

THE GAY BEATS:
CATS AT PLAY IN THE CLOSET

The other untraditional approach of the fifties was that of the beats, a group of young men initially popularized as just a bunch of unconventional, hip, but quite heterosexual holy barbarians. During the fifties the average gay reader could perceive little but wine, women, and song in Jack Kerouac's novels, and, the times being what they were, it is easy to see why the gay members of this milieu preferred the label "beat" to that of "queer." A beatnik was considered weird and maladjusted enough in those days, and the admission of being a queer beatnik would have caused unbearable consternation on all sides. Though the more literary gay activists now trace the start of the movement back to Allen Ginsberg's "Howl," most Americans still regard the beats as a band of hetero bohemians because of the myth-making provided by the critics and by the beat writers themselves, both in and out of their works.

Not all the beat writers were gay, and perhaps the most bisexual (or *least* sexual) of them all was Jack Kerouac, who in a 1968 interview tried to emphasize that he and his buddies had just been a bunch of regular fellows. "I mean, here I am," he said, "a guy who was a railroad brakeman, and a cowboy, and a football player—just a lot of things ordinary guys do. . . . We didn't have a whole lot of heavy abstract thoughts. We were just a bunch of guys out trying to get laid."[35] In his 1957 roman à clef *On the Road,* Kerouac had taken some pains to heterosexualize the characters—Sal Paradise (himself), Dean Moriarity (Neal Cassady), Carlo Marx (Allen Ginsberg) and Old Bull Lee (William Burroughs). Although in real life "Dean" and "Carlo" were lovers for a while, in the novel Kerouac tossed in enough "frosty fagtown" jokes to make it appear that his characters were normal and that they were just crisscrossing the country to see one another for the hell of it. Most literary critics have bought this interpretation, and their discomfort in handling beat homoeroticism is illustrated by the following passage from John Tytell's *Naked Angels: The Lives and Literature of the Beat Generation* (1976):

> That a writer's sexual condition is as important an aspect of his vision and sensibility as his social or theistic views is a post-Freudian commonplace. These instances with black or "Fellaheen" lovers [in Kerouac's *The Subterraneans*] reveal an ambivalence toward sexuality that links Kerouac with Ginsberg's fear of women and Burroughs' outright declaration of hatred for them. Indeed, the general attitude to women in Kerouac's books is a reminder of the homosexual orientation of the Beats.[36]

It is clear that Tytell would rather *not* be reminded of this orientation, however much he concedes its importance, because he quickly moves on to continue his interpretation of Kerouac as "Eulogist of Spontaneity." Meanwhile, however, through the revelations in Ann Charters' *Kerouac* and, more specifically, all of the *Gay Sunshine* interviews, the cats have been let out of the bag: the real truth is that Jack and the guys didn't always have to go *out* to get laid.[37]

Of this group it was, of course, Allen Ginsberg who was the most conspicuously homosexual in his writings of the fifties, but even in his outrageous "Howl" he took care to swathe gay sex in mystical-religious wrappings and to use the old Whitmanian device of dutifully including "a million girls trembling in the sunset."[38] Here again, many critics have preferred to sidestep the problem of homosexuality, and one of them has actually interpreted Ginsberg's view of brotherly love in terms that could be embraced by the Boy

Scouts of America. In "A Look at the 'Beat Generation' Writers," Wolfgang Fleischmann has written:

Beyond Ginsberg's bloody toilets . . . lie visions of a peaceful world made strong by the love of comrades and the joys of mystic insight. Zen Buddhism and a kind of comradeship reminiscent of the Wandervogel movement in the German Weimar Republic's days, are its ideals.[39]

Another gay writer—if not a "gay novelist"—who was at least sociogrammatically a member of the early counterculture was Paul Bowles. Rather than living in North Beach, Bowles spent most of the fifties living in North Africa, where exotic drugs and young men were even easier to come by. Gertrude Stein thought Bowles to be merely a "manufactured savage," and in his novels of the fifties (*Let It Come Down, The Spider's House*) there is a carefully controlled vagueness that keeps everything heterosexually respectable. In a recent *Gay Sunshine* interview, poet John Giorno said that Bowles and his wife "had this glamorous public image of themselves. It was Tangier and *Vogue* magazine and everyone was sublimely civilized."[40] Bowles hoped nobody would ever find out about his Arab boyfriends, Giorno said, adding that Bowles' response to someone asking him to contribute to a gay anthology was he did not believe in "literature engagee [*sic*]."

In the fifties none of the gay beats believed in littérature engagée —homosexuality could hardly be regarded in terms of a "problem" novel by a writer enveloped in drugs and boys in Morocco or Mexico City—and William Burroughs is a final case in point. Burroughs got his first novel, *Junkie,* published in 1953 by Ace Books, under the pseudonym William Lee, but significantly enough no one wanted to publish his second novel, *Queer.* The wild, jerking surrealism of Burroughs' more recent novels (*The Naked Lunch, Nova Express, The Soft Machine, The Wild Boys*) has made them somewhat offputting to the average gay reader in this country, while at the same time they have been praised by prominent literary critics for their bold and dazzling experiments in style.

The last word on the importance of gay sensibility in beat literature remains to be written. In *Naked Angels,* Tytell trots out the tags that have always been used in describing Ginsberg and Burroughs and Kerouac ("exiles," "foundlings," "outcasts"), but, viewed in the light of the *Gay Sunshine* interviews, these terms now seem to be nothing short of evasive euphemisms for the unutterable word "homosexual." As time goes on, a good portion of beat writing may well be classified as a variation of the gay literature of the fifties, however much it was not understood as such at the time by either heterosexuals or homosexuals.

SHORTER FICTION, SECONDARY THEMES, AND THE PULPS

The first anthology of gay short stories published in this country, Donald Webster Cory's *21 Variations on a Theme,* was brought out by Greenberg in 1953. Among the titles were Sherwood Anderson's "Hands," Charles Jackson's "Palm Sunday," Christopher Isherwood's "On Ruegen Island," John Horne Burns' "Momma," and Paul Bowles' "Pages from Cold Point."

Several gay stories were included in Tennessee Williams' 1954 collection, *Hard Candy,* published by New Directions. In both "The Mysteries of the Joy Rio" and "Hard Candy," a dirty old man goes to a shabby theater to have sex with shabby young men, and in the latter he chokes to death on hard "candy." "Two on a Party" described the successes and failures of a male-female team who cruise for "the lyric quarry" in New York and throughout the South. No longer being on the OK List, Gore Vidal apparently felt he had little to lose by including some gay stories in *A Thirsty Evil,* which was published by Zero Press in 1956. "Three Stratagems" was about a Princeton football player who hustles in Key West, and in "The Zenner Trophy" a student is expelled from a private school for having sex with his boyfriend. Vidal was not surprised at the negative reviews of *A Thirsty Evil:* "Not only was I out of fashion," he has explained, "but any writer who dealt with homosexuality could count on a particularly rabid press."[41] James Barr followed up *Quatrefoil* with *Derricks* (Pan Books, 1957), which is full of stories about finding down-to-earth men to love in the Midwest.

The publication during the fifties of so much fiction with a secondary gay motif can be interpreted from two points of view: heterosexuals were finding that the brief appearances of perverts added spice to their narratives, whereas homosexuals continued to downplay the subject so their books could be praised in terms of grander themes. Deserving special mention among the dozens of authors whose works contained some gay angle are James Purdy and Patrick Dennis.

The Deadpan World of James Purdy

James Purdy is now regarded as one of the more important men of letters in America, but his reputation has been won in spite of the ghostly homoeroticism that haunts much of his fiction. "They really are vicious," Purdy has said about the New York critics. "And they use all kinds of smears. They used to say my work was homosexual and therefore it had no validity, which is like saying if a Negro prepares food, the food is dirty."[42]

In the late fifties Purdy was just starting to get published, with *Color of Darkness* (short stories) coming out in 1957 and *Malcolm* in 1959. While critics may have been quick to sniff out the scent of sexual perversion in these books, most gay readers of the time were much less aware of what Purdy was about. In these books, homosexuality remained a shadowy undertone in a surreal landscape, and the gay reader looking for answers could find only puzzles expressed in deadpan language that offered no solutions at all.

Within the last fifteen years, some of Purdy's books have achieved underground cult status with a number of gay readers, notably his 1967 novel with the blockbuster ending, *Eustace Chisholm and the Works*. However, Purdy does not like to think of himself as a narrowly gay novelist and especially not as a gay-lib writer. "I . . . do not think I am a 'gay' writer in that my work has some political . . . message for liberation," he says. "I despise propaganda . . . love is terrible and tragic, whether it is between men and men or women and men or women and women. No political freedom will solve the agony of suffering."

The Campy Novels of Patrick Dennis

Strangely enough, British reviewers have pegged some of Purdy's novels (e.g., *I Am Elijah Thrush*) as camp, but, viewed in American terms, the writer of the fifties who was quite clearly King of the Camps was Patrick Dennis. Whether the main characters of campy novels are female (Auntie Mame) or "male" (Fay Etrange), this sort of writing has always had a special appeal to many gay men because of its brisk, witty theatricality and its breezy approach to love affairs and life. In short, the foundation for camp writing is the gay sensibility.

Even in his pre–Auntie Mame novels (*Oh, What a Wonderful Wedding,* 1953; *House Party,* 1954), Dennis was viewing life as a campy romp under the pseudonym of "Virginia Rowans." One reviewer complimented Miss Rowans for writing "with a fine feminine realism," and his special talent of enlarging gossipy chitchat into almost drag-queen melodrama helped Dennis to achieve enormous success with *Auntie Mame* (1955), *Guestward Ho!* (1956), *Around the World with Auntie Mame* (1958), to say nothing of *Little Me* and *3-D* and all the rest of the novels he has written since the fifties.

Gay characters have grown increasingly important in the Dennis novels over the years, although the subject is always conveyed with the same light touch. From the closeted Uncle Ned in *House Party* to the more obvious Hollywood directors in *Little Me* to the bisexual hero of *3-D,* Dennis has alluded to gayness as if he were a worldly-wise uncle winking at a knowing gay nephew.

Other Relevant Novels

The attitude of Holden Caulfield toward "perverts" in Salinger's *The Catcher in the Rye* typified the tone of many novels which featured a minor gay character. Rushing away from his old English teacher, Holden protests that he can't stand people being "perverty" when he's around and complains that he knows "more damn perverts, at schools and all, than anybody you ever met." The punk hero of Chandler Brossard's *The Bold Saboteurs* was even more negative than Holden: his gang rolled queers in the park, and he thought their being gay was a sign of "ineradicable sickness."

Being gay was considered as freakish in Norman Mailer's Hollywood novel *The Deer Park,* in Meyer Levin's fictionalization of the Leopold-Loeb case, *Compulsion,* and in the novel that Leslie Fiedler admired so much, Robert Phelps' *Heroes and Orators.* A gay episode was cause for regret and fear in Allen Drury's *Advise and Consent,* and in another novel set in Washington, D.C., gayness goes hand in hand with treason. This novel was Edward Ronns' *State Department Murders,* which was published in 1950 as a Gold Medal paperback to lacerate "the few effeminate diplomats who disgrace the Nation." Another mystery novel with a gay motif, *Death in the Fifth Position,* was written by Gore Vidal under the pseudonym of Edgar Box and published as a Signet paperback in 1953. According to the blurb, the hero is an engaging young straight detective who risks his reputation by going to a Harlem steam bath with a gay ballet dancer. With tongue in cheek, Box keeps his tough-guy hero untempted and untouched in the midst of a steam room orgy:

All around the steam room was a concrete ledge or shelf on which the various combinations disported themselves, doing a lot of things I never thought possible. It was like being in hell: the one electric light bulb in the steam room was pink and gave a fiery glow to the proceedings. For the first time that night I was tempted to give up, to run away, to let the whole damned murder case take care of itself. Only the thought of Jane kept me in that steam room.[43]

Mothers find out more than they want to know about their gay sons in Jack Dunphy's *Friends and Vague Lovers* and Grace Zaring Stone's *The Grotto.* In prison, gay things happen mainly to queens in Chester Himes' *Cast the First Stone* and Christopher Teale's *Behind These Walls,* while in Martin Mayer's opera novel, *A Voice That Fills the House,* almost everyone seems gay but the hero. Southern decadents are suicidal in Speed Lamkin's *Tiger in the Garden,* ineffably wispy in William Goyen's delicately written *The House of Breath,* and a little of both in John Weldon's *The Naked Heart.*

A San Diego schoolboy succeeds in seducing a friend at the start of Oakley Hall's *Corpus of Joe Bailey,* while a summer-camp counselor in William Goldman's *Your Turn to Curtsy, My Turn to Bow* succeeds in escaping from a crazy, homosexual former college jock. Esposito's creator, Russell Thacher, also continued writing during the fifties but his next novel, *The Tender Age,* hardly measured up to *The Captain* from a gay standpoint—its weird teenage misfit was, unlike Esposito, a real loser. The gayest thing about Alfred Chester's *Jamie Is My Heart's Desire* was its title.

The smart, often gay bohemian set in pre–World War II Europe was pictured in Eugene MacCown's *The Siege of Innocence* and in Gordon Merrick's chichi *The Demon of Noon.* In the latter, the adolescent son of a wealthy American couple falls for a bisexual French dancer, much to the obligatory disgust of his straight-arrow father. Another novel set in Europe was Alexander Randolph's *The Mail Boat,* an epistolary work which shows an American writer falling for a beautiful Italian boy, much to the nervousness of the writer's young American girlfriend. In a 1953 Padell hardback with the telltale title, *Dark Desires,* Wilma Prezzi inverted the plot of *Imre:* her bisexual Hungarian, Vanya, comes to America during World War II and finds blissful but only momentary "rest" in the arms of the put-upon heterosexual heroine.

Other gay motifs in novels of the decade ranged from hot-blooded bisexuality in the coy historical novels of Onstott/Horner[44] (*Mandingo* et al.) to a sexual exposé of Hollywood in Marita Wolff's *The Big Nickelodeon* to a possible low in Bud Clifton's *Muscle Boy,* in which depraved jock sniffers are depicted as villains. This thirty-five-cent paperback promised to bare "the naked truth about the Beefcake Kings" of Muscle Beach, and that truth was that they liked to whip ladies in garages.

In sharp contrast to most of these novels, the secondary gay theme in Warren Miller's *The Cool World* (1959) was interwoven into the plot without self-consciousness or sensationalism. Anticipating the themes of *Another Country,* Miller's novel contains several homosexuals who are as believable and compelling as all of the other black characters who are trying to cope with their dreary lives in Harlem. In many ways Duke, the hero of the novel, is the antithesis of Holden Caulfield, and it is "no big deal" when he has sex with another young black one night in Central Park:

> So I get up an go with Tommy. I don't know why. One of those times. Whut the hell. I went along. We walk for a while not talken. Tommy hummin to him self. Finely he say, "This here is the bridal path. You know where they ride the horses."
>
> He put his arm aroun me an I let him. He lead me off the path. "Over here." He say in my ear. "Over here. I know a real private place no one ever find us."[45]

Having sex with almost anyone is the cool thing to do in Miller's world, and thus there is no agonizing in his novel about people being "perverty."

Hardback Horrors and Paperback Originals

During the fifties a rash of pulps that were more homophobic than homosexual were published in both hardback and paperback. Written in the style of *Butterfly Man,* these books were edited and packaged to induce the straight reader to take a disdainful peek at those naughty, neurotic homosexuals.

One of the most execrable of the hardbacks was Hilton Rebow's *Oh, Dear,* whose hero was a window decorator who is always just *too* exhausted to commit suicide. This novel was published in 1951 by Key, whose line also included *Blonde Flame, Passion Pen,* and *Backstage Temptress.* Perhaps the most wretched novel ever written on the theme was published in 1958 by Bruce Humphries, Inc., of Boston. Its title was *The Flaming Heart,* its author was Deborah Deutsch, and its sentences read like something one might expect from a below-average high school freshman who is not well:

> The satyrs become grizzly, their contours drop or sag a little, they slow down a few paces, but they leap about the best they can, albeit the fields steadily become drier. . . . Some rich old aunties have a retinue of handsome young fellows trailing them—guess for what?[46]

The titles of the paperback originals tended toward the lurid— *Shadows of Shame, Strange Desires, Soul of Passion,* and *The*

Twisted Heart—and the publishers of these twenty-five-cent books included such undistinguished firms as Padell, Croydon, Star, and Pyramid. In 1954 Gold Medal published Dean Douglas' *Man Divided,* with the cover asking the question, "Could the strength of Sally's love give to him a manhood he had never known, bring him back from the shadows into the sunlight of a wholesome love?" The answer, of course, was yes. Featured on the front cover of Vin Packer's *Whisper His Sin* was an irrelevant picture of a man and woman in Central Park and the phrase, "How a strange and twilight love lighted the way to frenzied murder." The back cover gives the following rationale for straight folks reading queer novels:

> *This is one of the most shocking novels we have ever published.* It deals with a strange way of life that has become all too prevalent and is still spreading . . . a frightening picture of how the blight of sexual distortion spreads, corrupts, and finally destroys those around it. *We also believe this is one of the most morally enlightening books you will ever read.*[47]

The sin whispered about in this novel is Ferris Sullivan's falling in love with a dashing college upperclassman who turns out to be the notorious Cyanide-Cocktail Killer of New York City.

The illuminating "now it can be seen and said" quality of today's gay literary criticism sheds some light on the foredestined failure of homosexual fiction to win viability during the benighted fifties. It is immediately conceded that the atmosphere was murky: gay writers were still in the closet, and they were obviously engaging in camouflage in order to be published. But, granted this fact, it is now more to the point to ask some questions which will, however belatedly, place the homophobic critics of the fifties on the defensive, where they belong.

Can today's critics who were the detractors of the fifties excuse themselves by pleading, "Ah, well, everyone was homophobic in those days, and we just didn't know any better"? Can those who expressed bafflement over the start of homosexual fiction (it was "astounding," "most curious") expect anyone to believe they did not know that, just as Jews were writing Jewish novels and blacks were writing black novels, homosexuals were writing homosexual novels? (John Mitzel says what needs to be said in response to John W. Aldridge's professed puzzlement over all the gay characters in John Horne Burns: "Gee, do you think that JHB's writing in homosexual types and through a Gay Sensibility might have anything to do with the fact that he was a faggot himself?") Did the critics of the fifties not realize they were placing monstrously unfair demands on gay writers? If homosexuals were supposed to avoid "normal" fiction because they couldn't handle "normal passions" convincingly and at the same time avoid "abnormal" fiction because it was too "narrow" to be worthwhile and "great," what options were left?

In his 1951 *The Homosexual in America,* Donald Webster Cory offered a clue to why these questions were not asked during the fifties: "One is a 'hero' if he espouses the cause of minorities, but is only a suspect if that minority is the homosexual group."[48] Since not even Gore Vidal was ready to admit in the fifties that he was gay, the homophobic critics could attack with impunity, knowing that people would hesitate to defend gay writers lest they too be labeled fairies. But now that it is supposedly as OK to be gay as it is to be a Jew or a black or anything else, it is time for these questions not only to be asked but to be answered as well. As it stands today, the petty, imperceptive, and macho criticism of Aldridge, Cowley, Kazin, et al., brings far more discredit to themselves than to those novels of the fifties which they found so distressing.

NOTES

1. Vidal recalled the *anno mirabilis* and Tennessee Williams in "Selected Memories of the Glorious Bird and the Golden Age," *New York Review of Books* (February 5, 1976), p. 13.

2. The blurb announcing that Towne would continue to expose where others "whisper or fear to tread" appeared in the *American Mercury* (August 1951), p. 2. The other quote is from p. 6.

3. Malcolm Cowley, *The Literary Situation* (New York: Viking, 1954), p. 211. The "fairy–Freudian novel" is cited on p. 60.

4. Alfred Kazin's article, "The Alone Generation," was reprinted in Waldmeir's *Recent American Fiction* (Boston: Houghton Mifflin, 1963). Stanley Edgar Hyman's piece, "Trends in the Novel," in which he sniffed out the Albertine strategy in current gay literature, was the lead article in *College English* (October 1958).

5. Vidal discussed Aldridge during a lengthy interview printed in *Fag Rag* (Winter–Spring 1974). During the early fifties Vidal actually debated Aldridge at Princeton and Columbia, but the latter would not define what moral values literature needed to be "great."

6. John W. Aldridge, *After the Lost Generation*, pp. 101-2.

7. Vidal made this comment in an essay called "Love Love Love," which appeared in *Partisan Review* (Spring 1959), and Leslie Fiedler quoted the comment when he was giving his roll call of OK Jewish-American writers in "Zion as Main Street" (*Waiting for the End,* 1964). Omitting the reference to homosexualists and tagging Vidal as merely a WASP rather than gay, Fiedler affected to marvel at Vidal's "undertone of real bitterness."

8. David L. Freeman, "Literature and Homosexuality," *One* (January 1955), p. 13. The other quote is from p. 15.

9. Arthur Krell, "We Need a Great Literature," *One* (May 1954), p. 19. The other quote is from p. 22.

10. James Baldwin, *Giovanni's Room* (New York: Signet, 1959), p. 52. In going on to love Giovanni, David strikes the gay reader as far more homosexual than merely bisexual, and it is probably safe to say that gay people have met more "bisexuals" in fiction than they have in real life.

11. C. J. Rolo, *Atlantic Monthly* (December 1956). Hicks' review was in *The Times* book section, October 14, 1956. Esty's review appeared in the *New Republic* (December 17, 1956).

12. Anthony West's review appeared in *The New Yorker* (November 10, 1956).

13. William Talsman, *The Gaudy Image* (Paris: Olympia Press, 1958), p. 242. Although Tit often finds himself in bed with someone who embodies the "gaudy image," the novel never becomes pornographic, for reasons that are explained later on in this chapter in connection with the Jay Little novels. Other quotes are from pp. 69, 146-47, 41-43, 179, and 188.

14. Maurice Girodias, *The Olympia Reader* (New York: Grove, 1965), p. 405. Talsman's only other writing to be published was apparently *Notes from the Underground*, a collection of poems brought out by the William-Frederick Press in 1961. This book was copyrighted by James M. Smith, and Prof. Brom Weber, who taught Talsman in New York in the fifties, believes this was "Talsman's" real name. The book of poetry includes the information that the author was born and raised in the Midwest, took a "side trip" to New Orleans, was graduated from Iowa State in 1950, and at the time of publication was living in Cleveland.

15. James Barr, *Quatrefoil* (New York: Greenberg, 1950), p. 373. Barr discussed the writing of the novel in "Under Honorable Conditions in *Mattachine Review* (May–June 1955).

16. Loren Wahl, *The Invisible Glass* (New York: Greenberg, 1950), p. 100. The other quote is from p. 212.

17. Malcolm Cowley, *The Literary Situation*, p. 29.

18. Lonnie Coleman, *Ship's Company* (Boston: Little, Brown, 1955), p. 109. Other quotes are from pp. 120-21, 115, and 134.

19. Russell Thacher, *The Captain* (New York: Pocket Books, 1952), pp. 36-37. Other quotes are from pp. 287-88 and 311-12.

20. Mailer's article, "The Homosexual Villain," appeared in the January 1955 *One* and has since been reprinted in his *Advertisements for Myself*. The subject of villainous officers and victimized enlisted men was the theme of an essay written by the author for the gay *College English* issue (November 1974). Compared in "But for Fate and Ban" are *Billy Budd, Reflections in a Golden Eye, The Sergeant,* and *Eustace Chisholm and the Works*.

21. Ralph Leveridge, *Walk on the Water* (New York: Signet, 1952), p. 128.

22. James Jones, *From Here to Eternity* (New York: Signet, 1953), p. 357.

23. Leveridge, *Walk on the Water*, p. 192.

24. Harrison Dowd, *The Night Air* (New York: Avon, 1950), p. 137. Other quotes are from pp. 274 and 316-17.

25. Lonnie Coleman, *Sam* (New York: Pyramid, 1960), p. 44.

26. *The New York Times Book Review* (February 18, 1951); Vidal's review appeared in *The Saturday Review* (February 24, 1951). Peters recalled growing up in France in *Boyhood with Gurdjieff* (1964), which is altogether without a gay angle.

27. With very little basis, the reviewer in the *Library Journal* (November 15, 1956) lamented that "Tesch has seen fit to pepper his work with vulgarisms and lurid passages, no doubt in the interests of verisimilitude." The *Kirkus* review appeared September 1, 1956; the *Time* review, November 12, 1956.

28. This was a critic's comment on Goodman's 1946 novel, *State of Nature*. Since his death in 1972, Goodman has become better known as a writer of gay poetry than of gay fiction: Goodman's poems have been included in Eglinton's *Greek Love,* Ian Young's *The Male Muse,* and Winston Leyland's *Angels of the Lyre*. Goodman's experiences at Black Mountain College, which may well have provided the germ for *Parents' Day,* have been candidly described in Martin Duberman's *Black Mountain: An Exploration in Community* (New York: Dutton, 1972).

29. Paul Goodman, *Parents' Day* (Saugatuck, Connecticut: 5 x 8 Press, 1951), p. 202.

30. "Fuck stories" probably deserve a separate study—an essay if not a book—but the great problem is locating a sufficient number to provide a

representative view of all those that must have been typed up from, say, 1920 to 1960.

31. Vidal compared Texas to Italy in *Fag Rag* (Winter–Spring 1974), p. 3.

32. Jay Little, *Maybe-Tomorrow* (New York: Warner Paperback Library, 1965), p. 38. Other quotes are from pp. 41, 80, and 136.

33. Little, *Somewhere Between the Two* (New York: Pageant, 1956), p. 184. The other quote is from p. 185.

34. These reviews appeared in the October 1956 issues of the two magazines, and, according to the blurb on the back of the paperback edition of *Maybe-Tomorrow*, Little's first novel was praised in the San Diego *Navy News Review:* ". . . a book adults should read if they truly want to know more about one of the little-known segments of the human race."

35. Bruce Cook, *The Beat Generation* (New York: Scribner's, 1971), p. 87.

36. John Tytell, *Naked Angels* (New York: McGraw Hill, 1976), p. 204.

37. Charters' theory was that because of Kerouac's intense love for his mother, he had no real involvement in his heterosexual marriages or the romps at the Everard Baths, and in the *Gay Sunshine* interviews Kerouac seems to have been a rather complacent homosexual after drinking enough wine.

38. It is interesting to note that not only has Ginsberg traced his poetic style back to Whitman, but in his *Gay Sunshine* interview he also claimed to have a sexual tie: he had slept with Neal Cassady, who had slept with the grandson of President Arthur, who had slept with Edward Carpenter, who had slept with Whitman.

39. Fleischmann's article originally appeared in the *Carolina Quarterly* (Spring 1959) and was reprinted in Joseph Waldmeir's *Recent American Fiction* (1963), p. 112.

40. John Giorno, *Gay Sunshine* (Spring 1975), pp. 7-8. It might be added that some observers of the beats have engaged in fallacious thinking in their comments on gayness and drugs. In his *The Holy Barbarians* (1959) Lawrence Lipton falsely claimed that pot was as widely used among homosexuals as among the beats, and in *Waiting for the End* (1964) Leslie Fiedler theorized that there was a nexus between "dope and uranian love" since homosexuality implies a certain contempt for whiskey and a complementary taste for dope.

41. White, p. 129.

42. Purdy discussed the viciousness of his critics in his *Penthouse* interview (July 1974), and his comments about propaganda and love are from a 1973 letter he wrote to the author.

43. "Edgar Box," *Death in the Fifth Position* (New York: Signet, 1953), pp. 132-33. Box's other murder novels were *Death Likes It Hot* and *Death Before Bedtime;* the latter begins with a young lady saying she has never gone to bed with a man on a train before, and Vidal's hero responding, "Neither have I."

44. Noel I. Garde has worked out a complex chart which shows that there is a gay motif in every Onstott/Horner novel. Whether these books are set in times of Roman imperial decadence or the slavery days of the American South, they contain glowing descriptions of muscular male servants blessed with astounding sexual endowments. Even though their 1966 *Child of the Sun* (about a "perverted" Emperor) is almost entirely gay, Onstott and Horner have successfully avoided being tagged as gay novelists by setting their depravity in the past, "where it belongs."

45. Warren Miller, *The Cool World* (Boston: Little, Brown, 1959), pp. 94-95.

46. Deborah Deutsch, *The Flaming Heart* (Boston: Bruce Humphries, Inc., 1958), p. 149. It might be added that during the fifties there appeared a rash of trashy lesbian novels that were no more authentically gay than their male pulp counterparts (e.g., Artemis Smith's *Odd Girl,* "The Revealing Story of Life and Love Among Warped Women," and Dorine B. Clark's *Gutter Star,* "She Was a Hollywood Star, but Her Home Was the Gutter").

47. Another way these firms tricked straight readers into buying the more fundamentally gay fiction was to heterosexualize the cover art work on the paperback reprints. For instance, Bantam's 1950 reprint of *The Gallery* interprets the gay bar melee as a rugged, two-fisted brawl, with the sexual interest provided by a slim, beautiful girl who is supposed to be "Momma." More amusing is the cover of Avon's 1950 reprint of *The Bitterweed Path,* which shows a bare-chested sexy young man lying down in a barn. This would be Darrell Barclay, and although the phrase above the title reads "A Strange Relationship in a Small Southern Town," the other person with Darrell in the barn is neither Roger nor Malcolm Pitt but a beautiful bare-foot girl. About the only things to be said in defense of this picture are that the artist has shown her to be the aggressor and that Darrell has his eyes closed so he can imagine that the hand on his chest really belongs to Roger or Malcolm.

48. Donald Webster Cory, *The Homosexual in America* (New York: Greenberg, 1951), p. 14.

SINCE 1960

THE DECLINE AND perhaps even the "death" of traditional gay fiction over the past fifteen years is partially explainable by the developments that have made any sort of realistic problem novel seem old-fashioned and even anachronistic. Of course, the gay novelist is faced with the problems that confront all novelists: fewer novels are being bought and sold and read today because of the competition from nonfiction and the entertainment offered by other media. Too, the vanishing of sexual taboos in life and in fiction has undercut the shock value of sexual-problem literature, and the gay angle in a plot has become increasingly less compelling to many establishment publishers and editors. But perhaps the greatest counterforce in the literary world is that the "new" novel in America has been flouting all the traditions that used to underlie homosexual fiction. Many of the older gay novels were written to impose order on chaos and to make sense of the absurd: gay characters wrestled with the traumas of being odd men out in a heterosexual society, and gay readers wanted to laugh, love, and triumph with characters who were often just like themselves. In the more innovative fiction, however, non-heroes find themselves lost in surrealistic wastelands of nightmare and dread, powerless to control events in their chaotic lives. In addition, the new non-novel is usually mocking and anti-serious rather than sincere, and the reader is often left to conclude that life in general and these novels in particular add up to little more than a bad joke. Since the concept that life need be absurd is the point that older gay novelists set out to disprove, it is obvious that the premises of traditional gay writing and much of the more recent American fiction are antithetical.

However, the "death of the novel" has been excessively analyzed in this country for years, and it is of greater pertinence to view the decline of homosexual fiction in terms of what is now called "the gay community." During the last fifteen years, the revolutionary changes in the life styles of many homosexuals have produced dramatic shifts in self-definition: most of the favorite comforts of the early sixties are now regarded as quaint by the more self-assured gay males of today. The mid-seventies consensus appears to be that pornography is more "exciting" and nonfiction is more "real" than old-fashioned homosexual novels, and thus the traditional writer is now threatened not so much by the homophobia of establishment publishers and reviewers as by the lack of interest on the part of his preoccupied gay brothers. Ironically, there has been a tendency of some well-known critics to praise the special talents of gay writers, but this charitability is about twenty years too late to be of much help to the homosexual novel, having sunk as it has to the level of Laura Zametkin Hobson's *Consenting Adult* and Patricia Nell Warren's *The Front Runner* and *The Fancy Dancer*.

THE EARLY SIXTIES

Although Kennedy had replaced Eisenhower in the White House, there was never any Camelot for gay novelists in the early sixties—the country was still buttoned down, gay lib was still years away, and shaggy hair and shabby clothes tagged one not as a protester but merely as *declassé*. Queers, in short, were still queers, and no one thought it farfetched in *Advise and Consent* when Don

Murray shot himself rather than confess to his fellow Senators that he had once loved a buddy during the war. Most gay novelists, still in the closet, were forced to pretend their novels weren't really gay, a fact that did not go unnoticed when Stanton Hoffman wrote his 1964 essay, "The Cities of Night: John Rechy's *City of Night* and the American Literature of Homosexuality":

. . . homosexuality is never homosexuality . . . it is always something else. It is love, America, the failure of love, loneliness—always part of a case for something. . . .
Perhaps we are left then with the conclusion that the only real American literature of homosexuality exists in the underground of fantasy and pornography, where novels like those of Jay Little and K. B. Raul couple large sex organs with young beautiful boys to create young and beautiful boys with large sex organs.[1]

To a great extent, Hoffman's point about the masquerading aspects of homosexual fiction was well taken, and the early sixties saw the publication of four dark, brooding novels which had clear-cut messages on non-gay themes but were more equivocal in their attitudes toward homosexuality. The themes of loneliness in frightening American cities and the failure of love were basic to *Another Country*, *The Messenger*, *Last Exit to Brooklyn*, and *City of Night*, but in at least some of these novels the authors' evaluation of homosexuality remained fuzzy. Ian Young has quite rightly called *Last Exit to Brooklyn* and *City of Night* "quasi-exposé" novels, with the "quasi" factor clouding the issue of whether the exposer is a detached observer or a guilty insider.[2]

TO BE YOUNG, BISEXUAL, AND BLACK

James Baldwin and Charles Wright

In James Baldwin's *Another Country* (1962) and Charles Wright's *The Messenger* (1963), a racial theme was added to the problem of being a homosexual or bisexual in the lower depths of the big city. In Baldwin's more powerful, almost allegorical novel, the sex and race themes are tightly interwoven: as the author unfolds the story of Rufus (black/bisexual), Eric (white/basically gay), Ida (black/straight), Vivaldo (white/basically straight), and Cass (white/straight), the reader who accepts Baldwin's views on one of these topics is almost obliged to accept his views on the other. In Wright's novel about a handsome young black who delivers messages by day and sex by night to white people of all sexes in Manhattan, there is less of a problem on both counts; indeed, compared with *Another Country, The Messenger* is less of a problem novel and is closer in content to the more sensational works of Selby and Rechy. At least it was packaged as such in the paperback edition, where the blurb promised the story of a Negro youth adrift in a "subterranean world of junkies, prostitutes and perverts."

Neither *Another Country* nor *The Messenger* is a totally committed gay novel, but Baldwin comes closer than Wright to viewing homosexuality as an existential answer rather than as a kinky perversion. It is true that Rufus (who seems to be Baldwin's persona) and Eric are lovers only in retrospect—with Rufus' bedmate in Book One being a white woman—but it is also true that Vivaldo not only allows himself to be "rectally violated," to use Stanley Edgar Hyman's term, but afterwards whispers, *"Thank you, thank you, Eric, thank you."* In *The Messenger* Charles Stevenson hustles both men and women, but his hustling men can be regarded as something he does just for money and kicks, since he has a regular girlfriend. Altogether, gayness is more important and perhaps even redemptive in *Another Country,* while remaining just another seamy part of metropolitan life in *The Messenger.* On the surface, at least, Wright subordinates gayness to blackness, while Baldwin ultimately produces the reverse effect by having everyone go to bed with nearly everyone else.

In viewing the Big City as Jungle, however, Baldwin and Wright mince few words: their gay and straight characters are all victims of urban blight, with little hope of escape to any sort of pastoral refuge. Charles Stevenson sits on his stoop and wonders "Why am I here, why New York?" and "Do I really belong here?" The air was much less fevered, he remembers, in Sedalia, Missouri, where "small town folk had problems like people anywhere, but they faced them by looking them square in the eye, accepting them as they accepted changes in the weather."³ With his grandmother in Sedalia dead, however, Charles remains in Manhattan simply because he cannot think of any other place to go. Baldwin's characters stay in New York for about the same reason, and if there is any idyllic bower in his novel it is certainly not close at hand—Eric shares some blissful moments with his French lover in a rented Mediterranean villa, but this Eden proves to be as evanescent as any other. Both *Another Country* and *The Messenger* point to the emergence of New York City as a monstrous, brutalizing hell. By the 1960s, the old Carl Van Vechten assumptions of Manhattan being the ultimate in all that was chic and campy were replaced by the concept that if you're going to be gay in New York, you're going to have to steel yourself to cope with seediness, frustration, and despair.

The critical reaction to these novels was, as usual, mixed, with *Another Country* generating considerable controversy. Kay Boyle found *The Messenger* one of the most moving examples of the "new and ruthlessly honest literature" about the "lonely horror of the junkie and homosexual world of New York," and Baldwin praised Wright for his realism: ". . . no matter what the city fathers may say, this is New York; this is the way we live here now." The intertwined themes of race and sex in *Another Country* created a dilemma for reviewers who had previously praised Baldwin as a Negro writer, and for some critics the solution was to simply extract the sexual motif and complain about it. In *The Negro Novel in America,* Robert Bone viewed gayness as an "evasion" rather than an "affirmation of human truth"; in *Soul on Ice,* Eldridge Cleaver pronounced it to be a sickness like "baby-rape"; and *New Yorker* critic Whitney Balliett charged that the scenes of lovemaking between males in the novel suffered because they seemed "far larger than life."⁴ To his great credit, Norman Podhoretz sensed the homophobia behind many of the reviews in his article, "In Defense of a Maltreated Best Seller." Podhoretz first explained the implications of Baldwin's views on race and sex: "Putting the two propositions together, he [Baldwin] is saying, finally, that the only significant realities are individuals and love, and that anything which is permitted to interfere with the free operation of this fact is evil and should be done away with." Chiding his liberal colleagues for their hypocrisy, Podhoretz goes on to say that Baldwin's questions about race and sex deserve thoughtful consideration by anyone who thinks himself enlightened:

Do you believe, he demands of you again, that love is the supreme value and that sex is the most natural expression of love? Then you must realize that the stifling of your own impulses toward a sexual articulation of the love you feel for members of your own sex is unnatural, signifying a warping of the instincts and of the body that may end by destroying your capacity for any sexual experience whatever.[5]

DRUGS, DRAG QUEENS, AND PUNKS:
LAST EXIT TO BROOKLYN

Hubert Selby's narrow sketches of gay life in parts of *Last Exit to Brooklyn* (1965) are so bizarre and sordid that, by contrast, the daily lives of the gay characters in *Another Country* and *The Messenger* seem absolutely wholesome and cheerful. Most of Selby's pimps, whores, thugs, and queers seem far more victimized by the big city than anyone in Baldwin and Wright, and the style of *Last Exit to Brooklyn* is so wild and frenzied that everything totters on the brink of counterculture craziness.

Selby does provide one rather traditional, even old-fashioned touch that links his novel with some earlier gay works: there is the same subdivision of "shes" and "hes" that was so important in, for instance, *The Gaudy Image*. But there is little real tenderness between the drag queens and the ex-cons in Selby's novel, as the following passage from "The Queen Is Dead" chapter illustrates:

Whatta yasay sweetchips? Georgette turned and started opening her arms and Vinnie pinched her cheek, how about taking this inside and ringing it out, standing up slowly his hand clutching his crotch. Georgette lowered one hand (not now . . . later) and let the other one slide along his leg. Wanna help me empty this? wavering slightly then spreading his legs further apart and laughing as he bounced his balls with his hand. She leaned forward slightly (no no no! ! ! You will ruin everything) and he turned, still laughing, and went to the bathroom (his eyes are bugging out of his head. O Christ he is high. It will be beautiful! ! !) and roared as Camille leaped from the bathroom when he goosed her. . . .[6]

While Talsman was quite willing to identify himself with the "shes" in *The Gaudy Image,* it is hard to tell whether there is much authorial identification with anyone during the lurid sex scenes that take place in Selby's Brooklyn housing project. The average gay reader of this novel was probably not ready to identify with either the dizzy drag queens or the rapacious punks. The mere presence of these characters does not qualify *Last Exit to Brooklyn* as being a traditional gay novel, of course, and its special appeal was that Selby was able to "get away with so much" in his candid descriptions of homosexual lust.

Not surprisingly, critics were less indignant or threatened about fictional homosexuality when it was depicted as just another component of the macabre underworld and, as such, not presuming to make a claim for respectability. In *The New York Times,* the critic complained that there was too much "blood and gore and semen" in the novel, but at the same time concluded that *Last Exit to Brooklyn* was "an extraordinary achievement." But the *Time* reviewer was more blasé: "This is Grove Press's extra special dirty book for fall . . ."[7]

NO LOVE AN' KISSES, MAN: *CITY OF NIGHT*

In 1963 Grove Press published John Rechy's *City of Night,* perhaps the most ambitious and sweeping work of gay fiction to come out during the decade. The spirit of the novel is close to the romantic, wandering "O lost!" tradition of Thomas Wolfe, but Rechy's narrator-hustler is never quite so lost as the distraught gay people he encounters in large cities across the land. In contrast to these tenderloin transients, the hustler can and does go back home to El Paso, where, if he doesn't completely find himself, he can at least take some comfort in the knowledge that "spring is coming, with the yellow-green clusters of leaves budding on the skeleton trees, hinting of a potential revival—soon, soon." Jack Kerouac's writing probably influenced Rechy as well, but while the characters in *On the Road* are usually running around together, the "youngman" in *City of Night* is almost always alone. The only brotherhood in this novel is based on the flimsy ties that unite some hustlers for a while, and about the only thing that these male prostitutes share with the Kerouac gang is the reassuring thought that in spite of capricious lapses, they are all fundamentally heterosexual. In addition to Wolfe and Kerouac, a third influence at work in parts of *City of Night* seems to be Tennessee Williams, whose rhythmic qualities of distracted digressions and breathless exclamations are echoed in some of the gay characters' speeches. Here the Professor explains his "angels" to the young hustler, who is in the process of becoming one himself:

There are three chief categories of angels—though their areas are sometimes not so well defined: earthbound, seafaring, ethereal . . . the first, child, are the truck-drivers, the marines. One of my first loves was an All-American. The day he learned he'd been chosen, he came to me, he was my student, and he said: "Tante Goulu, I want you to be the first to know." He autographed a football for me. I detested football, but I adored him, and he had such a simplicity, such a desire to be on The Team—I helped him along, with his grades—Why, had it not been for my fondness for him, the world might have been deprived of one of its—What was he now? Oh yes, a tackle! The world would have been deprived of one of its great tackles! . . . And the next category of angels is the seafaring: the sailors. I suppose perhaps they are the original angels. I would watch them in San Diego—one summer I spent at La Jolla—as they invaded our streets, descending, all white, as if just arrived from Heaven, scattering themselves among the rest of us, unworthy, mortals! . . .[8]

City of Night also depicts big cities as hellish neon jungles, but at the same time it is the downtown squares that offer Rechy's hustler chances for kinky and remunerative sexual adventures. Furthermore, he can leave the city any time he wishes. He doesn't have to jump in the river, sit on the stoop, or escape through drag or drugs —there is always San Francisco or Chicago just a Greyhound bus trip away. But is Rechy's hustler gay? *City of Night* is a "quasi-exposé" novel because of its illusion that the hustler is going to bed with men more out of a sense of picaro resourcefulness than homosexual desire. In his review of the novel, Alfred Chester said that this pose "is very much in keeping with the nature of the hero who wants to limit his homosexual life to where he wears his BVD's— 'no love an' kisses, man, because I'm butch, man.' "[9] While Rechy has since explained that hustlers *had* to pretend to be straight in order to convince their clients they were going to bed with "real men," the particular point here is that *City of Night* and the other dark, brooding, lost novels of the sixties contained an out that allowed them, if necessary, to be interpreted as more than merely gay works. These were all rather "heavy" novels, and, in the expected American style, the authors were depicting queerness as a rather heavy burden which they were not quite ready to claim as their own. Meanwhile, Christopher Isherwood was sketching homosexuality with a light-fiction touch, and the difference between *Down There on a Visit* and *A Single Man* on the one hand and the quasi-exposé novels on the other is the difference between day and night.

THE LIGHTER TOUCH OF CHRISTOPHER ISHERWOOD

Isherwood's writing has been a refreshing exception in American gay literature because, rather than being born here, this author grew up in a British environment which gave a Bloomsbury benediction to all the bright young people who were in some way extraordinary. Isherwood was a part of the Auden-Spender circle, which agreed with the older Bloomsburyites that an androgynous nature was an important component of creative genius. "Most of my friends were either homosexual themselves or very relaxed in their attitude toward it," Isherwood has said. "They had been to upper-class schools and were therefore quite accustomed to it." In fact, he thinks heterosexuality would have fatally cramped his style: "I have been perfectly happy the way I am. If my Mother was responsible for it, I am grateful. . . . My life has been extremely lucky."[10] It is thus not surprising that Isherwood maintained a cavalier disregard of the puritan game of "Let's Pretend That I Am Not a Homosexual," even when he left England and moved to our less enlightened shores.

That Isherwood was generally immune from slashing homophobic attacks in this country may be because he wrote about homosexuals in British upper-class rather than American middle-class terms. In some of his earlier works, he had so interwoven gayness as quietly supplemental to other themes that homophobes were left with very little to attack. Even in his bolder novels of the sixties, *Down There on a Visit* and *A Single Man,* his homosexuals were sketched with such happy nonchalance and intelligence that they provoked little alarm, inside or outside of the covers. The tone in many Isherwood novels has been that of the bemused British sophisticate who finds gay characters as delightful as the tweedy Margaret Rutherford types or retired Anglican bishops who are stock characters in fiction about the international set. As a writer with ties to the debonair tradition of Noël Coward and Graham ("May We Borrow Your Husband?") Greene, Isherwood has usually sketched his gay scenes with a light touch, knowing that his readers were going to be either tolerant of or even charmed by the idiosyncrasies of human behavior.

Isherwood's lighthearted approach to the subject is especially apparent in *Down There on a Visit* (1962), which takes place more abroad than in America. In the first three portraits, the facts that Ambrose is gay, Waldemar is trade, and Hans is a sadist are conveyed in terms that are amusing rather than shocking. In "Ambrose," for example, the setting is a Greek island where rats run wild, the Greeks jabber in pidgin English, Geoffrey heckles Ambrose as a "Bugger man" and "Catamite keeper," and Madame Constantinescu arrives in grand style to visit and seduce Waldemar. It is a sense of feyness rather than gayness that characterizes "Ambrose," with its clash of international temperaments creating the tension rather than who may be sleeping with whom. Even in the final portrait of "Paul," which is a bit more serious and set mainly in America, Isherwood conveys gayness in quite a breezy style: when Christopher and Paul embark on their regime of Vedantic renunciation, they confine themselves to the hills for their afternoon walks, as the beach is "too dangerously sexy."

A Single Man (1964) is set entirely in America, but Isherwood never allows the homosexuality of this novel's hero to become a heavy theme; it is never a burden to be wished away but merely a facet of everyday animal existence. At the start of the book, George seems so average that anyone could identify with him as he wakes up, goes to the bathroom, eats breakfast and does all of the unremarkable things everyone has to do in the morning. As he goes through his day, George's gayness does emerge here and there—he admires the bodies of two tennis players, he talks of love and loathing and minorities to his literature class, he copes with a seductive young man who "splits" rather than stay the night with him, and he finally drifts off to sleep after imagining the tennis players having sex with each other. Compared with the tone of the quasi-exposé novels, however, homosexuality in *A Single Man* remains understated and unsensational. The *One* reviewer called this novel "the most honest book ever written about a homosexual," and it is ironic and yet understandable that the unmelodramatic novel about an American gay man called for by David Freeman in the fifties was finally written by someone who was born elsewhere.

OTHER RELEVANT WORKS, 1960–1965

The atmosphere of the other explicit fiction of the early sixties ranged between the disoriented, troubled midnight of the *City of Night* approach and the autumnal sunlight of Isherwood. Many of these novels illustrate the "domestic versus foreign" theme: the hero may have a bit of liberated fun if he can escape to France or Japan or Korea, whereas wariness is the watchword if he is forced to remain in the forty-eight contiguous states.

Two delightful novels by Thomas Doremus were published in 1961 by Clarkson Potter, the less gay taking place in Boston and the more gay set mainly in Paris. *To Beaucock, with Love* is the story of a nominally heterosexual half-bright handyman, Ambrose Groden, whose Irish charm brings out the latent homosexuality of his psychiatrist, Dick Beaucock. A further gay motif is provided by the male couple who hire Ambrose to tend their flower gardens and who occasionally put him up for the night after some heavy drinking all around. Doremus is as slyly witty as Talsman in this sentence about one of the gay men giving Ambrose something to cover his spectacular nakedness:

He handed him a dressing gown, his hospitality taking the form of both reluctance to cut off the view and the promise of Ambrose inside something that belonged to him.[11]

Latitudes of Love is a more forthright novel told through the eyes of an urbane teenager named Hector who gets adopted by an outrageously understanding couple named Mary and Bill. It is 1939, Bill is dying, and Mary sends Hector off with her husband on a voyage to Paris, asking him to make "an honest effort to love Bill. Even though he's not your sort, try it. . . . Think of the reward in heaven. It will be a pearl in your crown." Hector agrees to try, quoting Lady Mary Wortley Montague ("Where love is, there is *always* something to say") to himself, but it is mainly Bill who talks of love. "I love you powerfully and would go broke for you in a trice," the stepfather says in their stateroom. "You can have a piece of my meat anytime." In Paris, the two love each other as best they can, Bill dies, and Hector returns to New England to pick up his affair with a beautiful Greek laborer and finish prep school. In a lovely parody of J. D. Salinger, Hector announces that he is really more sporty than sensitive:

Tommyrot! How do you think I managed the old man in Paris? By artistic means? I attract gutty men. Men of action and daring. I'm a very daring person myself. . . . In spite of my speech, I'm a very masculine person. It's time everybody woke up and realized that. I don't know where I got this reputation for being an Emily Dickinson. I'm not. I'm sporty. Physically, I'm very strongly motivated.[12]

A better-known title of the sixties was Sanford Friedman's *Totempole,* published by Dutton in 1965 and reprinted as a Signet paperback. Friedman's tale of a New York Jewish boy who goes to camp, college, and Korea and finds sexual satisfaction only with a Korean POW seems to be almost too psychoanalytically autobiographical. In *The Saturday Review,* Granville Hicks said that the novel seems "a little too much like a case study," but he went on to say that some episodes were "developed with unusual imaginative power."[13] Although Friedman's theme of an American finding love in the arms of a foreigner is not new, he does succeed in bringing a certain freshness and sharpness in his final scenes between Stephen Wolfe and Dr. Pok.

Another novel with a West-meets-East motif is John Goodwin's *A View of Fuji,* which was published by Neville Spearman, Ltd., in England in 1963 (and more candidly gay than his 1952 novel about Haiti, *The Idols and the Prey*). *A View of Fuji,* written with an appropriately "Oriental" style of spareness and restraint, focuses on a middle-aged American tourist who meets, loves, and finally leaves a much younger Japanese. "This touching book will not offend the most sensitive reader," the book jacket copy promises. "It does not set out to titillate or excite; the tragedy and hopelessness inherent in the relationship provide its compelling theme."

Gay people of all nations have a rather adventuresome time in *Behold Goliath,* Alfred Chester's collection of short stories set mainly in Europe, which was published in 1964 by Random House. One of the gay stories is "In Praise of Vespasian," a Genêtesque piece which details the adventures of Joaquin in the Paris pissoirs, brought to a climax with this recherché paragraph:

Hands now on hips, the swaggerer stands at the urinal revealing himself to all and accepting reverence. From both ends, like the lines of a cathedral, attention focuses toward the center, toward the swaggering giant with gleaming hair who, as in Joaquin's dream, seems now invested in a robe of gold, shot through with red and silver. Twenty pairs of devout eyes genuflect and twenty hearts bring tribute. The eyes chant. The hearts carol. Undine sings. Aphrodite hums. Now, in this frozen night of joy, there are no swords between men. There are no secret jealousies, no envies, no rivalries, no rancor against the hero's choice against him who will know the ultimate accomplishment of love. And Joaquin, beside the swaggerer, closes his eyes, drops to his knees violently as if suffering a conversion or a revelation and, throwing wide his arms to grasp him who comes to them, opens his lips upon Life Everlasting.[14]

Another relevant book was Paul Goodman's 1963 *Making Do,* which was sufficiently multifaceted to escape being called a "gay novel," just as Goodman himself was by this time regarded as versatile enough to be thought of as much more than merely a novelist. Nonetheless, the love interest for the Goodman-like hero in this novel is a young male student named Terry, and, in this regard, *Making Do* parallels a central concern of *Parents' Day.* A chief difference is that the author's persona in *Making Do* had developed into a married man, a father of two, a nationally regarded nay-sayer who passes out antiwar literature, and therefore readers could interpret the novel's bisexuality as just one more manifestation of Goodman's wide-ranging and indefatigable iconoclasm. Indeed, the 1964 paperback edition encouraged readers to accept the novel in this light—the opening blurb (which is mistitled "The Misfits" and which introduces the main characters, who form a "community" in Vanderzee, N.J.) says that the "tired, middle-aged" hero, "impartially bisexual in his affections . . . sees in their deviant behavior a rebellious reaction to the Cold War, conservatism, and a bomb-happy world."

Paperbacks, Secondary Themes, Gay Publishing

Among the better selling paperbacks of the early sixties was K. B. Raul's *Naked to the Night,* published by Paperback Library in 1964. Tracing Rick Talbot from everyday life in Iowa to an ultimately disastrous hustling career in New York and Hollywood, this novel gives every indication of being derived from the greatly superior *City of Night,* which came out a year before. The back cover screams, "A NOVEL THAT WILL OPEN YOUR EYES TO THE HIDDEN WORLD OF TWILIGHT MEN," and promises "SURE TO BE THE MOST TALKED-ABOUT NOVEL OF THE YEAR!" As it happened, it was not. Some gay paperback originals were still being packaged as straight love stories, with pictures of essentially irrelevant women on the covers. An example is *Always Love a Stranger* by "Roger Davis," published by Hillman Books in 1961. This story of a bisexual torn between marrying a woman and staying with his Sugar Daddy was accepted by a new editor at Hillman who was later told that the firm did not accept gay manuscripts because they had no market.[15]

A number of novels of the early sixties featured a minor gay motif, and it is interesting to see in retrospect that some gay writers still felt compelled to pretend that they were no more interested in homosexuality than they should be. Merle Miller's semi-autobiographical *A Gay and Melancholy Sound* (1960) was more melancholy than gay (it relied on the Albertine strategy, the author has told me), and Miller's readers would have to wait a decade for the more candid *On Being Different* and *What Happened*. The veil is removed in James Kirkwood's *There Must Be a Pony!* only in brief flashes, as, for instance, when the young hero dwells overlong on the sexiness of Cary Grant. In *Stations* Burt Blechman obscured his narrative through the ploy of zigzag surrealism, but the story seems to be about cruising lavatories in New York subways.

Susan Sontag made some of the same points in *The Benefactor* that she was to make in "Notes on Camp" when she has her gay character expound on the usefulness of masks:

> Why should we all not exchange our masks—once a night, once a month, once a year? . . . Most men, without resisting, put them on and wear them all their lives. But the men around you in this café do not. Homosexuality, you see, is a kind of playfulness with masks. Try it and you will see how it induces a welcome detachment from yourself.[16]

Other novels of the early sixties were less sympathetic. One of the most sordid and melodramatic pictures of gay life was presented through the eyes of a virtuously heterosexual family lawyer in Carley Mills' *The Nearness of Evil*. In Bart Spicer's *Act of Anger*, Roderick Duquesne is a vicious rapist of heterosexual boys; in R. V. Cassill's *The President*, Winfred Mooney peroxides his hair and engages in campus skulduggery as the rival of a college president; in Philip McFarland's *A House Full of Women*, a decadent artist takes advantage of a twelve-year-old boy in the South; and in

Charles Gorham's *McCaffrey*, gay men are seen as fair game for street punks in New York. Homosexuality turns out to be a trumped-up charge in Bruce Cameron's *The Case Against Colonel Sutton,* which is sympathetic to the extent that the real villain is a Pentagon "queer chaser."

Meanwhile, gay publishing for the slowly growing, gradually more visible gay market was finally getting underway. Perhaps in the wake of Jay Little's success, some people concluded that straight publishers could be sidestepped altogether by gay presses turning out gay fiction. However, problems still loomed: simpleminded post-office inspectors, court rulings on obscenity, and sale and distribution at a time when few gay readers wanted their real names and addresses on mailing lists. As a result, much of the earlier gay underground fiction was, just to be on the safe side, about as understated as that being published by establishment presses. For instance, the stories in the 1960 paperback, *Harry's Fare,* are more "literary" than unabashed, and the illustrations of young men wearing shorts and sailor caps seem prim by today's standards. This anthology was published as a part of the Dorian Vignette series by Pan-Graphic Press in San Francisco, which in 1961 brought out Harry Otis' *Camel's Farewell,* a fictional travelogue almost as discreet as those of Prokosch.

As the sixties progressed, though, the trend was toward greater explicitness. By 1965 the Argyle Book Company of Los Angeles, which had published Lou Rand's tepid *Rough Trade* and James Colton's equally mild *Strange Marriage,* was promoting comparatively lurid novels. In Joe Leon Houston's *The Gay Flesh,* readers were promised a look at "the full bloom of unleashed savage passion," and "strange forbidden acts occur on the moonlight beach" when Edwin Fey probed "into the very depths of masculinity and virility" in *Summer in Sodom.* And, of course, those pathetic anti-queer paperbacks continued to spill forth. On the cover of Lynton Brent's 1965 *Sir Gay* is the teaser, "When the Limp Wrist set took over, the power structures trembled," and, inside, the reader was treated to sentences such as: "He plied his want upon me for a long time . . . and I could not help wondering frantically if he had harmed my innards."[17]

THE LAST TEN YEARS

The Decline of Traditional Novels

With the upsurge of pornographic and gay-liberation literature, there has been a corresponding decline in both the quantity and quality of homosexual fiction written in the more traditional realistic style. Many of the better gay novels came out during 1965–1970, when the competition from other types of gay writing was still rather negligible.

One of the most unusual titles published in 1966 was Casimir Dukahz' *The Asbestos Diary,* claiming to be "the *first* fictional work to demonstrate conclusively that boy-love can and should be fun." Also published in 1966 was James Barr's second novel, *The Occasional Man,* which featured a rather refined teacher-pupil relationship again, with a moving man thrown in for animalistic contrast. Other titles published during the year included Tom Lockwood's novel of gay Atlanta, *The Ugly Club;* Charles Wright's *The Wig,* which includes an amusing movie-star-struck drag queen; and James Ramp's *The Love Smeller,* set in Possum County, Tennessee, and full of Lum 'n' Abner dialogue.

In 1967, John Rechy's *Numbers* proved to be nearly as frantic as *City of Night,* with the hero having to make it with a set number of other young men in Griffiths Park during a certain period of time. The ending of James Purdy's *Eustace Chisholm and the Works* is dominated by the sado-masochistic relationship between Captain Stadger and Private Daniel Haws in an army camp in the South. Daniel eventually submits to the ultimate humiliation to atone for not having loved a young man back in Chicago as he should have. Another master-slave theme was that of an epistolary novel written in 1968 by William Carney, *The Real Thing,* which ends on an equally devastating note.

One of the most important books to be published during the past ten years was, significantly enough, not a traditional novel at all. In his 1968 *Myra Breckinridge,* Gore Vidal was illustrating the point he had made in the afterword to *The City and the Pillar* (Revised): ". . . there is of course no such thing as a homosexual . . . categorizing is impossible."[18] To get away with it in this novel, Vidal shifted from earnest realism, which was vulnerable to critical attack, to camp, which was much less so. In 1964 Susan Sontag had noted that camp "is a solvent of morality. It neutralizes moral indignation . . ." and to a great extent she was right.[19] Could anyone become *morally* indignant over all the dizzy metamorphoses into and out of androgyny that occur in *Myra* and its sequel, *Myron?* The homophobic critics were generally foiled because they knew that if they attacked these novels on the same grounds they had attacked *The City and the Pillar*, they would risk branding themselves imperceptive curmudgeons who had not read Sontag's "Notes on Camp." Surely one of Vidal's goals in writing *Myra Breckinridge* was to wreak revenge on the John W. Aldridges of his past.

If there is any trend that characterizes much of the fiction published in more recent years, it is that of deproblemizing homosexuality, at least from the point of view of the gay male. Gordon Merrick has made a splash with his glossy love stories (*The Lord Won't Mind, One for the Gods, Forth into Light*) which are pleasant escape fiction for the Gay and Gray set. Some writers have had success with a mystery story featuring a hero whose gayness is important but not overriding—for instance, George Baxt's *A Queer Kind of Death, Swing Low, Sweet Harriet,* and *Topsy and Evil,* Joseph Hansen's *Death Claims* and *Fadeout,* and Richard Hall's *The Butterscotch Prince.*[20] In the recent well-reviewed quasi-fiction, the implication is that it's rather cozy to be gay in prison (James Blake's *The Joint*) and fun to be gay in Boston and New York (John Reid's *The Best Little Boy in the World*). The best-publicized and best-selling gay novels of the last few years have been penned by women in whose view the problem must not be solved by gay men but rather by such national institutions as the Amateur Athletic Union, the Roman Catholic Church, and the Jewish Mother. Patricia Nell Warren's *The Front Runner* is at heart jock lib, exuding a scent of Absorbine, Jr., and retaining a sense of authenticity as long as the subject is track, but turning into an idealized love story when she sends coach and miler out into the greenwood. Warren's plea in *The Fancy Dancer,* a Catholic gay western, is that the Church come to terms with homosexuality as felicitiously as has her Montana priest-hero. The problem in Laura Z. Hobson's *Consenting Adult* is whether or not the agonizing mother ("My son, my son") can give homosexuality the Good Housekeeping Seal of Approval, and of course by the end of the novel, bless her heart, she does.

Some correlation exists between the deproblemization of homosexuality and the decline of the more traditional homosexual novel. Inherent in many of the older gay novels was the "Oh God I'm queer" syndrome, and as coming out becomes ever less traumatic for American males, the gay problem novel will no doubt continue to fade. This trend has been viewed apprehensively by one gay novelist, Dan Curzon, whose *Something You Do in the Dark* was published several years ago. In his recent essay, "The Problems of Writing Gay Literature," Curzon says that acceptance and assimilation are threatening the future of distinctively homosexual fiction:

If we give up our history as outcasts (our No Names), and become Joe or Jane Citizen, we will run into a very real problem—or at least gay literature will. That problem will be that our distinctiveness, our great diversity of temperament and personality will be lost. With greater respectability in society will come the pressure for even more, pressure to play down our eccentricities and uniqueness. . . . But of course real artists must go on saying what they see . . . because the worst problem is writing falsehood and banality.[21]

Banality seems to be selling, however, and Curzon's conclusion is that unless present circumstances change dramatically, genuinely gay literature written by real artists "may have already seen its day."

The Explosion of Pornography

Irving Buchen has noted in his book, *The Perverse Imagination,* that since 1965 pandemonium has reigned in the world of avant garde publishing, as what was once underground has surfaced for all to see. Part of this pandemonium is the huge number of pornographic paperbacks that come out year after year as pulp publishers take advantage of the confusion over what constitutes obscenity. The relaxation of standards has been so complete that the "daring" novels of the mid-sixties (e.g., *Summer in Sodom*) now seem tastefully written when compared with the mindless sexual excesses in such current titles as *Lifeguard for Lunch* and *Sucker for Seafood*.

Younger gay readers who can buy a pornographic novel in any "adult" bookstore may not be able to appreciate the welcome given to the candid fiction that came out about ten years ago. When Richard Amory's *Song of the Loon* appeared in 1966, those who had previously been granted only fleeting glances at exposed chests and thighs were thunderstruck by such passages as this:

> Ephraim stood up and began to unbutton his breeches. He hesitated, knowing that his cock was swollen. The breeches hung at his hips below the silky, copper-shining hair of his lower belly. Quickly, he pulled his breeches off and threw them on the ground by his boots.
> Singing Heron gazed casually at Ephraim's cock, thick and muscular like an oak tree.[22]

The most famous of the early near-hardcore gay fiction, Amory's "Loon" novels carried the wish-fulfillment world of Jay Little to its ultimate conclusion. While it had been allowable for Jay Little to have one unlikely character such as the Cotton High halfback become marvelously gay, nearly everyone else in the novel had to be, realistically enough, heterosexual. Richard Amory helped to change these rules: in his nineteenth-century "pastoral" novels of burly white trappers and lusty Indian braves, everyone is not only masculine and sexy but also absolutely gay! Thus the moment sought for in much American gay fiction—the return to some idyllic past where your buddy becomes your lover—is magically captured and sustained in Amory's novels. In *Song of the Loon* and *Listen, The Loon Sings,* muscular white men and muscular red men love and fuck each other with such intensity that if Leslie Fiedler ever read these novels—and to complete his education he should—he would have to sit down and weep.

The quality of writing in the increasingly explicit novels published by underground gay presses during the sixties was uneven, but the writer of the more softcore porno was expected to be able to handle characterization and dialogue and keep sex scenes subordinate. For instance, in Amory's "Loon" novels, an attempt is made to be primitively poetic, even though the publisher, Green-leaf Classics of San Diego, has not been known for its insistence on literary niceties. Of notably high quality are the fictional adventures of the handsome Greek hustler, Phil Andros, in such works as *$tud,* whose author ("Phil Andros") holds a Ph.D. in English. In the more brazen hardcore fiction, however, writing quality is sacrificed in order to create an atmosphere of almost constant sexual tremulousness and in the pornographic novels being published today (*The Cops Are Comin'!; My Teacher, My Lover; Little Big Horny; Locker Room Lads; Gaius Maximus; Military Orgy; Trucker's Chicken;* et al.) there is little pretense to literary excellence. Orgasms now tend to start on page one, and the publishers are no longer relying solely on the "hot" scenes to excite the reader—in many of these "novels" drawings or photos are now included lest the written word alone not succeed in moving the reader to the desired state of lasciviousness.

Gay pornography has quite obviously attracted a number of men who in previous decades might have been tempted to write or buy traditional gay novels. Writers can hack out these books in a short time, and although they can't expect much pay, they can at least expect to be published if they have thrown in enough sex. More importantly, from a marketing point of view, it appears that the plethora of bad fiction has helped to drive out the good or at least the better. Gay men now buy novels more for titillation than for story line and, like their straight counterparts, are willing and even eager to subsidize fiction that descends to the eternally compelling common denominator of sex. As a result, the more serious and literate gay writer has found himself the victim of a paradox: with the wide-open acceptance of frankly homosexual fiction, the future of his sort of novel is threatened by its lurid competition.

The Implications of Gay Liberation

The gay liberation movement has directly affected the consciousness of all gay men in this country and has also affected indirectly what they are interested in writing and reading today. In a number of ways, the gradual shift from homosexual guilt and shame to Gay Pride has turned everything upside down. Many of the old premises of the traditional gay writer, whose ordinary-guy hero was more outraged than outrageous, have been undercut: that which was once regarded as embarrassingly outlandish is now applauded as up front, and some of today's activists delight in being as bizarre as anything Carl Van Vechten could have imagined. Ten years ago, the radicalism of Ginsberg and Burroughs was regarded with some chagrin by the middle-class Mattachine accommodationists, whose motto was "Look, we are just as normal as anyone else." In the mid-sixties gay leaders were politely requesting rather than demanding acceptance by straight society, and flamboyant poems and books about blowing and being blown were regarded as less than helpful to their public relations campaign. Since the Stonewall riots, however, there has been a gradual recognition in the minds of many gay men that radicalism is necessary to effect social change, and during the last few years the movement has had considerable influence on nearly everything published with a gay theme.

One of the most obvious results of the politicalization of gayness has been the publication of scores of nonfiction books which have quite dramatically overshadowed the output of traditional gay fiction. Merle Miller's recent writing is a good case in point: although he was finally able to publish his frankly gay novel *What Happened* in 1972, it has been his long essay "On Being Different" which has been more widely read, praised, and sold. As closet doors have been flung open, men who have had neither the time nor the talent to write novels have not hesitated to dash off personal reminiscences, and altogether the movement has produced very little fiction but an avalanche of confessions, interviews, essays, diaries, and polemics.[23] Samples of this sort of writing include Dennis Altman's *Homosexuality: Oppression and Liberation,* Arthur Bell's *Dancing the Gay Lib Blues,* Nichols and Clarke's *I Have More Fun with You than Anybody,* Peter Fisher's *The Gay Mystique,* John Murphy's *Homosexual Liberation: A Personal View* (which contains a strong chapter on "Queer Books"), and Donn Teal's *The Gay Militants.* In recent years gay people have been getting published on everything from religion (Gearhart and Johnson's *Loving Women/Loving Men*) to legal rights (Walter Barnett's *Sexual Freedom and the Constitution*), and other nonfiction runs from Bruce Rodgers' omniscient *The Queens' Vernacular* to John Mitzel's appreciative biography of John Horne Burns to Laud Humphrey's *Tearoom Trade*, which tells who cruises men's rest rooms and how. Furthermore, the rise of the counterculture sensibility has aided the blossoming of gay poetry in periodicals, mimeographed volumes and paperback anthologies, and all across the country hundreds of gay men are now writing and having published verses that are frankly celebrative of male love. Also competing for the gay reader's attention today are a number of quarterlies, national and regional newspapers, local bar throwaways, and magazines catering to every gay subculture. Finally, it might also be said that the gay-liberation movement has helped to spark the development of competing media (gay theater, gay films, gay radio and television programs) which lure homosexuals away from reading altogether.

It is obvious that the writer of traditional gay fiction finds himself in a world markedly different from the one that witnessed the birth of homosexual fiction in America. Forty years ago, about the only way one had of discovering what it meant to be a homosexual —especially if one were in the closet—was to somehow find a copy of an underground gay novel. One man recalls that in those years "the classic Gay Novel was passed around like the Eucharist, with moist eyes and a warm endorsement. In high school or the first year of college, you were likely to be introduced to somebody with great knowledge and experience who kept a bookshelf of forbidden or 'particular' books."[24] But now, with no one having to rely on gay fiction for information, amusement or encouragement, nearly everyone agrees that the "moist eyes" era is over.

Some Critics Begin to See the Light

The logic behind gay liberation has not been lost on a number of open-minded and thoughtful reviewers, and recently an ironic crisscross has begun to emerge in connection with gay literature and the critics. At least among some of the younger intellectuals there has been a tendency to give the homosexual artist the benefit of past doubts. As they look around for novels to praise today, however, all they see are the ersatz works of Laura Z. Hobson and Patricia N. Warren.

Of course, literary homophobia has not completely disappeared. Within recent memory *Time* was dismissing gay novelists as mere "chroniclers of faggotry and fellatio," and in an academic quarterly several years ago an English professor dismissed all gay novels as "quaint."[25] As late as 1968 Ronald Berman was still twitting Gore Vidal over the question of sexual norms, suggesting that "cultural beliefs" provided incontrovertible proof that it was better to be heterosexual. "It may be regrettable, although I do not find it so," Berman wrote with macho headiness, "but most of us do have some belief in what is normal."[26] But praising heterosexual norms and jumping aboard queer-baiting bandwagons is not being done so much anymore, and today one is likely to be suspect not for defending gay literature but rather for stamping one's foot and attacking it with the ritual homophobia that went out with the Eisenhower years.

One of the earliest writers to question the superiority of what Berman would call "normality" and to predict the coming of gay liberation was Seymour Krim. In his "Revolt of the Homosexual," Krim's gay character debates a straight man who believes normal people are better because they are normal:

> You're smug in your superiority to the homosexual because you have average tastes while mine are comparatively rare. You use the word normal to congratulate your averageness and the word abnormal to smear my individuality. You look down on myself and other homosexuals as being freakish or repulsive because our way of life is foreign to you—like a schoolboy who throws rocks at a synagogue window. You refuse to see beyond our uniqueness to our *universality* just as your grandfather and great-grandfathers choked the life out of the minorities of their time. . . . But I tell you in complete honesty that this pathetic half-existence of homosexuals is ending because we will no longer accept your version of ourselves. . . . When homosexuality achieves legitimacy, it will be seen as a branch of a river rather than a contamination of the

source. When it is given unity, homosexual culture will be seen as constituting a unique view of experience, offering insights to all people. The homosexuality of great figures of the past—not only our Prousts and Whitmans—will be revealed, as Byron's is beginning to be, and he the outstanding popular symbol of the Don Juan! All the dearly-bought insight that has come out of a closed-door suffering which can no longer bear its isolation will be given to society at large.[27]

Expanding on Krim's concept that gay writers can offer unique insights of interest to all, Theodore Solotaroff has more recently claimed that it is the gifted gay writers who are best able to perceive and define the "character of the age." In an essay on Hubert Selby, reprinted in *The Red Hot Vacuum,* Solotaroff goes a step beyond the concessions made by Susan Sontag in her "Notes on Camp." Claiming that Sontag was too backhanded in praising gay writers for only their aestheticism, Solotaroff points out that gay writers are doing as well as the Jewish humanists in grappling with "moral" issues:

. . . Sontag suggests that two minority groups are making the only significant contributions to contemporary culture: the Jews, who impart moral seriousness, and the homosexuals, who impart aesthetic style and playfulness. But it seems to me the homosexual imagination is having a more decisive effect in defining the moral as well as the aesthetic character of the age. . . . The darkest (deepest) truths about drug addiction come from William Burroughs, about Negro-white relations from Genêt and Baldwin, about modern marriage from Albee and Tennessee Williams, about the disaffected young from Allen Ginsberg.[28]

A writer who has helped to challenge some clichés about how red-blooded men should write has been Carolyn Heilbrun, whose *Toward a Recognition of Androgyny* was published several years ago. In this book her polarities are not so much heterosexual versus homosexual as they are extreme femininity versus extreme masculinity, and she says we in America have discouraged the androgynous vision that added a civilized balance to the works of such writers as Virginia Woolf and Lytton Strachey. The stout insistence that men write like *real men,* Heilbrun notes, has brought us, in James Dickey's *Deliverance,* the book "for which the novel of masculinity has been preparing us. Out in the 'territory,' beyond the bounds of culture, the men rape each other."[29] (*Deliverance* was not belittled as a gay novel, of course, for we are led to believe that the sex wasn't quite as much fun for the rapee as it was for the raper and on the basis of this redeeming quality the novel was accepted as perfectly straight.) Altogether, Heilbrun's arguments attack the American tradition of applauding women for writing like women, rewarding men for writing like men, and of being embarrassed and confounded by the androgynous (often gay) author who cannot be fitted neatly into either category.

Perhaps the most eloquent defender of the special contributions made to literature by homosexual writers was Benjamin DeMott in his essay "But He's a Homosexual . . . ," which was included in his *Supergrow* (1970). Analyzing why critics have been so mean or condescending to the gay artist in America, DeMott both attacks the unwarranted smugness of heterosexuals and praises gay writers for their singularly perceptive and compelling writing. In the middle of his essay DeMott names five gay writers, goes on to praise them, and he concludes with an admonition about failure to hear out the homosexual artist:

With a few other poets and dramatists, they are the only compelling writers of the postwar period who seem to know anything beyond the level of cliché about human connectedness, whose minds break through the stereotypes of existential violence or Nietzschean extravagance into recognizable truths and intricacies of contemporary feeling. They are not purveyors of situation comedy or Bond banalities or *Playboy* virility or musical-marital bliss (*I Do! I Do!*) or mate murders. A steady consciousness of a dark side of love that is neither homo- nor heterosexual but simply human pervades much of their work; they are in touch with facts of feeling that most men do not or cannot admit to thought.
. . . Failure to hear out the homosexual artist with a seriousness matching his own, overeagerness to dismiss him as ignorant or perverse, assurance that we know what we are . . . this is worse than senseless. It is a mockery not only of art and of the suffering that art rises out of and seeks to comprehend: it is a mockery of our famous, preening new liberation as well.[30]

While it is entirely conceivable that some gay artists are "in touch with facts of feeling that most men do not or cannot admit to thought," no claim is being made that the American gay novelist has been able to speak to and for humanity in mysterious ways denied all others. What *does* seem to be clear is that the homosexual novelist has been trying to speak to and for the millions of homosexuals in this country, often with a surprising amount of pluck and grace, and that his official nonstatus or second-class status is not the result of his being ungifted but rather of Americans remaining homophobic to a degree that they are no longer anti-Semitic or racist. That present circumstances of homosexual fiction are rather bleak is obvious, and whether or not it has a future will depend on the willingness of both homosexuals and heterosexuals to reward talented gay men for telling all the stories that remain to be told. But that the homosexual novel has a past—and that this past contains some of the most poignant writing in twentieth-century American literature—can no longer be denied.

NOTES

1. Stanton Hoffman, "The Cities of Night," pp. 205, 206.
2. Young discusses these novels in "The Flower Beneath the Foot: A Short History of the Gay Novel," which was reprinted in his *The Male Homosexual in Literature.* Another quasi-exposé novel he cites is James Herlihy's *Midnight Cowboy* (New York: Simon & Schuster, Inc., 1965).
3. Charles Wright, *The Messenger* (New York: Farrar, Straus, 1963), pp. 190-91. Also present in *The Messenger* and *Another Country* is the theme of the young man being spiritually lost in contrast to the saved and sanctified church members safely within the fold. This theme is rarely mentioned by white writers of modern gay fiction.
4. Kay Boyle's comments on *The Messenger* are taken from the 1963 Crest paperback reprint of the novel. The Bone and Cleaver comments on *Another Country* appear in Kenneth Kinnamon's collection of essays titled *James Baldwin* (Englewood Cliffs, N.J.: Prentice-Hall, 1974). Balliett's review appeared in *The New Yorker* (August 4, 1962).
5. Podhoretz' review first appeared in *Show* (October 1962), and these quotes come from its reprint in Richard Kostelanetz' *On Contemporary Literature* (New York: Avon, 1969), pp. 235-36.
6. Hubert Selby, *Last Exit to Brooklyn* (New York: Grove Press, 1964), pp. 69-70.

7. The *Time* reviewer justifiably complained that "what Selby scrupulously elides are all the pleasant moments in life." The novel was reviewed in *Time* (October 30, 1964) and in *The Times Book Review* (November 8, 1964).

8. John Rechy, *City of Night* (New York: Grove Press, 1963), pp. 69-70.

9. Chester went on to say that the hero "wants to be loved and wanted, but he doesn't want to love or want—he doesn't, in fact, want to be queer, though this is much too chic a book to admit that except backhandedly." Chester's review appeared in the *New York Review of Books* (May 1963). Rechy discussed hustlers' poses in *Gay Sunshine* (November–December 1974).

10. *Gay Sunshine* (September–October 1973). More recently, Isherwood has set forth the gay key to much of his earlier fiction in *Christopher and His Kind* (New York: Farrar, Straus, Giroux, 1976).

11. Thomas Doremus, *To Beaucock, with Love* (New York: Clarkson Potter, 1961), p. 29.

12. Doremus, *Latitudes of Love* (New York: 1961), pp. 142-43. An earlier novel, *Flaw Dexter* (1947), was not particularly gay. Unfortunately, this talented and promising writer died in Portugal in 1962.

13. Granville Hicks (*The Saturday Review*, August 21, 1965).

14. Alfred Chester, *Behold Goliath* (New York: Random House, 1964), p. 182. In this story Chester tries to explain the inability to love which he criticized in Rechy's hustler. Joaquin finds that Manhattan is an eerie, tombstoned island full of robots who cannot love, cannot know they are robots, and cannot know they cannot love.

15. "Davis" gave this background information in a letter to the editor in the *Mattachine Review* (December 1962).

16. Susan Sontag, *The Benefactor* (New York: Avon, 1965), p. 56.

17. Lynton Brett, *Sir Gay* (Hollywood: Brentwood, 1965); *The Gay Flesh* and *Summer in Sodom* are described on the dust jacket of James Colton's *Strange Marriage* (Los Angeles: Argyle, 1965).

18. Of course there is such a thing as a homosexual, but *Myra Breckinridge* was written just before the gay liberation movement proclaimed that equivocation about being gay was no longer necessary.

19. Susan Sontag's "Notes on Camp," which originally appeared in *Partisan Review* and was reprinted in her *Against Interpretation,* provoked a storm of pro-gay and anti-gay controversy. Later in the sixties she was chided by such people as Theodore Solotaroff and Benjamin DeMott for implying that homosexuals excelled only in campy writing.

20. In "The Flower Beneath the Foot," Ian Young calls these detective novels a gay "sub-genre" and mentions such other titles as Larry Townsend's *The Long Leather Cord,* Richard Amory's *Frost,* and Robert Bentley's *Here There Be Dragons.* Other sub-genres mentioned by Young include science fiction and juveniles, and perhaps another would be the S&M novels that Townsend turns out so prolifically.

21. Dan Curzon, "The Problems of Writing Gay Literature," *Margins* (20), 1975, p. 12. It should be added, however, that other observers of the literary scene are more optimistic. In his *The End of Intelligent Writing: Literary Politics in America* (1973), Richard Kostelanetz predicts that gay writers may replace the current New York "Literary Mob" as the next powerful super-militant minority: "As public attitudes and libel laws change, what was once a source of shame will become, in literary discourse at least, a mark of pride . . ." More recently, Richard Hall has mentioned (in his book column in the *Advocate*) that some major publishing houses now seem to be either willing or eager to publish at least one book on a gay theme per year.

22. Richard Amory, *Song of the Loon* (San Diego: Greenleaf, 1966), p. 12. A frequent contributor to the San Francisco gay magazine *Vector,* Amory has written that he grew up in Columbus, Ohio, "the capital of superma-chismo in the form of the Ohio State football team," and it could well be that his burly trappers and Indians are simply Ohio State football players in disguise. Although Amory says the model for the Loon novels was Gaspar Gil Polo's *Diana Enamorada,* these books are very much a part of a gay Wild West pastoral tradition which (according to the latest Elysian Fields catalog) goes back to Andy Adams' *The Log of a Cowboy* (1903) and Badger Clark's *Sun and Saddle Leather* (1919) and *Sky Line and Wood Smoke* (1935).

23. An exception to this trend was Irving Rosenthal's counterculture novel *Sheeper* (1967), a rambling, self-indulgent autobiographical book in which the author recalls unsuccessful conversations with Allen Ginsberg and Peter Orlovsky and speculates on the sex life of Melville and the members of the Red Army in Russia.

24. Angelo d'Arcangelo, *The Homosexual Handbook* (New York: Ophelia Press, 1969), p. 228.

25. Strangely enough, the professor who belittled gay novels as "quaint" (in "The Origins of Homosexual Fiction," *Colorado Quarterly,* Spring 1974) is the very person who has written so sympathetically about Gore Vidal in *The Apostate Angel*—Bernard Dick.

26. Ronald Berman, *America in the Sixties: An Intellectual History* (New York: Harper & Row, 1970), p. 256.

27. Seymour Krim, *Views of a Nearsighted Cannoneer* (New York: Dutton, 1968), pp. 141-42. Krim's views are extraordinary for two reasons. Not only is he apparently a heterosexual (as are the other defenders cited at the end of this chapter) but "Revolt of the Homosexual" was actually written during the deadly 1950s, being first published in the *Village Voice* in 1959.

28. Theodore Solotaroff, *The Red Hot Vacuum* (New York: Atheneum, 1970), pp. 165-66.

29. Carolyn Heilbrun, *Toward a Recognition of Androgyny* (New York: Harper & Row, 1974), p. 170.

30. Benjamin DeMott, *Supergrow* (New York: Dell, 1970), pp. 25, 34.

Selected Bibliography (1870-1965)

Anderson, Sherwood, "Hands," in *Winesburg, Ohio,* New York: Huebsch, 1919.

Anon., *The Strange Confession of Monsieur Mountcairn,* J. A. Norcross, 1928.

Baldwin, James, *Giovanni's Room,* New York: Dial, 1956.

————, *Another Country,* New York: Dial, 1962.

Barnes, Djuna, *Nightwood,* New York: Harcourt, Brace, 1937.

Barr, James, *Quatrefoil,* New York: Greenberg, 1950.

————, *Derricks,* New York: Greenberg, 1951.

Benton, Stuart, *All Things Human,* New York: Sheridan House, 1949.

Blechman, Burt, *Stations,* New York: Random House, 1964.

Bolton, Isabel, *The Christmas Tree,* New York: Scribners, 1949.

Boyle, Kay, *Gentlemen, I Address You Privately,* New York: Smith & Haas, 1933.

Brinig, Myron, *This Man Is My Brother,* New York: Farrar & Rinehart, 1932.

Bruce, Kennilworth, *Goldie,* New York: William Godwin, 1933.

Burns, John Horne, *The Gallery,* New York: Harper, 1947; Bantam, 1950 (paperback).*

————, *Lucifer with a Book,* New York: Harper, 1949.

————, *A Cry of Children,* New York: Harper, 1952.

Burt, Nathaniel, *Scotland's Burning,* Boston: Little, Brown, 1953.

Cain, James, *Serenade,* New York: Knopf, 1937.

Calmer, Edgar, *Beyond the Street,* New York: Harcourt, Brace, 1934.

Cameron, Bruce, *The Case Against Colonel Sutton,* New York: Coward-McCann, 1961.

Capote, Truman, *Other Voices, Other Rooms,* New York: Random House, 1948.

Chandler, Raymond, *The Big Sleep,* New York: Knopf, 1939.

Chester, Alfred, *Jamie Is My Heart's Desire,* New York: Vanguard, 1957.

————, *Behold Goliath,* New York: Random House, 1964.

Coleman, Lonnie, *Ship's Company,* Boston: Little, Brown, 1955.

————, *Sam,* New York: McKay, 1959.

Colton, James, *Strange Marriage,* Los Angeles: Argyle, 1965.

Cory, Donald Webster, *The Homosexual in America,* New York: Greenberg, 1951.

————, ed., *21 Variations on a Theme,* New York: Greenberg, 1953.

Creekmore, Hubert, *The Welcome,* New York: Appleton-Century-Crofts, 1948.

Dale, Alan, *A Marriage Below Zero,* New York: Dillingham, 1889.

Davis, Fitzroy, *Quicksilver,* New York: Harcourt, Brace, 1942.

Davis, Roger, *Always Love a Stranger,* New York: Hillman, 1961.

De Forrest, Michael, *The Gay Year,* New York: Woodford Press, 1949.

Doremus, Thomas, *To Beaucock, with Love,* New York: Clarkson Potter, 1961.

————, *Latitudes of Love,* New York: Clarkson Potter, 1961.

Douglas, Dean, *Man Divided,* New York: Fawcett Gold Medal, 1954.

Dowd, Harrison, *The Night Air,* New York: Dial, 1950.

Edmunds, Murrell, *Sojourn Among Shadows,* Caldwell, Idaho: Caxton, 1936.

Evans, John, *Shadows Flying,* New York: Knopf, 1936.

Fey, Edwin, *Summer in Sodom,* Los Angeles: Argyle, 1964.

Ford, Charles Henri; and Tyler, Parker, *The Young and Evil,* Paris: Obelisk, 1933.**

Frank, Waldo, *The Dark Mother,* New York: Boni & Liveright, 1920.

Friedman, Sanford, *Totempole,* New York: Dutton, 1965.

Fuller, Henry Blake, *Bertram Cope's Year,* Chicago: Alderbrink, 1919.

Goodman, Paul, *Parents' Day,* Saugatuck, Connecticut: 5 x 8 Press, 1951.

————, *Making Do,* New York: Macmillan, 1963.

Goodwin, John, *The Idols and the Prey,* New York: Harper, 1953.

————, *A View of Fuji,* London: Neville Spearman, 1963.

Houston, Joe, *The Gay Flesh,* Los Angeles: Argyle, 1965.

Isherwood, Christopher, *The Berlin Stories,* New York: New Directions, 1946.

————, *Down There on a Visit,* New York: Simon & Schuster, 1962.

————, *A Single Man,* New York: Simon & Schuster, 1964.

Jackson, Charles, *The Fall of Valor,* New York: Farrar, Straus, 1946.

Kent, Nial, *The Divided Path,* New York: Greenberg, 1949.

Levenson, Lew, *Butterfly Man,* New York: Macauley, 1934.

Leveridge, Ralph, *Walk on the Water,* New York: Farrar, Straus, 1951.

————, *Somewhere Between the Two,* New York: Pageant, 1956.

McAlmon, Robert, *Distinguished Air (Grim Fairy Tales),* Paris: Three Mountains Press (for Contact Editions), 1925; paperback reprint under the title *There Was a Rustle of Black Silk Stockings,* New York: Belmont Tower Books, 1963.*

McCullers, Carson, *Reflections in a Golden Eye,* Boston: Houghton Mifflin, 1941.

————, *The Ballad of the Sad Café,* Boston: Houghton Mifflin, 1951.

McIntosh, Harlan, *This Finer Shadow,* New York: Lorac Books, 1941.

Maxwell, William, *The Folded Leaf,* New York: Harper, 1945.

Mayne, Xavier, *Imre: A Memorandum,* Naples: The English Book-Press, 1906.**

Meeker, Richard, *Better Angel,* New York: Greenberg, 1933.

Melville, Herman, *Billy Budd, Sailor: An Inside Narrative,* Chicago: University of Chicago Press, 1962.

Merrick, Gordon, *The Demon of Noon,* New York: Messner, 1954.

Millar, Kenneth, *The Dark Tunnel,* New York: Dodd, Mead, 1944.

Mills, Carley, *A Nearness of Evil,* New York: Coward-McCann, 1961.

Murphy, Dennis, *The Sergeant,* New York: Viking, 1958.

Niles, Blair, *Strange Brother,* New York: Liveright, 1931.**

Otis, Harry, *Camel's Farewell,* San Francisco: Pan-Graphic, 1961.

Packer, Vin, *Whisper His Sin,* New York: Fawcett Gold Medal, 1954.

Paul, Elliot, *Concert Pitch,* New York: Random House, 1938.

Peters, Fritz, *Finistere,* New York: Farrar, Straus, 1951.

Phillips, Thomas, *The Bitterweed Path,* New York: Rinehart, 1949.

Prezzi, Wilma, *Dark Desires,* New York: Padell, 1953.

Purdy, James, *Malcolm,* New York: Farrar, Straus & Cudahy, 1959.

Rand, Lou, *Rough Trade,* Los Angeles: Argyle, 1964.

Raul, K. B., *Naked to the Night,* New York: Warner Paperback Library, 1964.

Rechy, John, *City of Night,* New York: Grove Press, 1963.

Rivette, Marc, *The Incident,* Cleveland: World, 1957.

Schane, Janet, *The Dazzling Crystal,* New York: Reynal & Hitchcock, 1946.

Scully, Robert, *A Scarlet Pansy,* New York: Royal Publishers, n.d.

Selby, Hubert, Jr., *Last Exit to Brooklyn,* New York: Grove Press, 1964.

Sontag, Susan, *The Benefactor,* New York: Farrar, Straus, 1963.

Starr, J. P., "Boys, Men, and Love," 1925(?) in One, Inc., library, Los Angeles.

Stoddard, Charles Warren, *South-Sea Idyls,* Boston: James Osgood and Company, 1873.

————, *For the Pleasure of His Company: An Affair of the Misty City,* San Francisco: A. M. Robertson, 1903.

Talsman, William, *The Gaudy Image,* Paris: Olympia, 1958.

Taylor, Bayard, *Joseph and His Friend: A Story of Pennsylvania,* New York: Putnam, 1870.

Tellier, André, *Twilight Men,* New York: Greenberg, 1931; New York: Pyramid, 1957 (paperback reprint).*

Tesch, Gerald, *Never the Same Again,* New York: Putnam, 1956.

Thacher, Russell, *The Captain,* New York: Macmillan, 1951.

Thomas, Ward, *Stranger in the Land,* Boston: Houghton Mifflin, 1949.

Van Vechten, Carl, *The Blind Bow-Boy: A cartoon for a stained glass window,* New York: Knopf, 1923.

Vidal, Gore, "A Novel," 1943, ms. owned by Wisconsin State Historical Society, Madison.

————, *The City and the Pillar,* New York: Dutton, 1948.

————, *A Thirsty Evil,* New York: Zero, 1956.

————, *The City and the Pillar Revised,* New York: Dutton, 1965.

————, pseud. Edgar Box, *Death in the Fifth Position,* New York: Dutton, 1952.

Wahl, Loren, *The Invisible Glass,* New York: Greenberg, 1950.

Williams, Tennessee, *One Arm,* New York: New Directions, 1948.

————, *Hard Candy,* New York: New Directions, 1954.

Willingham, Calder, *End As a Man,* New York: Vanguard, 1947.

Wright, Charles, *The Messenger,* New York: Farrar, Straus, 1963.

Wright, Stephen, ed., *Different: An Anthology of Homosexual Short Stories,* New York: Bantam, 1974.

*Edition/version quoted when two are cited.
**Reprinted in 1975 as a volume in the "Lesbians and Gay Men in Society, History and Literature" collection published by Arno Press, New York.

INDEX

PS
374
.H63.A9
MEYER

Stanford University Libraries

3 6105 003 782 153

BC23

DATE DUE SPRING 1982

MAY 1 9 1982

APR - 8 1984

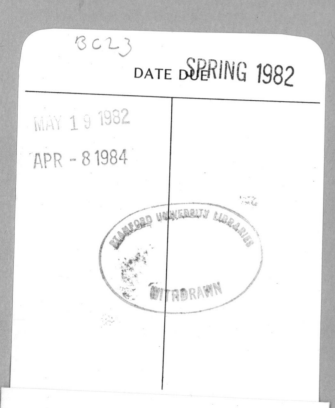

STANFORD UNIVERSITY LIBRARIES
STANFORD, CALIFORNIA
94305